Slavery, Indenture and the Law

This book addresses historical issues of colonialism and race, which influenced the formation of multicultural society in Mauritius. During the 19th century, Mauritius was Britain's prime sugar-producing colony, yet, unlike the West Indies, its history has remained significantly under-researched. The modern demographic of multi-ethnic Mauritius is unusual as, in the absence of an indigenous people, descendants of colonists, slaves and indentured labourers constitute the majority of the island's population today. Thus, it may be said that the Mauritian nation was "assembled" during the period in question. This work draws on an in-depth examination of the two labour systems through which the island came to be populated: slavery and indenture. In studying the relevant laws, four legal events of historical importance within the context of these two labour systems are identified: the abolition of the slave trade, the abolition of slavery, private indentured labour migration and state-regulated indenture. This book is notable in that it presents a legal analysis of core historical events, thus straddling the line between two disciplines, and covers both slavery and indentured labour in Mauritian history. Mauritius, as an originally uninhabited island, presents a rare case study for inquiries into colonial legacies, multiculturalism and race consciousness. The book will be a valuable resource to scholars worldwide in the fields of slavery, indenture and the legal apparatus of forced labour.

Nandini S. Boodia-Canoo is a lawyer and an academic, currently teaching at Bloomsbury Institute London. Her scholarship is interdisciplinary, covering law, history, international relations and sociology.

Routledge Research in Legal History

The Royal Prerogative and Constitutional Law
A Search for the Quintessence of Executive Power
Noel Cox

Socialism and Legal History
The Histories and Historians of Law in Socialist East Central Europe
Edited by Ville Erkkilä and Hans-Peter Haferkamp

A History of Divorce Law
Reform in England from the Victorian to Interwar Years
Henry Kha

The League of Nations and the Development of International Law
A New Intellectual History of the Advisory Committee of Jurists
Edited by P. Sean Morris

Transforming the Politics of International Law
The Advisory Committee of Jurists and the Formation of the World Court in the League of Nations
Edited by P. Sean Morris

Transitional Justice in Italy and the Crimes of Fascism and Nazism
Paolo Caroli

Slavery, Indenture and the Law
Assembling a Nation in Colonial Mauritius
Nandini S. Boodia-Canoo

Justice and International Law in Meiji Japan
The María Luz Incident and the Dawn of Modernity
Giorgio Fabio Colombo

See more at www.routledge.com/Routledge-Research-in-Legal-History/book-series/RRLEGHIST

Slavery, Indenture and the Law

Assembling a Nation in Colonial Mauritius

Nandini S. Boodia-Canoo

Routledge
Taylor & Francis Group
LONDON AND NEW YORK

First published 2023
by Routledge
4 Park Square, Milton Park, Abingdon, Oxon OX14 4RN

and by Routledge
605 Third Avenue, New York, NY 10158

Routledge is an imprint of the Taylor & Francis Group, an informa business

British Library Cataloguing-in-Publication Data
A catalogue record for this book is available from the British Library

ISBN: 978-1-032-32201-8 (hbk)
ISBN: 978-1-032-32205-6 (pbk)
ISBN: 978-1-003-31336-6 (ebk)

DOI: 10.4324/9781003313366

Typeset in Galliard
by Apex CoVantage, LLC

Dedicated to my Ancestors,
who started the journey,
and my Descendants,
who will continue it.

Contents

Acknowledgments

This work is based on my doctoral thesis, which I completed at SOAS, University of London.

I am grateful to my former supervisor, Professor Matthew Craven, who allowed me to experience the true meaning of academic freedom and provided the support to progress at critical junctures.

Many thanks are due to the members of my family, for assisting and enduring the process that is involved in producing original research. I wish to express my gratitude to both of my parents for raising me in consciousness of my roots, thereby providing the original inspiration for this study. In particular, I am deeply grateful to my father for his unfailing support and belief in me, the value of which cannot be put in words.

Special thanks are due to my children Raunakh and Maheera, for giving up much of the time and attention they would have been entitled to over the years. This work represents their heritage in more ways than one and is my gift to them.

I am grateful to the sister of my heart, Dr Yuko Kanda, who did not grow up with me, but was with me when I had to grow up. Her presence brought joy in the darkest moments.

I wish to thank Mr Peter Lampier, former tutor and colleague, who had been my mentor since undergraduate days, and Dr Chaloka Beyani, my LLM supervisor, for his support of my PhD application.

My gratitude extends to all the helpful staff at the various libraries and archives where I conducted my research, especially Mr Vishwanaden Govinden of the Mahatma Gandhi Institute in Mauritius.

Most of all, I thank the empyrean guidance, which in its various manifestations is ever present in my life.

Figures and Tables

Preface

Scholars of colonialism are accustomed to having to defend the relevance of their work. While the past few years have seen a surge of interest in this area, the question "Why does it matter?" remains, even if unspoken. In the context of law, colonial studies may appear even more as an anomaly; after all, the practice of law is primarily concerned with the law as it is, not as it was, particularly centuries ago.

The research presented here examines the role law played in influencing Mauritian society. The main matter of concern is the social effect of law, as initially introduced and developed during the colonial period. This study is thus not a positivist legal account, but rather seeks to answer the question as to how legal structures influenced culture, identity and entitlement, leading to the empowerment of some and the deprivation of others.

A gap was perceived to exist in form of a legal examination of historical events, which has remained largely missing from the scholarly discourse. The perspective of a legal analysis upon primary sources has allowed this study to subvert certain accounts previously deemed canonical in Mauritian history. Through this synecdoche, using Mauritius as a looking-glass through which colonial legacies are examined, it is hoped that there are wider conclusions to be drawn for the study and understanding of imperialism and international law.

To be sure, colonial rule remained an experience for various countries around the world well into the 20th century. Mauritius achieved independence from Britain in 1968, and as such, during the lifetime of this author's parents, who were both born there.

Colonialism is thus not as ancient a subject as sometimes implied by commentators, yet whether regarded as a bygone or recent era, its problematic relationship with the present remains. Resistance to fully integrating it as part of Britain's imperial legacy became evident again when it transpired that the Home Office had commissioned a course on colonialism for its 36,000 employees, yet seemed more concerned they were not "browbeaten" by the content, and reportedly asked academics involved in the development of the material to "tone down" parts of it.[1] Evidently this counters the purpose of commissioning the course in

1 Gentleman, Amelia, 'Home Office Tried to "Sanitise" Staff Education Module on Colonialism', *The Guardian* <www.theguardian.com/politics/2022/jun/10/home-office-tried-to-sanitise-staff-education-module-on-colonialism> [accessed 10 June 2022].

the first place, to which the Home Office committed after a report established that the Windrush scandal was the result of racist ideology traceable back to the British Empire.[2]

A full analysis of the concept of racism as a social phenomenon is beyond the scope of this work. Its focus are the two major labour systems which supported the colonial project, namely slavery and indentured labour. Yet much can be gleaned from 19th century practices which dehumanized and commoditized workers for exploitative ends. In the words of Aimé Césaire, "colonization works to decivilize the colonizer, to brutalize him in the true sense of the word."[3] They find illustration in the pages of this book, which demonstrate how colonization operated, in the context of both unfree and free labour, with consequences which resonate far beyond the boundary lines of an island in the Indian Ocean. If considered attentively, the reader will be in a position to answer the question posed at the beginning: why the study of colonialism matters.

Nandini S. Boodia-Canoo
London, 2022

2 Gentleman, Amelia, 'Windrush Scandal Caused by "30 years of Racist Immigration Laws" – Report', *The Guardian* <www.theguardian.com/uk-news/2022/may/29/windrush-scandal-caused-by-30-years-of-racist-immigration-laws-report> [accessed 29 May 2022] Notably, the Home Office has refused to make the report, compiled by a historian, available to the general public.

3 Césaire, Aimé, *Discourse on Colonialism*, trans. by Joan Pinkham (New York: Monthly Review Press, 1972), p. 35.

1 Introduction

1.1 Overview

1.1.1 Background

Mauritius, a group of islands commonly referred to in the singular form, is situated in the Indian Ocean southeast of Africa, and has during its history been a colony of several imperial powers. It belonged successively to the Portuguese, the Dutch and the French, before in 1968 achieving independence from Britain. Mauritius became a British possession in 1810, obtained by conquest in local battle against France. Originally uninhabited and at the turn of the century mainly occupied by French plantation owners and African slaves, the island was initially more of strategic interest to Britain. By the mid-19th century however, Mauritius had risen to become the Empire's prime sugar-producing colony. Figure 1.1 shows a map of the main island.

The procurement and retention of cheap and effective plantation labour presented a significant concern for Britain. The abolition of slavery through the Imperial Act of 1833 was expected to cause a drastic reduction in available workers. The anticipated shortfall lead to the recruitment of contract workers predominantly from India, first on a private basis at the initiative of plantation owners, and later under a government-backed scheme. Among the sugar colonies adopting this system, Mauritius became the first and largest recipient of indentured labourers from the subcontinent.

Descendants of colonists, slaves, indentured labourers and certain other groups arriving at the time make up the population of Mauritius today. The Mauritian demographic is unique and it may be said that it was "assembled" during the era in question. Modern Mauritian society presents an amalgam of different cultures and ethnicities, each seeking to protect their interests and jockeying for power, an enduring feature of life on this multi-ethnic island which effectively began in the 19th century.

1.1.2 Focus

The research involves a consideration of both law and history. Part of the endeavour is to reframe relevant historical events as legal processes as a way of gaining deeper insight into the underlying dynamics. The general scope of this work

DOI: 10.4324/9781003313366-1

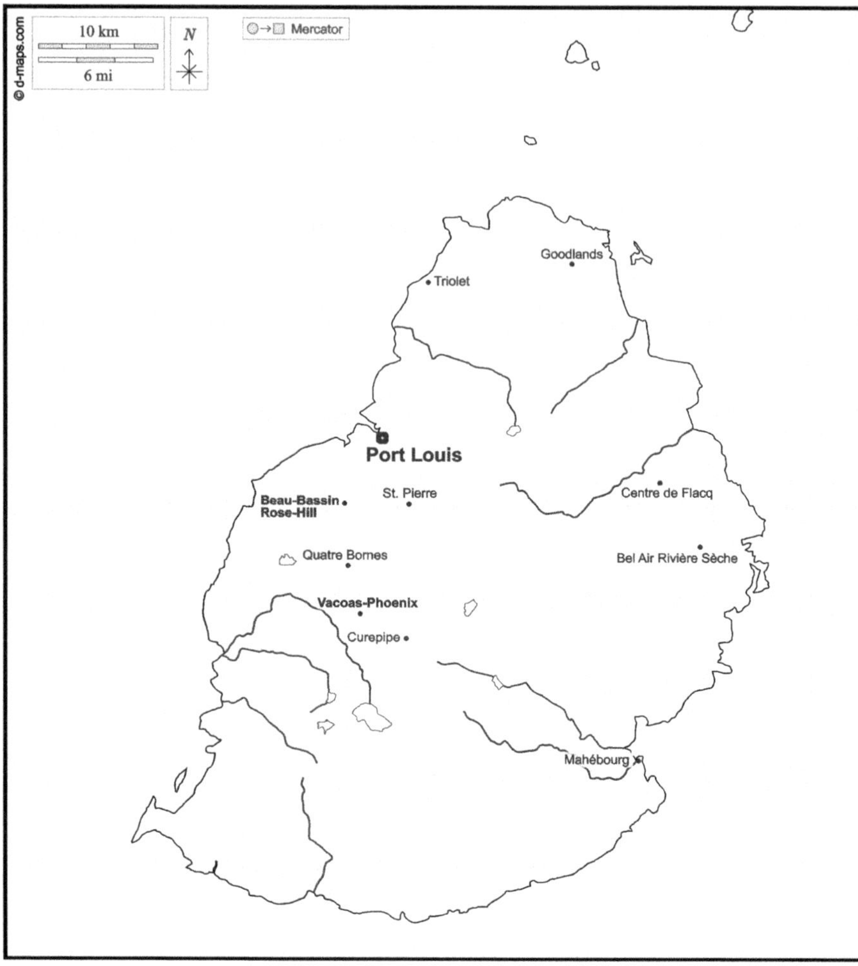

Figure 1.1 Map of Mauritius[1]

can be described as laws affecting plantation labour in 19th-century Mauritius, but within that wide area four concrete legal events have particular historical importance: (1) the abolition of the slave trade; (2) the abolition of slavery and the introduction of apprenticeships; (3) the introduction of indentured labour from India on an informal basis; and (4) the beginning of state-regulated labour migration from India. To some extent, these mark out distinct "eras" of rule – the first spanning the period between 1810 and the abolition of slavery in 1835, at which point the second period begins. However, they are also overlapping, as

1 Mauritius map, d-maps.cowwm. <https://d-maps.com/carte.php?num_car=27487&lang=en> [accessed 8 August 2021].

post-emancipation apprenticeships coincided with the informal recruitment of indentured labourers from the Indian subcontinent.

This work contends that each of these events are linked: each was conceived as a result of the effects of the preceding one. Just as the abolition of slavery responded to the problematic that emerged in the aftermath of the abolition of the trade in slaves, so also did the informal recruitment of indentured labour from India respond to the shift from slavery to apprenticeship. The later government-backed scheme was conceived to respond to the failures of private labour migration. To best address the processes involved, each event is accorded a separate chapter in which, in addition to the research questions set out below, one particular segment of 19th century Mauritian society is investigated. Thus, Chapter 3 examines the effects of the abolition of the slave trade, which provides insight into the conditions the slave population laboured under. Chapter 4, which addresses the context in which the abolition of slavery was effected, allows for a closer examination of the white ruling class who felt their interests were threatened. Chapter 5 deals with the informal introduction of indentured labourers from India, and thus permits an assessment of certain cultural issues that were important in the context of an increasingly multi-ethnic society. Chapter 6, which discusses state-sponsored indenture immigration, addresses the last part of the process, which saw Mauritian society being assembled during an eventful 19th century.

1.1.3 Aims

In the 21st century, Mauritius remains a country which has largely retained the markers of its diverse ethnic origins, and retains significant levels of social segregation. In the absence of an indigenous population, race consciousness has been integral to the construction of social identity on the island. This is evident in private as well as public life, where politics continue to be broadly demarcated along racial and religious lines. Further, the general perception of history is riddled with stereotypes, conceiving the modern nation to be made up of identifiable, separate groups of descendants of certain colonial archetypes, such as "the African slave", "the French plantation owner", and "the Indian indentured labourer".

These are rough and simplified demarcations. Other relevant minorities include Sino-Mauritians as well as Muslims of Indian heritage, whose ancestors were part of the indentured labour migration or arrived as independent traders during the same period.[2] These categorizations do have a basis in history, however a rigid adherence to this conception obscures the complexity of the processes by which the island came to be populated. Neither the experience of slavery nor of that of indentured labour was uniform, which by itself is responsible for

2 See Carter, Marina, and James Ng Foong Kwong, *Forging the Rainbow* (Mauritius: self-published, 1997).

further fragmentation in societal composition.[3] Additionally, it is worth pointing out that in reality a great degree of *métissage* occurred in Mauritius. This is prima facie evident from the basic gender imbalance among the ethnicities in early census numbers, and has further been substantiated by anthropological and genealogical studies under the aegis of the Truth and Justice Commission.[4] As its report states: "Mauritians have much more in common than they think they have and are much more united than they think they are".[5] Nevertheless, as is also observed, this unity is more "than they care to admit".[6] The unwillingness to confront personal histories, it is submitted, is detrimental to a common national consciousness.[7]

While the parameters of this study prevent it from conducting a comprehensive investigation of the various genealogical facets of society and their socioeconomic reality, it seeks to establish a common history by examining both slavery and indentured labour during the 19th century. With the need for coercible labour to cultivate the island being the prime reason for how Mauritius came to be populated, the vast majority of Mauritians today are descendants of imported workers of one description or another. The experience of arriving in Mauritius in support of the imperial project was a shared one by both slaves and indentured labourers.

This study's focus on the labour question also prevents a detailed analysis of other minority groups which were not directly involved in the query, such as traders of various ethnicities who settled as well as the resident *gens de coleur*, the free people of colour. However they too are part of the process which gave birth to the Mauritian nation, and their role is noted where relevant to the issues discussed.

It has been observed by scholars that academics have a tendency to construct separate histories of Mauritius that are demarcated along ethnic lines,[8] with much scholarship singularly focused on either slavery or indentured labour. It is submitted that this approach is at least partially the result of the broadly separable "epochs" evident in the historical timeline of Mauritius. This research, however, aligns itself with scholarship which consciously seeks to counteract the trend of separate histories.[9]

3 Teelock, Vijaya, 'The Influence of Slavery in the Formation of Creole Identity', *Comparative Studies of South Asia, Africa and the Middle East*, 19 (1999), 3–8.
4 Truth and Justice Report, Volume I, p. 44. (full citation below).
5 Ibid., p. 17.
6 Ibid., p. 145.
7 It also has practical ramifications for the conduct historical research, discussed below at 1.3.
8 See for example Carter, Marina, and James Ng Foong Kwong, *Forging the Rainbow* (Mauritius, 1997); Teelock, Vijayalakshmi, *A Select Guide to Sources on Slavery in Mauritius, and the Testimony of Slaves in the Era of Sugar* (Bell Village: African Cultural Centre, 1995); and the Truth and Justice Report, Volume I, p. 82.
9 See 1.3 below for a full discussion.

1.1.4 Purpose

The research presented here seeks to transcend a conception of law as merely a body of rules which is to be evaluated solely by reference to its successful implementation. The desire is to demonstrate the constitutive power of the law in shaping society in a way that is not only responsive but also formative. The study is designed as a legal analysis, but given the historical setting there is necessarily a descriptive dimension, with exploratory aspects arising as a consequence of the under-researched nature of the subject. The purpose is not to present a comparative analysis of slavery and indentured labour (which, as explored in detail below, is considered an ill-conceived endeavour). Instead, both types of plantation labour are set into their legal contexts, with any comparative elements limited to general observations only.

1.1.5 Proposition

The intention of this work is to suspend the ethical judgements that inevitably arise from a superficial comparison between slavery and indentured labour and instead consider "desired" and "undesired" outcomes by examining the mechanics of these deeply legal regimes. The question here is: How did law create the labour markets and thus the emerging identities in 19th century Mauritius? The overarching argument advanced in this work is that Mauritian society emerged as a result of contradictions inherent in the British colonial endeavour which manifested as a series of contestations between various stakeholders. Slavery and indentured labour cannot be merely understood in the conventional historical view as separate political constructs, each born out of the economic necessities of their period. In this study both types of labour are understood as essentially legal relationships, which evolved with changing conditions. The research seeks to demonstrate that during the period of either system, the legal and political dimensions constantly interacted in a process whereby one continuously influenced and reshaped the other. As such, it is argued that the experience of indentured labour in Mauritius was very much the result of preceding experience of slavery. The successive labour systems did not simply supplant one another, but interconnected. Their effect on Mauritian society was not merely formative but in fact constitutive.

1.2 Theory and method of colonial research

1.2.1 Particularities of the Mauritian context

It is submitted that any discussion of colonialism in Mauritius must be acutely aware of the idiosyncrasies the island presents as a case study. Hereby, the observation that Mauritius does not possess an indigenous population is not merely a factual note, but presents a salient issue in understanding the setting in which colonization was carried out, and ultimately, how different segments of society came to relate to each other.

The particularities of the Mauritian context are illustrated by considering Jürgen Osterhammel's frequently quoted definition of colonialism:[10]

> **Colonialism** is a relationship of domination between an indigenous (or forcibly imported) majority and a minority of foreign invaders. The fundamental decisions affecting the lives of the colonized people are made and implemented by the colonial rulers in pursuit of interests that are often defined in a distant metropolis. Rejecting cultural compromises with the colonized population, the colonizers are convinced of their own superiority and of their ordained mandate to rule.

This definition throws up a number of questions in the context of Mauritius. During the French period, slaves were introduced, which would arguably fall into Osterhammel's classification of a "forcibly imported" majority, but the relationship cannot with certainty be so characterized during British occupation, when slavery was soon abolished and former slaves gained the status of "apprentices". The incongruence is even stronger in the case of indentured labourers, who despite the varied shortcomings in the recruitment process, were in legal terms contract workers and cannot collectively be described as "forcibly imported". And what of the unseated French colonist, who remained the ruling class? Given their continued influence post British capture, which was indeed the result of cultural compromises with the new colonists, their characterization as "the colonized" is hardly convincing.

How then should a relationship be described that involved domination of a people who were neither forcibly retained nor indigenous? It falls outside Osterhammel's definition of colonialism, and even though he identifies colonies without it, he limits that paradigm to societies which, lacking an indigenous population, were "homogenously 'white' ", namely "colonies of the 'New England' type."[11] Mauritius, of course, was no such colony.

It is evident that the colonial situation as it existed in Mauritius does not fall within the more common paradigms of European colonialism. Colonialism however is more than a "relationship" as defined by Osterhammel. More accurately, it is a system of various components. "And when we talk of the 'colonial system', we must be clear about what we mean. It is not an abstract mechanism. The system exists, it functions; the infernal cycle of colonialism is a reality. . . . For the colonist is fabricated like the native; he is made by his function and his interest", as observed by Jean-Paul Sartre.[12] What then, is the function and interest of the colonist? With the concern being primarily economic, the colony is regarded as a source of supply for the empire. The tandem of capitalist and colonial expansion

10 Osterhammel, Jürgen, *Colonialism: A Theoretical Overview*, trans. by Shelley L. Frisch (Princeton, NJ: Markus Wiener Publishers, 1997), pp. 16–17.

11 Osterhammel, op. cit., p. 17

12 Sartre, Jean-Paul, *Colonialism and Neocolonialism* (London; New York: Routledge, 2001), p. 44

caused this perception to become institutionalized, with "the colonizer and colonized locked into a rigid hierarchy of difference deeply resistant to fair and equitable exchanges, whether economic, cultural or social."[13]

This is indeed how the imported workers in Mauritius, irrespective of their legal status or ethnic origin, became fixed into the position of being "colonized": defined largely by their function to toil on the plantations, whether as field-hands or in the households, they were economically and socially beneath the "colonizers", meaning those who represented imperial interests, whether they were British administrators or French oligarchs. Thus, employing Sartre's terminology above, the Mauritian "native" was indeed "fabricated" by the colonial system. A very clear distinction between the "colonizers" and the "colonized" existed and was maintained. The decisive characteristic of the dynamic, as Osterhammel himself noted, is the notion of domination.[14] A binary concept central to imperialism like other binaries, it involves power being exercised by one side over the other.[15] Mauritius may have lacked a native people, but domination was most certainly a part of the colonial experience.

Mauritius as a nation is a "direct result of its colonial history, . . . having been entirely created by European colonisation", as Jean Houbert observed.[16] "In Mauritius, colonialism was not something which came from outside; it was built into the fabric of the whole society."[17] Mauritius was a colony constructed not through the subjugation of an indigenous population but through subordination of an imported one. Ethnic divisions underpinned the relations of capital and labour which drove the system designed for profit extraction, creating in the process a new society ex nihilo.

The case of Mauritius embodies in the truest sense the abused concept of "uninhabited territory". The idea exerted such a pull on the European imagination that elements of it can be traced in nearly every aspect of colonialism, and consequently also in the beginnings of an organized body of international law, the backing of which was employed to rationalize the colonial endeavour.[18] In the context of "land belonging to no-one", the term *terra nullius* has become fairly common, however it must be distinguished from the concept of *territorium nullius.*[19] The former, Andrew Fitzmaurice explains, signifies "a complete absence of

13 Ashcroft, Bill, Gareth Griffiths, and Helen Tiffin, *Post-Colonial Studies: The Key Concepts*, Routledge Key Guides (London: Routledge, 2000), p. 46, "Colonialism".

14 Osterhammel, op. cit., p. 17.

15 Other binaries include "white" and "black", or "civilized" and "primitive", see Ashcroft et al., op. cit., pp. 24–27.

16 Houbert, Jean, 'Mauritius: Independence and Dependence', *The Journal of Modern African Studies*, 19 (1981), 75–105, p. 75.

17 Ibid.

18 Dolin, Kieran, '"A Beautiful Fiction of Law": Rhetorical Engagements with Terra Nullius in the British Periodical Press in the 1840s', *Journal of Victorian Culture*, 18 (2013), 498–515, p. 498.

19 Fitzmaurice, Andrew, 'Liberalism and Empire in Nineteenth-Century International Law', *The American Historical Review*, 117 (2012), 122–40, pp. 131–132.

rights", whereas the latter "denied rights only of territorial sovereignty."[20] While neither term gathered much popularity in the either the 18th or 19th century,[21] the idea was used to dispossess indigenous populations of their land, creating a legal fiction which provided justification for European occupation. While its actual legal application has been limited to Australia and New Zealand, the symbolic power of *terra nullius* drove colonization in many regions, and arguably remains an undercurrent of modern globalization to this day.[22]

Whitney Bauman has highlighted the biblical foundations of the concept, viewing it as an "re-enactment of the Christian European beginning", since it builds on the view embedded in the civilizing mission that God created the world ex nihilo, and that "the Europeans were heirs to this knowledge, whether as divine law or natural law".[23] Part of the civilizing mission was also the perceived duty to cultivate lands, particularly where they were deemed under-utilized. The alleged absence of proper cultivation was used to weaken the claim natives had to their own territory. *Terra nullius* therefore provided "legal justification for re-creating the world in the European Christian image; that transcendent space of nothing, needing to be filled, created and made useful."[24] Bauman observes: "Of course the problem is that a country without any history of human inhabitants rarely (if ever) existed, much less a country without non-human inhabitants."[25] Pre-colonial Mauritius however, almost exactly fulfils that condition: a true and full expression of *terra nullius*, a fertile island awaiting cultivation.

The European colonizer in Mauritius thus fulfilled his directive, acquiring new territory and making it his own. But lacking an indigenous population to exploit or civilize, the colonizer had to create the colony from ground up, importing a "native" population so the colony could be managed "as if" they had always been there. How relevant, if at all, is this to the French colonists who were the first permanent residents?

The production of the Mauritian "native" was such as to enable the colonist to assume the role of "settler", because as Mahmood Mamdani points out, "you cannot have one without the other, for it is the relationship between them that makes one a settler and the other a native."[26] Since, however, both settler and native were themselves imports, this raises the important question: when does a settler become a native, and when do they remain a settler? Mamdani answers

20 Ibid.

21 Fitzmaurice, Andrew, 'The Genealogy of Terra Nullius', *Australian Historical Studies*, 38 (2007), 1–15.

22 Bauman, Whitney, *Theology, Creation, and Environmental Ethics: From Creatio Ex Nihilo to Terra Nullius* (New York: Routledge, 2009), p. 89.

23 Ibid.

24 NIbid., p. 94.

25 Bauman, op. cit., p. 97.

26 Mamdani, Mahmood. 'When Does a Settler Become a Native? Reflections of the Colonial Roots of Citizenship in Equatorial and South Africa', *Inaugural Lecture, University of Cape Town*, 13 May 1998, <https://citizenshiprightsafrica.org/wp-content/uploads/1998/05/mamdani-1998-inaugural-lecture.pdf> [accessed 26 June 2022].

that question by differentiating between civic and ethnic citizenship.[27] Whilst according to him, the former status can be acquired swiftly, depending solely on relevant legislation, the latter remains forever elusive. Ethnicity is that which accounts for the permanent division between settler and native, colonizer and colonized.

The dichotomy of civic and ethnic citizenship does not sit well in the context of Mauritius. The absence of an indigenous people disturbs the settler-native dynamics that Mamdani employs in his account, not because ethnicity was irrelevant (indeed, as is suggested in this work, it has become an enduring marker in Mauritian society), but because the relationship between settler and native in Mauritius was first and foremost a juridical and economic one – one conditioned by the importation of slaves and later indentured labourers.

It is clear, in that sense, that Mamdani's reasoning must be limited to the context of the more common paradigm which involves foreign settlers and indigenous populations. In the case of Mauritius, while the situation may have replicated the usual power balance, the "settler" was in fact no more foreign than the worker cast as a "native". By the same token, the "settler" was also no more "native" than the worker who accompanied him.

The above considerations are particularly relevant from an epistemological point of view and serve to reveal certain biases present in Mauritian historiography. It is not uncommon to encounter scholarship of the period in question wherein the French inhabitants are referred to as "Mauritians", to the exclusion of other racial groups.[28] This choice, while seemingly innocuous, is of serious consequence. The implication is one in which greater legitimacy is conferred upon one segment of society, which in the context of an originally uninhabited island populated solely through the process of colonization is profoundly difficult to sustain. Given that their arrival was more or less simultaneous, it is submitted that white inhabitants had no greater claim to ethnic citizenship than black inhabitants. To confer early Mauritian citizenship to the colonists at the exclusion of the slaves is to subscribe to the legitimacy of the colonial project which sought to appropriate uninhabited territory by divine right. While the fallacy of European claims may be more readily apparent in the case of a fictional *terra nullius*, in the instance of an actual *terra nullius* too, at least in the case of Mauritius, European claims to "nativeness" cannot be supported.

Sensitivity in this matter is required, for through the use of language, different images and messages are conveyed. Thus the choice may be to view the deserting field worker as a "maroon" menacing "Mauritian" plantation owners,[29] or he may be identified as a slave who escaped the conditions in which he was

27 Ibid.

28 Referring to black inhabitants, local historian Vijaya Teelock has used the term "Afro-Malagasy Mauritian", which is a more accurate, but rather cumbersome designation.

29 See the description in Allen, Richard B., *Creoles, Indian Immigrants and the Restructuring of Society and Economy in Mauritius, 1767–1885 (PhD Thesis)* (Ann Arbor, MI: University Microfilms International, 1987).

held and now seeks to reverse the power balance by engaging in law-breaking behaviour. This work seeks to be conscious of the use of language and imagery. As a consequence, the terminology of "slave-holding" is preferred as opposed to "slave-ownership", amongst other choices. The reference to "slaves" has been maintained for coherence with original source materials quoted, though the author fully recognizes the validity of some scholars preferring the term "the enslaved" in general discourse.

1.2.2 Theoretical basis

A study of the colonial context from a legal point view rapidly reveals a multitude of strata within the organization of an empire governed from a main metropolis. According to Lauren Benton and Richard Ross, empires were "invariably" legally plural, suggesting that these layered aspects were intrinsic to colonial governance.[30]

In the case of Mauritius, the concept of legal pluralism endures in a modern hybrid French-English legal system which owes its origins to the colonial period.[31]

Lauren Benton has researched the various manifestations of legal pluralism extensively, and while the work at hand is not concerned with the idea of legal pluralities as such, it employs one of Benton's conceptualizations to support its central argument. In an approach which moves the study of legal pluralism away from its traditional focus on the complexities or structure of legally pluralistic systems, Benton draws attention to broader issues by placing attention on what she describes as "jurisdictional tensions" or "jurisdictional conflicts".[32] The appeal of Benton's concept lies in its inclusiveness. Making no distinctions related to the sources of law, its ambit covers "clusters of conflicts" as they arose in the exercise of power.[33] "Jurisdiction" is hereby understood very broadly and does not differentiate between public or private types of authority. As a consequence, the notion of a "jurisdictional tension" is methodologically not limited to normative content, but permits wider historical investigation into structural shifts which occurred as a result of "legal strategies" employed by the "parties to jurisdictional conflicts".[34] According to Benton, these conflicts had

30 Benton, Lauren, and Richard J. Ross, 'Empires and Legal Pluralism: Jurisdiction, Sovereignty and Political Imagination in the Early Modern World', in *Legal Pluralism and Empires, 1500–1850*, ed. by Lauren Benton and Richard J. Ross (New York ; London: New York University Press, 2013), p. 1.

31 Discussed in Chapter 2.

32 Benton, Lauren, *Law and Colonial Cultures: Legal Regimes in World History, 1400–1900* (Cambridge; New York, NY: Cambridge University Press, 2001); Benton, Lauren, 'Historical Perspectives on Legal Pluralism', in *Legal Pluralism and Development: Scholars And Practitioners In Dialogue*, ed. by Brian Z. Tamanaha, Caroline Sage, and Michael Woolcock (Cambridge: Cambridge University Press, 2013); Benton and Ross, op. cit., pp. 5–6.

33 Benton and Ross, op. cit., p. 6.

34 Ibid.

the potential to powerfully influence both strategy and institution-building in the colonial setting.[35]

The absence of rigid classifications, whether in respect to the conflicts per se, or to those who may be party to them, makes the concept highly suitable to the subject matter of this research. As indicated in the previous section, this study suggests that Mauritian society emerged out of a series of contestations between various parties. These contestations may indeed be regarded as "jurisdictional conflicts", which were not only subject to the frequently contradictory aims of the British colonial project (manifesting jurisdictional tensions within itself), but involved parties so varied that their encounters, if to be studied in conjunction, must be framed broadly. The question of labour in 19th century Mauritius engaged many stakeholders. British involvement was not unified: more often than not, the metropolitan government took a view which was quite remote from, and even at odds with, the concerns of the local British administration, which found itself more aligned with the requirements of the resident French oligarchy. Slaves and indentured labourers were both the object of, and party to, these contestations. The arrival of the latter also brought a further stakeholder to the mix: the Indian government. It is clear that the application of a strict categorization of types of conflict or authority would not serve the research at hand. For these reasons, Benton's concept of jurisdictional conflicts is employed and built upon.

This study conceptualizes slavery and indentured labour as essentially legal relationships, the precise configuration of which is a significant part of the discussion contained in this study.

More fundamentally however, the research seeks to examine these labour relations to investigate the relationship between law and identities. The central hypothesis is that Mauritian society (meaning the various identities it contains), emerged out of the contestations around laws relating to labour. And it shares, in that sense, the same concern with the relationship between law and human identity that Samera Esmeir explores in her seminal work.[36] Studying the effect modern law had on colonial Egypt, Esmeir examines the processes which in turn, first dehumanized and then humanized colonial subjects, specifically peasant labourers during British occupation, endowing them with what she has termed "juridical humanity".[37]

This work does not directly utilize any of Esmeir's concepts, or seek to theorize the concept of "humanity" in the same way. Nevertheless, many of the queries she raises in the Egyptian colonial context are instructive and relevant for the Mauritian colonial context as considered in this research:

35 Benton, Lauren, 'Colonial Law and Cultural Difference: Jurisdictional Politics and the Formation of the Colonial State', *Comparative Studies in Society and History*, 41 (1999), 563–88, pp. 563–564.

36 Esmeir, Samera, *Juridical Humanity: A Colonial History* (Stanford: Stanford University Press, 2014).

37 Ibid.

> How was the concept of the human cemented in the legal processes of colonizing projects? . . . How does modern law make possible and activate the moment of decision over the human? . . . Could this decision, in attempting to mold a human that is always chained to the law, be part of a legal technology that functions to prevent revolution against the law and to assert state power?[38]

These questions, posed with reference to 19th century peasant labourers working on Egyptian cotton fields, are considered relevant to the conditions of 19th century indentured labourers toiling on Mauritian sugar-cane fields as well. As will be discussed in the subsequent chapters, the rules underpinning labour management on the island at the time configured not only the political economy, but also constructed identities through the distributive effects of law by fixing certain groups into particular roles.

1.2.3 Issues within existing scholarship

In this work, slavery and indentured labour are framed along their most basic common denominator in the Mauritian context, namely as sugar-plantation labour systems. In scholarly contributions on indentured labour, references to slavery are abundant. As a consequence, a level of comparison between the two systems is inevitable. A large part of scholarship falls into one of two "camps": one maintaining that indentured labour was "better" than slavery, the other that it was merely a "new type" of the same. Scholars who favour the former view tend focus on one particular dimension of those relationships to support their argument that indenture is not to be equalized with the slavery, such as for instance, the question of legal status. The discussion can then be brought to a swift close – for, of course, slaves were nominally chattel while indentured labourers were not. On the other hand, scholars who persist in arguing that indentured labour was a continuation of slavery will go to great lengths to establish the similarities found within the two systems, with instances of duress and deception in recruitment as well as similar living and working conditions commonly cited as examples.

To the extent that both these arguments appear equally plausible – that indentured labour was "better" because it did not involve the "ownership" of labour, and that it was "no better" because the conditions of exploitation were largely the same – is to frame the enquiry as a purely ethical or utilitarian one (good/bad, better/worse), which is not particularly enlightening and arguably draws attention away from the dynamics and contradictions that attended to each system of labour. By looking at these relations as essentially complex legal relationships, this work seeks to examine the distributive consequences of in both systems of labour, uncovering the logics and the mechanics that drove them. This is not to say that an ethical or evaluative analysis is entirely irrelevant. It tends however to block out more fine-grained analysis if taken as the starting point of the enquiry.

38 Ibid., pp. 1–3.

While the suggested approach is considered a more useful one, it requires awareness of the drawbacks an emphasis on law may potentially entail. Legality is frequently, at least in common parlance, conflated with legitimacy – a conflation sustained, in large part, in the language of law itself, when it draws upon notions of right or justice. Law and legitimacy, of course, are not covalent concepts, and it is quite feasible to understand that the enslavement of, and trade in, human beings was once upon a time sanctioned by law, whilst holding out the view that such acts were nevertheless reprehensible. Hindsight enables this, as does the idea that our contemporary "moral compass" is more mature, liberal or cosmopolitan than that of our forebears. A certain moral complexity thus attends to any evaluative examination of the practice of slavery, but it is one which can be scarcely avoided if only to prevent lapsing into the kind of apologetic or justificatory discourse that might be entailed were the practice to be examined in the light of the moral discourse of its own time. Contextualism, in other words, has its obvious limits.

What of the perpetual discussion around the concepts of free and "unfree" labour? Are they of any continued relevance? While the setting of this study is an Indian Ocean island in the 19th century, certain dynamics are being reproduced in the 21st century in places with high migration flows, and most notably so in the Gulf states, as examined in a separate publication.[39] Certainly, contemporary discussions on the working conditions of migrants often are redolent of references to slavery and forced labour, an occurrence which Cathryn Costello states cannot be outright dismissed as simply "political rhetoric".[40] Rather, she suggests the phenomenon of "vulnerability to forced labour" are persistent characteristics of immigration and labour market regimes.[41]

Emphatically rejecting a simple dichotomy of free and "unfree" labour, Costello asserts that the latter is a political, not a legal concept. Accordingly, she stipulates that the frequently perceived link between slavery and forced labour as "sub-sets"[42] of unfree labour may be inappropriate, given that the notions of "'forced labour,' 'servitude' and 'slavery' belong in the legal realm."[43] In the context of labour migration, Costello sees the process as creating two types of vulnerability in particular. As a costly undertaking, involving significant expenditure, migrants may be required to make a considerable investment to support their emigration. Additionally, in the process there are in-built "information

39 Boodia-Canoo, Nandini S., 'Researching Colonialism and Colonial Legacies from a Legal Perspective', *The Law Teacher*, 54 (2020), 517–546.

40 Costello, Cathryn, 'Migrants and Forced Labour: A Labour Law Response', in *Autonomy of Labour Law*, ed. by Alan L. Bogg et al. (Oxford; Portland, OR: Hart Publishing, 2015), p. 189.

41 Ibid.

42 As for example articulated by Strauss, Kendra, 'Coerced, Forced and Unfree Labour: Geographies of Exploitation in Contemporary Labour Markets', *Geography Compass*, 6 (2012), 137–48

43 Costello, op. cit., p. 199.

asymmetries", which may be exploited to create dependency as well as a level of uncertainty. According to Costello, "indebtedness, and misinformation about likely life-conditions and earnings can together lead to conditions of vulnerability to forced labour, in that exit options may be foreclosed."[44] As will be seen, these two aspects regarding debt and limited knowledge of local conditions were indeed highly relevant to the conditions in which indentured labourers found themselves in Mauritius in the 19th century. What makes a particular system of labour "unfree" is examined in Part II ("Indentured Labour") of this work, and while it cannot aspire to be a conclusive statement on the matter, it hopes to broaden the frequently theoretical discourse through analysis of concrete legal mechanisms and their effects.

1.2.4 Conceptualizations of law within social contexts

This work is at a cross-section of several disciplines, drawing on more fields than may be assumed at first glance. Initially conceived as a project combining law and history by virtue of the colonial context, the research's emphasis on law's effect on society requires attention also to be given to sociological theories. Further, the focus on labour relations demands that economic issues be brought into the equation. As a consequence, this research, far from presenting merely a legal history, is concerned with the economic sociology of law.

The field is a well-established one. Sabine Frerichs identifies three generations of socio-legal thought, clarifying the various conceptualizations of Law which may arise when it is placed in relation to other disciplines.[45] Frerichs observes that the idea of "Law and Society", frequently applied as an all-encompassing label for scholarship on this subject, is in fact "misleading", for it already assumes the two to be separate.[46] Underpinning her identification of three generations within sociological legal theory is her classification of three approaches, which she condenses into the following headings: "Law in . . .", "Law and . . ." and "Law as . . .".

The first generation was, according to Frerichs, concerned with "law in society", and characterized by a generally historical approach wherein law was predominantly conceived as an integral part of society.[47] Scholars such as Emile Durkheim, Karl Marx and Max Weber dominate this era. Most relevant to this research is the work of Karl Polanyi, who in his seminal contribution expounded upon the idea of "embeddedness", which is discussed in more detail below.[48] Frerichs deems the second generation, the "law and society" approach, as realist,

44 Ibid., p. 208.

45 Frerichs, Sabine, ***Studying Law, Economy, and Society: A Short History of Socio-Legal Thinking*** (Rochester, NY: Social Science Research Network, 2012) <http://papers.ssrn.com/abstract=2022891> [accessed 26 June 2022].

46 Ibid., p. 16.

47 Ibid., p. 17.

48 Polanyi, Karl, *The Great Transformation: The Political and Economic Origins of Our Time* (Boston, MA: Beacon Press, 2001).

influenced primarily by positivism, wherein sociology and jurisprudence are studied with emphasis on how the two areas relate to each other. At the forefront here is Richard Posner's work, in the specific area of law and economics.[49] Lastly, Frerichs regards the third generation of scholars as constructivist, falling under the "law as" heading, for whom the "question is . . . not what law really is – if it is embedded or autonomous – but how it is conceived and performed".[50]

This development towards a more constructivist approach in socio-legal thought has also been observed by other commentators. According to Roger Cotterell, progressive legal scholars have been become less concerned with the traditional perspective which queries how society produces law and instead ask how law produces society.[51] This work finds itself falling into this category – for how colonial laws have shaped Mauritian society is indeed the overarching theme of this study. The question arises whether such research is sociological or legal. Cotterell observes that the field of socio-legal studies lacks clear demarcation, being not a definite sub-set of either discipline. However, he believes this ought not to be regarded as a shortcoming of the field, for "disciplinary boundaries should be viewed pragmatically; indeed with healthy suspicion. They should not be prisons of understanding."[52] According to Cotterell the issue is not whether socio-legal scholarship is valuable, but rather, what the benefits of such inquiries are, specifically for lawyers and others involved in legal processes.

Cotterell provides three "postulates" for a sociological interpretation in the legal context:[53] firstly, law is to be regarded as "an entirely *social* phenomenon", in the sense that it gives expression to social relationships. Secondly, that understanding must be underpinned *empirically*, that is, through an examination of "historical patterns". Finally, the assessment must be *systematic*, as opposed to anecdotal, for the aim is to draw broader conclusions from the specificities of a study. The work at hand follows this approach in method, if not by design. The subject of this research inevitably requires an analysis of trends in the colonization of Mauritius, satisfying Cotterell's second postulate. The first one is a given for any inquiry that ventures to assess law's impact on society. The third postulate finds expression in the final chapter of this work.

1.2.5 Law: separate from or intertwined with politics?

The tendency to perceive law and politics as a single, unified system is an old one, and according to Niklas Luhmann, largely the result of the concept of the

49 See for example Posner, Richard A., and Francesco Parisi, eds., *Law and Economics* (Cheltenham: Edward Elgar, 1997).

50 Frerichs, op. cit., p. 18.

51 Cotterell, Roger, 'Why Must Legal Ideas Be Interpreted Sociologically?', *Journal of Law and Society*, 25 (1998), 171–92.

52 Ibid., p. 177.

53 Ibid., p. 183.

state, which is simultaneously a legal and political entity.[54] He makes, however, an interesting argument for keeping the two systems separate. Drawing on a concept borrowed from the natural sciences, autopoiesis,[55] he conceives of the legal system as one which "is able to draw a distinction between itself and other functioning systems."[56] The operative element in his theory is indeed that of function, which, in the instance of law and politics, must be differentiated. He does not negate the strong causal connection between the two, but rather asserts that precisely in order to find these causal links, distinctions between the two must be drawn. Luhmann states thus that "the hypothesis of the separation of the system provides a better explanation for the finding that systems are dependent on each other in their . . . structural development."[57]

Luhman's conceptualization not only enables one to highlight the interdependence of the systems, but also to notice the frequently unanticipated and possibly unintended outcomes from political decisions and legal rules. Since the aim of this research is to investigate the mechanics of the law relating to 19th century plantation labour and thus trace certain patterns of cause and effect, a certain provisional demarcation between the legal and political fields is necessary, even if, on another analysis, both may be found to be saturated with the other. This, above all else, allows one to conceptualize law as a political stratagem.

As will be seen, law was frequently used by the British administration, whether locally in Mauritius or as directed from London, as a tactic to achieve certain ends. Such an approach to governance and law-making has been theorized by Michel Foucault in his seminal lecture on "Governmentality". There, Foucault draws on the definitions of La Perrière and frames the idea of government as the "right manner of disposing things so as to lead not to the form of the common good, . . . but to an end which is 'convenient' for each of the things that are to be governed."[58] He states that there are a number of specific aims to be achieved, which he refers to as "finalities", meaning the objectives of government. According to Foucault, in order to achieve these objectives, the exercise of sovereignty is inseparably linked to law. Hereby, "it is a question not of imposing law on men, but of disposing things: that is to say, of employing tactics rather than laws, and even of using laws themselves as tactics – to arrange things in such a way that, through a certain number of means, such and such ends may be achieved", and therefore "the instruments of government, instead of being laws, now come

54 Luhmann, Niklas, *Law as a Social System*, ed. by Fatima Kastner et al., trans. by Klaus Ziegert (Oxford; New York: Oxford University Press, 2004), p. 357.

55 Autopoiesis refers to a system that is closed and self-maintaining, see Maturana, Humbert R., and Francisco J. Varela, *Autopoiesis and Cognition: The Realization of the Living* (Dordrecht; Boston, MA: D. Reidel Publishing Company, 1980).

56 Luhmann, op. cit., p. 357.

57 Ibid., p. 368.

58 Foucault, Michel, 'Governmentality', in *The Foucault Effect: Studies in Governmentality*, ed. by Graham Burchell, Colin Gordon and Peter Miller (Chicago: The University of Chicago Press, 1991), 87–104, p. 95.

to be a range of multiform tactics." The idea of laws as tactics finds particular application in this work, on both a metropolitan level and local level. It is argued that the abolition of the slave trade and slavery had served multiple aims across the empire, while at the same time their local implementation was yet subject to another set of considerations. In Mauritius, these were more often than not of an economic nature, with profound effects for the development of society. This echoes Karl Polanyi's concept of "embeddedness". With economic considerations being imperative to the existence of society, he argues: "Instead of the economy being embedded in social relations, social relations are embedded in the economic system."[59]

The underlying supposition of this study is that law is both embedded as well as relatively autonomous, and may therefore be examined as such. This is exemplified by an analysis of the effects of the law, which, as will be seen in the subsequent chapters, had both intended as well as unintended consequences. The latter can only be perceived if the relative autonomy of law is taken as a starting point. Thus, Luhmann's theory of perceiving politics and law as separate in order to highlight their causal effects is very much applicable, while at the same time Polanyi's postulate that a society is inextricably linked to its economic system also finds validation.

1.2.6 Theories of labour law

This work does not address general labour law concerns as such, but is concerned with the legal regulation of labour as it was conceived when "free" labour was to replace slavery in a political economy. As such, the scope includes both economic considerations as well as the personal conditions of the workers, whether slaves or labourers. Since the period at hand effectively marks the introduction of labour laws in Mauritius, a brief consideration of the theories underlying the area is provided.

Contemporary attention to labour law is directed at a wide range of issues, such as wages, working time, discrimination and trade union membership. However, it is the perspective one assumes which fundamentally affects the how challenges in this area are theorized. Two angles appear to be pervasive: human rights on the one side, and political economy on the other.[60] Within the framework of the former, the focus largely falls upon the relationship between local labour regulation and the international legal environment, such as the binding directives issued by the EU or statements by the International Labour Organization, in which considerations as to the competitive undercutting of labour standards are brought to the fore.

59 Polanyi, op. cit., p. 60.

60 See for example Davies, A. C. L., *Perspectives on Labour Law*, 2nd Edition (Cambridge: Cambridge University Press, 2009).

In the context of the latter, labour law is examined from the perspective of its distributional effects within a national political economy. Kerry Rittich, for example, conceives labour and employment law as constituting, in their most basic form, a social contract, reflective of the political visions of the day, and notes that they are effectively the mechanism by which resources are distributed and the benefits and costs of economic activity shared by society.[61] Her concern with the distributional consequences of economic arrangements is shared by Duncan Kennedy who has provided an insightful analysis on the distributive function of law in the context of creating, or re-creating, social injustice.[62] Contrasting a realist analysis of the capitalist system with the traditional economic point of view, Kennedy states that the notion of "freedom" has no part the in the realist's interpretation of the agreement between capital and labour. While the idea of freedom (whether in relation to markets, labour or contract) has often been employed as a justification for the capitalist system, according to Kennedy, realists hold the view that "capitalism was as coercive in its way as socialism."[63]

Importantly, the coercion paradigm illuminates the role of law. As Kennedy explains, the state becomes implicated in the distribution of income simply by its use of force to assure compliance to the bargain agreement, even though that agreement might have been entered into "freely" by the parties.[64] Legislatures and judges establish the "ground rules", meaning the legal framework, within which labour relations take place. Drawing on Robert Hale's theory on the distribution of wealth and power, Kennedy states that these ground rules play a significant "causal" role, contrary to standard Marxist analysis (in which the law was frequently regarded as "superstructural").[65] The reason why the distributional effects of law are largely invisible is, according to Kennedy, because ground rules of permission are generally not perceived as such, unlike those of clear prohibition. However, these are not omissions in the law, but "conscious decisions" by legislators. Commonly "when lawmakers do nothing, they appear to have nothing to do with the outcome", yet it is also possible to conceive of "inaction" as being the consequence of "a policy", and legal rules to have active effect, in the sense that they always could prohibit the conduct in question.[66]

Kennedy's attention to the distributive effects of the law, whether as a consequence of permission or prohibition, is particularly relevant to the current

61 Rittich, Kerry, 'Between Workers' Rights and Flexibility: Labor Law in an Uncertain World', *Saint Louis University Law Journal*, 54 (2010), 565, p. 565.

62 Kennedy, Duncan, 'The Stakes of Law, or Hale and Foucault!', *Legal Studies Forum*, XV (1991), 327.

63 Ibid., p. 328. In this assessment, Kennedy draws on arguments articulated by Warren Samuels, see Samuels, Warren J., 'Adam Smith and the Economy as a System of Power', *Review of Social Economy*, 31 (1973), 123–37.

64 Kennedy, ibid., p. 329.

65 Ibid., p. 332.

66 Ibid., p. 334. Kennedy draws on the idea of legal permissions as expounded by Wesley Hohfeld in Hohfeld, Wesley, 'Fundamental Legal Conceptions as Applied in Judicial Reasoning', *Yale Law Journal*, 710 (1917).

research in respect of the analysis of the effects of each labour system. It is argued throughout that the legal arrangements prevailing within each labour system, not only distributed property (including, most visibly, what "counted" as property), but also had distributional effects in terms of what kinds of activities they enabled or closed down. They created (or distributed) not only rights, duties, privileges or immunities, but also incentives and inducements that were to give each regime a certain dynamic. For example, the respective options made available to former slaves and indentured labourers, specifically in terms of access to property, placed each group on a definite trajectory in terms of their place within the political economy of the island.

One qualification here should be noted. As Kennedy himself observes, the main objection to the pervasiveness of the distributive effects of law is that it may arguably overstate how much law may be seen to influence social behaviour. He states, however, that a distinction should be maintained between plain ineffectual enforcement on the one hand, and actual permission on the other hand, a distinction which may be easily overlooked when noncompliance is discussed. Furthermore, Kennedy notes that social norms may also play a role in distribution, and it may be argued that it is these norms which most greatly effect distribution. In this context, judicial and legislative law-making must also be differentiated.[67] Whilst taking these objections into account, the distributive paradigm provides a useful starting point for assessing the impact of slavery and indentured labour in the subsequent formation of social strata in Mauritius as this work, it is hoped, will illustrate.

1.2.7 Characterizations of labour

In the context of labour law, Mark Freedland and Nicola Kountouris define "legal construction" as "the whole process of ascribing legal form and structure to personal work relations", which includes determining the applicability of legal, or legally recognized, norms.[68] A significant part of this process is, they aver, the classification (or taxonomy) of personal work relations, which is carried out to ascertain the particular applicability of a set of norms to a particular personal work relation. This aspect is not a self-contained element within the process, but according to Freedland and Kountouris, "part of a very complex activity which we identify as the 'legal characterization' of personal work relations."[69] Legal characterization, according to them, is the combination of taxonomy with regulation, which is the pronouncement of certain norms as applicable to a particular work relation. As a consequence, the scholars point out, legal characterization

67 Kennedy, ibid., p. 345.

68 Freedland, Mark, and Nicola Kountouris, 'The Legal Characterization of Personal Work Relations and the Idea of Labour Law', in *The Idea of Labour Law*, ed. by Guy Davidov and Brian Langille (Oxford; New York: Oxford University Press, 2011), 190–208, p. 192.

69 Ibid.

demonstrates how closely "legal categories of personal work are bound up with particular sets of norms in particular legal systems at particular moments in time", and that " 'legal characterization' depicts an activity which is very contingent upon the particular legal and practical context in which it takes place, and very dependent on the path by which that context was created."[70] Freedland and Kountouris state that legal characterization may be descriptive or prescriptive, with the former being concerned with pure application of norms and the latter with fundamental re-classification and re-regulation. Depending on the role of the legal actor in question, there may be a tendency to choose a single mode, such as judges predominantly choosing the descriptive mode and legislators frequently, though not exclusively, operating in the prescriptive one. For theorists and policy makers, the scholars observe, the choice may be difficult, and they suggest a combination of the two, using descriptive mode for analysis and in prescriptive mode, offer conscious criticism.[71]

For this study, these definitions of the legal characterization of personal work relationships offer interesting guidance. Slavery, as explored in detail in Part I, is not usually conceptualized as a work relationship, but in historical discourses commonly regarded as a system of oppression, integral to early colonialism, which itself has been conceptualized as a scheme of domination. Characterizing slavery as a system of plantation labour, as proposed here, is a re-classification which allows for critical analysis of the relationship between plantation owners and their workers, and the effect of that relationship not only in the context of the contemporary economy, but also in shaping the emerging multi-ethnic society. This re-classification of also places slavery within the same framework of analysis as that of indentured labour, and thus helps to bring out and elucidate the commonalities of both systems, not simply at the superficial level of working conditions, but more fundamentally as the structures upon which Mauritian society was erected.

A brief example might suffice here. A major issue in the way in which indentured labour operated in Mauritius was through the commodification of labour, the negation of which is the principal tenet behind the idea of labour law.[72] Polanyi argues against the idea that labour is a commodity, stating that to describe it as such, as with land or money, is "entirely fictitious", while also stating that it is this fiction which enables the market economy to operate.[73] But is it labour which is bought on and sold? Karl Marx elucidates this point when discussing the "price" of labour. The price is of course the wages, defined by Marx as "the sum of money paid by the capitalist for a particular labour time or for a particular output of labour."[74] He stipulates however that the transaction merely appears to

70 Ibid., p. 193.

71 Ibid., p. 194.

72 Dukes, Ruth, 'Hugo Sinzheimer and the Constitutional Function of Labour Law', in *The Idea of Labour Law*, ed. by Guy Davidov and Brian Langille (Oxford; New York: Oxford University Press, 2011), 57–68, p. 64.

73 Polanyi, op. cit., p. 76.

74 Marx, Karl, 'Wage Labour and Capital', in *Wage Labour and Capital & Wages, Price and Profit* (Revolutionary Classics; London: Bookmarks, 1996), p. 23.

be a sale of labour, and asserts that it is in fact the "labour power" that is being sold. Marx explains that it is the labour power which is equivalent to any other commodity, and may be substituted for such. Hereby, the labour power is the worker's commodity, which is exchanged for another commodity, namely money. However, within that framework, labour power understood in terms of "labour time" was not that which was commodified in the case of slaves – rather it was the slaves themselves who were the commodity, unlike the free labourer who sells the "hours of his life".[75] The shift from slavery to indentured labour, can thus be analyzed through an examination of the extent to which there is a transformation in the character of the "commodity" being exchanged – whether, for example, the system of indentured labour could be understood as one concerned with the exchange of labour time as opposed to the body of the labourer.

In the case of Mauritius, it is submitted, such a transition is not discernible. Indentured labour continued to be redolent of slavery precisely because workers continued to be treated as expendable commodities. This, it is argued in the work, is partially the result of the island's geographical proximity to India and Africa, providing an endless reservoir of workers during the periods of indentured labour and slavery respectively, the availability of which incidentally also acted as a brake upon amelioration policies of any kind.

1.2.8 The interplay of disciplines: law and history

Legal colonial research throws up a number of theoretical and methodological challenges, which are linked to the interplay of the disciplines involved. These have been discussed in detail and published elsewhere,[76] though certain points bear mentioning here.

Drawing on historical evidence is necessarily a constructive activity; the material is transformed into a coherent narrative with the intent to support the argument being advanced.[77] An author's predispositions, themselves the result of culture, background and circumstances, cannot be discounted, for they inevitably colour both the account and the analysis thereof.

A compounding factor is the Eurocentric emphasis in Western historiography, which not only assumes European superiority but renders it normative.[78]

It is submitted that awareness of these influences as well as contextualization are essential to a rigorous scholarly discourse on colonialism.

75 Ibid., p. 26.

76 Boodia-Canoo, Nandini S., op. cit.

77 Rigney, Ann, 'History as Text: Narrative Theory and History', in *The SAGE Handbook of Historical Theory*, ed. by Nancy Partner and Sarah R. I. Foot (Los Angeles: SAGE Publications Ltd, 2013), p. 190.

78 See Blaut, James M., *The Colonizer's Model of the World: Geographical Diffusionism and Eurocentric History* (New York; London: Guilford Press, 1993); and Ashcroft, Bill, Gareth Griffiths, and Helen Tiffin, *Post-Colonial Studies: The Key Concepts*, Routledge Key Guides (London: Routledge, 2000), p. 90.

Christopher Tomlins suggests that contextualist historiography does not present the best approach in illuminating our understanding of law, since "the contemplated object is not enlivened by the relationalities within which it allegedly belongs, the relationalities of its time, but by the fold of time that creates it in constellation with the present, the moment of recognition."[79] Thus, according to Tomlins, it is the present, rather than the past, which adds to the actual understanding of historical phenomena. Tomlins highlights, here, historicism's links to teleology, arguing that by fixing events and objects in the setting they occurred, their meaning becomes entirely dependent upon it, making their significance changeable according to context, thus rendering historicism "an antifoundational philosophy of history."[80]

Whilst Tomlins' critique of contextual history is helpful insofar as it liberates the scholar from an injunction to remain, at all moments, in the past, it is a critique which arguably goes further than it needs. The current project, it is admitted, takes as its starting point an enquiry that is animated by a contemporary field of reference (informed by an underlying ethical and political critique of colonialism), but in practice, its concern is not to impute to the agents and actors within the account a contemporary sensibility, but understand them in their own terms, by reference to the currents of thought pervading at the time. A further point to observe here is that the main danger may not be that of projecting the present on the past, but of an inability to shake off a past that may be seen to envelop the present. Indeed, it is the intuition that the past continues to structure and shape contemporary Mauritian society that is the main concern of this work.

In a broad appraisal of colonial discourse theory, David Washbrook draws on Aijaz Ahmad's work, who claims that critics of colonialism are in fact the main beneficiaries, and points out that most such theorists are residing in the West and not (or no longer) in the former colony.[81] Their motivation and portrayal of victimization is thus, he claims, linked to the political agenda of the West. This assessment may be correct to some extent, but it does not render the critique futile. It is submitted that the ability to observe and make value judgements requires a certain level of detachment, as well as exposure to differing circumstances, which act as contrast and by reference to which new conceptions are formed. Further, the ability to make such judgement, and more importantly, to vocalize it and have it heard, represents a privilege that is accorded by time and place. While a level of elitism is no doubt present, it does not render a discourse inherently illegitimate.

79 Tomlins, Christopher, 'Historicism and Materiality in Legal Theory', in *Law in Theory and History: New Essays on a Neglected Dialogue*, ed. by Maksymilian Del Mar and Michael Lobban (Oxford: Hart Publishing, 2019), p. 59.

80 Tomlins, op. cit., p. 60.

81 Washbrook, D. A., 'Orients and Occidents: Colonial Discourse Theory and the Historiography of the British Empire', in *The Oxford history of the British Empire*, ed. by Robin W. Winks and Alaine M. Low, *The Oxford History of the British Empire, Volume 5: Historiography* (Oxford; New York: Oxford University Press, 2001), citing Ahmad, Aijaz, *In Theory: Nations, Classes, Literatures* (London ; New York: Verso, 2008).

Washbrook's assessment of colonial discourse critique is provoking, but falls foul of the very issues he highlights. He bemoans the common image of colonizers as reduced to "almost to the point of caricature, . . . representatives of the manly, the civilized and the white."[82] (In making that claim, he cites exclusively the work of well-known feminist scholars: Antoinette Burton, Anne McClintock and Mrinalini Sinha.) But in his own objections towards this school of thought, Washbrook draws an even more peculiar caricature: that of the colonizer as an impressionable foreigner who merely learns about power relations from the locals. He makes the following observation:

> Colonial rule was often thinly stretched and could scarcely have sustained itself without the "collaboration" of local power structures, whose relations of conflict and domination became incorporated into its own constructs. Again, such incorporation certainly reconfigured such structures. But it hardly reconstituted them entirely anew . . . The power relations of colonialism were inextricably bound up with the power relations between colonial subjects themselves.[83]

The "collaboration" of the colonized is an important element in the discourse on colonialism, and will be revisited in subsequent chapters. But as a general argument, it fails to address the question of how settlers exploited local power systems to their own advantage. The role played by colonizers themselves is minimized, who in Washbrook's paradigm are portrayed as merely perpetuating the status quo, rendering them essentially blameless.

This idea is thrown into sharp relief particularly in the context of Mauritius, which, when Britain took over, was populated by imported slaves and the previous colonists. The only cooperation that took place was extended from the British to the French, despite the latter being in the minority, because it was the only association that was perceived to yield benefits to the new colonists. The precise nature of that relationship and how it evolved will be discussed in detail in the main body of this work, but it should be noted here that while colonial critique may be steeped in clichés, in dismantling those, arguments with apologist overtones should be avoided.

1.3 Colonial legacies and contemporary concerns

1.3.1 When past and present meet

Primary research has been predominantly carried out in London. In Mauritius, various access issues were encountered which however have not proved an obstacle for the current research as nearly all relevant documents are also held

82 Washbrook, op. cit., p. 599 (footnote omitted).
83 Ibid., p. 604.

in at the Public Records Office, including correspondences, Blue Books,[84] and the Protector of Slaves Reports. Similarly, for the research on Indian indentured labour, research has been carried out at the British Library, which now houses the India Office Reports as well as many manuscripts formerly held at the British Museum.

The Mauritius National Archives were consulted, but were found difficult to navigate, not least because of the absence of a searchable catalogue onsite. The Mauritius Archives are in the process of being digitalized, but the process has proved slow. Explorative research appears to be discouraged, since retrieval of documents is only by way of specified request. This may be due to preservation issues, which other scholars have commented upon.[85]

The Mahatma Gandhi Institute (MGI) in Mauritius houses relevant records to Indian immigration to the island, however here too, documents are not directly searchable. Like the National Archives of Mauritius, a digitization process has been underway for years, but is not yet accessible, even upon request. There are certain administrative constraints to access the "Indian Immigrants Archive" section at the MGI which the Truth and Justice Commission has deemed "political".[86] For individually identifiable data, one needs permission from a descendant of the immigrant one wishes to investigate, which in practice limits possible enquiries to persons of the relevant heritage, and only by reference to their own ancestor.[87]

The Truth and Justice Commission has called this requirement for permission "ridiculous", for it calculates that from the nearly half-million immigrants who arrived from India, roughly a third returned without settling, while another third did not survive the indenture experience, thus not leaving descendants.[88] If these estimates are correct, and the MGI's policy does not change, the personal history of the majority of Indian immigrants will remained locked away and fall into neglect. While the frustration as articulated by the Truth and Justice Commission is understandable, the MGI's stance is based on relevant concerns that cannot be easily dismissed.

During a visit, staff at the MGI explained to the author of this work the private nature of the data available, which includes information such as caste and occupation of the arriving immigrants. As set out above, race consciousness is an important part of identity construction in Mauritius. On a further level, within the Indian diaspora, this extends to caste. Chapter 5 discusses how "loss of caste"

84 "Blue Books" are essentially reports containing data relevant to local colonial management.
85 See Teelock's research guide, op. cit.
86 Truth and Justice Commission Report, Volume I, p. 154. For the purposes of the report, the MGI provided samples of depersonalized data to aid the research.
87 The process is complex, for the records are not searchable by name, but by an immigrant arrival number only. This necessitates the researcher to know the full name of the original immigrant (through tracing of family trees, unless known) and to obtain the arrival number by enquiry at the Civil Status Office in the capital Port Louis.
88 Truth and Justice Commission Report, Volume I, p. 154.

was often part of the process of emigrating, and it would not be unusual for this to become officialized in the records, whether by purposeful misstatement of the immigrant or as the result of administrative errors.

Staff at the MGI stated that descendants frequently express disappointment, even rage, at the outcome of their research if the data shows their ancestor of a different caste or background than expected. As a result, staff have experienced intimidation from enquirers, and on several occasions the Institute has even been accused of falsification of records, an accusation reportedly even perpetuated by the local media.

There is thus an element of privacy for descendants which requires sensitive handling. As noted before, Mauritians are not entirely accepting of all the possible aspects of their heritage. It is to be hoped that at some point Mauritians may be more comfortable with their personal histories, which will not only allow their common history to be acknowledged, but also their common identity to be embraced.

1.3.2 Challenging paradigms

The lack of a native people in Mauritius presents a variation on the more common colonial paradigm in which settlers graft a community on top of an indigenous population. The development from a created plantation society, inhabited by colonists and their imported workforce, to modern multi-ethnic state invites detailed analysis, not at least because colonial history remains evident in every aspect of Mauritian life.

Despite Mauritius' advances as a largely industrialized and politically stable country, the island's inhabitants continue to experience the legacy of their colonial past strongly and are, consciously or not, even repeating certain colonial patterns. Social migration and economic diversification notwithstanding, the white minority still exerts a disproportionate amount of influence in the private sector, with the black population largely continuing to suffer manifest disadvantage in terms of progress and opportunities. The Indo-Mauritian experience has been overall on a more upward trajectory, but nevertheless represents an arduous journey. As can be inferred, the issue of "race" remains an important one because of an informal segregation that is evident in Mauritian society, politics and economy.

This work examines the role law played in influencing Mauritian society. The main matter of concern is the social effect of law, as initially introduced and developed during the colonial period. Carlo Ginzburg argues that the relevance of microhistory is intrinsic to the object of study and therefore provides "an opportunity to subvert pre-existing hierarchies".[89] Achieving a subversion of canonical Mauritian history is certainly among the aims of this work.

89 Ginzburg, Carlo, 'Our Words, and Theirs – A Reflection on the Historian's Craft, Today', in *Historical Knowledge: In Quest of Theory, Method and Evidence*, ed. by Susanna Fellman and Marjatta Rahikainen (Newcastle upon Tyne: Cambridge Scholars Publishing, 2012), p. 115

1.3.3 The Truth and Justice Commission

In November 2011, a Truth and Justice Commission (TJC) that had been established to enquire into the legacies of slavery and indentured labour submitted its final report.[90] Constituted in March 2009, subsequent to the Mauritian Truth and Justice Act 2008, the Commission understood its mandate as an investigation of "the continuities in history up to the present", specifically "from an economic and social perspective" and with a particular focus on issues relating to "colonialism, slave trade, slavery and indenture".[91]

Alexander Boraine, who took over as chairman of the Commission in 2010, stated in an interview that what distinguished the Mauritian TJC from other commissions was the remoteness in time of the issues under scrutiny. According to him, "many would argue that there is no absolute tie between slavery and indentured labour and the situation today, but others say there is. So what we are doing is researching that."[92] Boraine appeared to discount the possibility of assigning blame, either to the descendants of slave-owners or the current government, for the events of the past. Instead, he saw the Commission as an instrument to question policy. His professed aim was "to hold a mirror to the Mauritian society".[93]

The author of this work similarly does not favour seeking to attribute blame for the past, which in the Mauritian context is considered inappropriate. This shared epistemological standpoint notwithstanding, it is submitted that the lack of rigour in seeking to clearly identify, where possible, root causes of certain inequalities, is problematic. The document largely reads as a reiteration of the situation as it is today. The findings recognize the disproportionate disadvantage suffered by Afro-Malagasy Mauritians, the concentrated influence of Franco-Mauritians in the private sector and the broad success enjoyed by Indo-Mauritians in forming a large swath of the middle-class. Yet the links to the colonial period, or indeed to the post-independence developments as identified by the TJC, are weak, and as a consequence perpetuate stereotypes which are partly responsible for the organization of modern social strata.

For instance, in its Executive Summary, under the rubric "Indentured Labour" the TJC's report states: "To the credit of the Indian immigrants and later on their descendants is the faith which they had in the promotion of their children through education. Education was and continues to be the priority. The

90 *Report of the Truth and Justice Commission* (Mauritius, November 2011), Volume I (primary submissions) <www.usip.org/sites/default/files/ROL/TJC_Vol1.pdf> [accessed 3 June 2015].

91 Ibid., p. 1.

92 Boudet, Catherine, 'Alex Boraine: "For Many, Mauritius Is Still Undemocratic and Racist"', *Analyse Sociopolitique de L'île Maurice*, 2010. <https://catherineboudet.wordpress.com/2010/07/02/alex-boraine-for-many-mauritius-is-still-undemocratic-and-racist-2/> [accessed 26 June 2022].

93 Ibid.

privileged position held by people of Indian origin in government institutions is due to investment made in higher education for their children."[94]

This statement raises more questions than the one it purports to answer. How the development is "to the credit" to those of Indian origin is not clear. Is it to the "discredit" of the other groups of society, that a similar achievement for their posterity has not been attained? Did they not have an equal "faith" in education? Were they not able to make a likewise investment for their children? If so, why?

In the same section, under "Economy", the TJC provides the following list of reasons for why certain inequalities have endured: "Land speculation, poverty, greed of some family members, the corruption of officials and professionals, an ever-encroaching sugar industry and laws that protect the traditional economic structure".[95] Who are these "family members", "officials" and "professionals"? Broad and emotive concepts such as "poverty", "greed" and "corruption" require explanation and rational dissection, however these findings are not clearly identifiable in the main submissions and it is only upon closer inspection of the supporting materials that the context of these claims can be deduced.[96]

It is submitted that Professor Boraine and his fellow commissioners succeeded in precisely their aim noted above: the production of a mirror. The report does reflect the face of Mauritian society, with all its prejudices and inequalities. Unfortunately, it fails to provide convincing answers as to why Mauritian society was to emerge and remain so divided both economically and politically, and why ethnicity, or origin, appears to remain so fundamental as an explanatory trope.

The work at hand cannot hope to remedy this gap entirely, focused as it is specifically on the issue of labour during the 19th century, and not covering in any detail the issues which have arisen since then. This research does however aim to provide some insights, through its investigation of how Mauritian society was assembled, as to the mechanics by which social segregation was established and maintained in the early years, and from which one might speculate as to what kind of social and legal change was needed for it to be unravelled. The detailed findings of the TJC report are hereby given due consideration and are discussed in Chapter 7.

1.3.4 Chapter summaries

Chapter 2 provides the historical backdrop of the work, situating the events of the 19th century which form the main timeframe for the subjects considered in this research in their wider context by tracing the history of Mauritius from its discovery to recent events of the 21st century. It presents a detailed legal history

94 TJC Report, Volume I, op. cit., p. 3.

95 Ibid., p. 4.

96 The report consists of six volumes. Unfortunately, the TJC does not have its own dedicated website, but has made Volume I available through a webpage of the United States Institute of Peace, see the link provided above. Volumes 2 to 4 have been made available through the Research Gate website at <www.researchgate.net>. Volumes 5 and 6 which contain database materials and oral testimonies are not available.

of the island unique in breadth and depth. Starting with theories related to the island's first sighting and the initial claim of the Portuguese, the chapter provides an appraisal of the Dutch attempts at occupation before addressing the period of French colonization. Since British colonization of Mauritius is the main subject of this work, this section does not discuss that era in detail, but introduces the overarching themes which are relevant to the analysis contained in subsequent chapters, particularly the position of Mauritius in the wider British Empire and the role of the sugar industry in the 19th century. The chapter concludes with an overview of certain developments which form part of the legal history of Mauritius in the 20th and 21st century.

Since the research is principally concerned with two labour systems, the work is divided into two parts: Part I (Chapters 3 and 4) covering slavery, and Part II (Chapters 5 and 6) addressing indentured labour.

Chapter 3 is concerned with the abolition of the slave trade in Mauritius. After a discussion of the imperial Act abolishing the trade and its genesis, an analysis of the context of Mauritian slavery with specific reference to (a), its geographical situation in the Indian Ocean, and (b) French occupation, is provided. These two aspects, as elucidated in the chapter, fundamentally influenced the enforcement of the ban on slave trading. It must be understood that in Mauritius, abolition of the trade is closely linked to issues relevant to British conquest, the latter having occurred in 1810, three years after the Imperial Act was passed. Soon after British takeover, the question arose as to the applicability of the 1807 Act on the island, given that the Terms of Capitulation preserved the local French laws, under which the trade continued to be legal. There continues to be a level of uncertainty in the current historical discourse on the legal aspects of the trade's abolition, and the chapter provides a full discussion of questions that have arisen. The remainder of Chapter 3 examines theoretical and practical aspects to enforcing the ban, as well as specifically the challenge faced by administrators with respect to judicial enforcement, by having to implement a British policy in a French legal system. The abolition was largely circumvented, leading to serious consequences for the slave population. This chapter can therefore be regarded as dealing primarily with the black segment of 19th century Mauritian society.

Chapter 4 looks at the abolition of slavery itself. The wider notions of slavery and freedom are discussed, leading into an analysis of the markedly low manumission numbers during the first two decades of British occupation in Mauritius. The legal requirements for manumission are examined, as well as motivations for slave retention. The role of the sugar industry in the 1820s hereby emerges as pivotal. Importantly, this part of the work reveals how certain British policies permanently placed Mauritius on a very specific economic trajectory which would influence labour relations for decades, or arguably even centuries, to come. The broader focus of this chapter lies with the position of the slave-holders in Mauritius as the party most strongly affected by the passage of the 1833 Act abolishing slavery. Their attitudes are particularly revealed in context with the amelioration policies that preceded abolition as well as the subsequent compensation process.

This Chapter is thus primarily devoted to the white segment of society in 19th-century Mauritius.

Moving on to indentured labour, Chapter 5 of the work addresses the first phase of indenture migration from India. Coinciding with the period of post-emancipation apprenticeship, this chapter simultaneously addresses the immediate aftermath of the legal abolition of slavery. Examining in the first instance colonial labour migration more broadly, the first introduction of Indian indentured labourers, which took place on a private basis, is placed under scrutiny. The 1830s marked the transition from slavery to indenture in Mauritius, and an analysis of the legal frameworks for both apprentices and indentured labourers respectively is provided. A legal evaluation of early indenture highlights the shortcomings of the system which lead to a two-year suspension of indenture emigration from India, and the nature of coercion in a "free" system of labour is addressed, which also covers cultural issues relevant to Indian labour migration specifically. This analysis provides the context in which the second phase of indenture must be understood.

Chapter 6 addresses that second phase of indenture migration, which took place under a government-backed scheme from 1842 onwards and was adapted to the needs of a burgeoning sugar industry in very obvious ways. Over the coming decades, the indenture concept underwent several changes in design, moving from a "bounty" system to a "contingent" system, which are analyzed in detail in the chapter. The regulation of labour reflected an increasingly coercive setting which with the passage of new labour laws in 1867 did not ease the situation but rather sharpened it. A legal distinction between Old Immigrants and New Immigrants was introduced, designed to bind a greater number of available workers to the sugar industry. The chapter ends with an examination of the process that saw the end of indenture and the emergence of a local Indian peasantry engaged in sugar production in a process which overall maintained the power structures of the sugar economy, but on a different footing. Both Chapter 5 and 6 deal with the Indian segment of society during the relevant time period, and further, how all the different segments related to each other at a time when all parts of Mauritian society had been "assembled".

Chapter 7 presents the conclusion of the work. A summary of the findings from the preceding chapters is supplied and the contemporary relevance of such research to modern Mauritius is discussed. The report of the Truth and Justice Commission, published in 2011, which sought to address the legacies of slavery and indentured labour in Mauritius is examined and a detailed critique is provided, highlighting the shortcomings and missed opportunities in the processes of that once-in-a-lifetime project for the Indian Ocean nation.

2 Historical background

2.1 Introduction

Mauritius became a British possession in 1810 and remained as such until achieving independence in 1968. The research at hand is concerned with a particular period in Mauritian history: British colonial rule during the 19th century. As previously indicated, the study focuses primarily on two processes: slavery and indentured labour. The purpose of this chapter is to outline the broader history of Mauritius and the context in which the abolition of slavery and the introduction of indentured labour must be understood. The ambit of this section is purposefully limited to general points only, with a detailed discussion of issues reserved for the relevant chapters. The following therefore traces the early history of Mauritius before providing a brief overview of the sugar industry which acted as the engine which drove the political economy of the island during the 19th century. The chapter concludes with an outline of important events of the 20th and 21st century which, while not examined in detail in this study, inform of the island's current trajectory.

2.2 Discovery

Mauritius is situated in the southwestern part of the Indian Ocean, roughly 800 kilometres east of Madagascar. Figure 2.1 shows its position to Africa and Asia. With 2,040 square kilometres of mainland, it is further composed of a number of smaller islands,[1] as well as claiming Tromelin and more controversially the Chagos Archipelago as its territory.[2] For ease of expression, as commonly cited, Mauritius is referred to throughout this study in singular form.

Among historians it is generally speculated that Mauritius may have been known to the Phoenicians and visited by Malay and Polynesian sailors, though

1 Agalega Islands, Saint Brandon (Cargados Carajos Shoals) and Rodrigues.

2 The island of Tromelin is administered by France, but claimed simultaneously by Mauritius and the Seychelles. The Chagos Archipelago was retained by Britain when Mauritius achieved independence in 1968 and has held the designation "British Indian Ocean Territory" ever since. Mauritius has persistently claimed sovereignty over the islands, and though this has yet to be recognized, some vindication was obtained in the recent arbitration case of *The Republic of Mauritius v. United Kingdom of Great Britain and Northern Ireland*, discussed below.

DOI: 10.4324/9781003313366-2

there is no concrete evidence to sustain that speculation.[3] The first record of the existence of Mauritius has often been derived from Arab sources, namely an early 12th-century map of the Indian Ocean drawn by ancient Arab cartographer Al-Idrisi.[4] A link was established between the map and the 1502 Cantino planisphere, which seemingly shows Mauritius with the Arabic name "Dina Arobi". There has been some dissent to these hypotheses,[5] with the idea of an early Arab discovery refuted quite emphatically in a detailed study of the period.[6] This is further supported by seminal research on sea trade routes of that epoch, which makes no mention of Mauritius.[7] Accordingly, an early discovery by Arabs seems unlikely, and even if it did occur, any later connection appears to have been superficial and closely followed by Portuguese arrival.

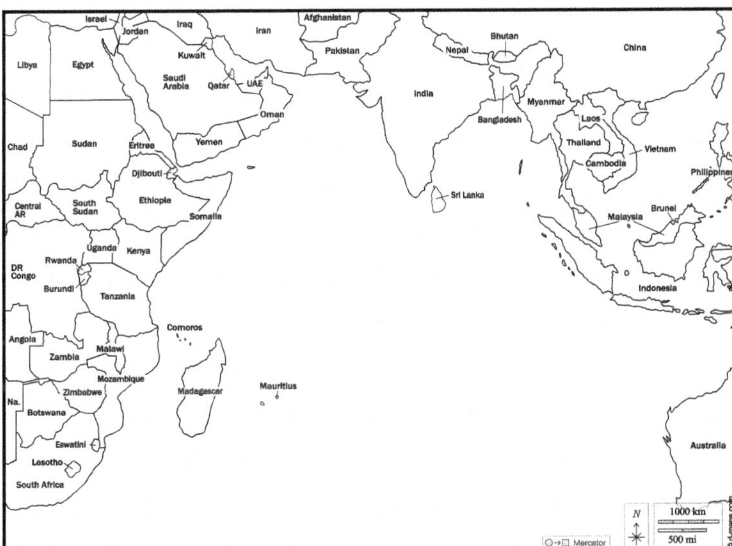

Figure 2.1 Map of the Indian Ocean[8]

3 In 2009, Archeologist Antoine Gigal was in the early stages of investigating pyramids in Mauritius which may indicate visits by an early travelling civilization, see <www.gigalresearch.com/uk/pyramides-maurice.php> [accessed 26 June 2022].

4 Emrith, Moomtaz, *History of the Muslims in Mauritius* (Vacoas: Editions Le Printemps, 1994), p. 7. Emrith spells the name "Al-Edrissi".

5 See Teelock, Vijayalakshmi, *Mauritian History: From Its Beginnings to Modern Times*, 2nd Edition (Moka: Mahatma Gandhi Institute, 2009), p. 23.

6 North-Coombes, Alfred. *La Découverte Des Mascareignes Par Les Arabes et Les Portugais : Rétrospective et Mise Au Point : Contribution À L'histoire de L'océan Indien Au XVIe Siècle* (Port Louis: Service Bureau, 1979).

7 See Hourani, George Fadlo. *Arab Seafaring in the Indian Ocean in Ancient and Early Medieval Times*. Revised and expanded. (Princeton, NJ: Princeton University Press, 1995), which makes no mention of Mauritius.

8 Indian Ocean map, d-maps.com. Available at <https://d-maps.com/carte.php?num_car=3255&lang=en> [accessed 8 August 2021].

The first concrete date, commonly cited to mark the beginning of the Portuguese period, is 1507. On 20 February of that year, Diego Fernandez Pereira sighted Mauritius, but despite his intention to disembark and explore, he was unable to do so due to a hurricane.[9] Over four years later, on 28 December 1511, Domingos Fernandez arrived, becoming the first European to set foot on the island.[10] During that period, Mauritius was known as "Cirne",[11] or less commonly "St. Apollonia".[12] But while Portugal retained the island until 1582, using it as a stopover during their voyages in the Indian Ocean, no permanent settlement was established during these many years.[13] An enduring heritage from the Portuguese period remains in the designation applied to the entire group of islands (comprising Mauritius, Rodrigues and Réunion) as the "Mascarenes", after Portuguese navigator Pedro Mascarenhas.[14]

2.3 The Dutch

The Dutch sought to establish settlements in Mauritius on two occasions, though both instances were ultimately unsuccessful. On 17 September 1598, under the direction of Admiral Wybrandt Warwijck, the Dutch took possession of and gave the island the name "Mauritius", in honour of their Stadtholder, Mauritius Van Nassau,[15] later known as the Prince of Orange. In 1638 the first settlements were erected and Governor Cornelius Gooyer took his position with 24 men under his command.[16] While initially administered from Batavia,[17] Mauritius later fell under the control of the Dutch Cape Colony after its establishment in 1652.[18] In 1658,

9 Chelin, Antoine. *Une Ile et Son Passé* (Port Louis: Claude Marrier d'Unienville – The Mauritius Printing CY. Ltd, 1973), p. 1.
10 Ibid. It should be noted that the idea of "Discovery", from its earliest inception, was a legal concept, its underlying doctrine arguably "one of the earliest examples of international law", see Miller, Robert J., 'The Doctrine of Discovery', in *Discovering Indigenous Lands: The Doctrine of Discovery in the English Colonies*, by Robert J. Miller, Jacinta Ruru, Larissa Behrendt, and Tracey Lindberg, Reprint Edition (Oxford: OUP, 2012), p. 9. In practical terms, Discovery commonly involved: (1) a landing; (2) the authorization to make discoveries; (3) a symbolic taking of possession; see Simsarian, James, 'The Acquisition of Legal Title to Terra Nullius', *Political Science Quarterly*, 53(1) (1938), 111–28, p. 111. Applying the doctrine of Discovery, Mauritius became a Portuguese possession in 1511, not 1507 as commonly stated in historical accounts. The absence of a landing and a symbolic taking of possession left the formalities of Discovery incomplete on the previous occasion.
11 Sometimes spelled "Cerne".
12 Macmillan, Allister, *Mauritius Illustrated: Historical and Descriptive, Commercial and Industrial, Facts, Figures and Resources, Printed in 1914* (New Delhi: Asian Educational Services, 2010 Reprint), p. 12.
13 Varma, Moonindra Nath, *The Making of Mauritius* (Mauritius: Editions Le Printemps, 2013), p. 12.
14 Addison and Hazareesingh, op. cit., p. 3; Macmillan, op. cit., p. 13.
15 Ibid.
16 Addison et al., op. cit., p. 5.
17 Modern Jakarta, Indonesia.
18 Jahangeer-Chojoo, Amenah, and Diana Bablee, 'Outer Islands of Mauritius, Historical Overview', *Journal of Mauritian Studies*, 3 (2) (2007), 2–43, p. 22.

however, the island was abandoned, only to be re-settled in 1664, and remained from that point on a Dutch possession until 1710.

Historians generally frame the Dutch period in exceedingly negative terms, not least because their final abandonment of the island, as on the first occasion, involved the demolition of all constructions that could have been of use to later inhabitants.[19] The settlement attempts are regarded as having damaged Mauritius' ecology irremediably, for several parts of flora and fauna became extinct.[20]

While the Dutch along with the French are the only Europeans to have attempted settlements in Mauritius, their experience contrasts significantly with the latter. The encounter is however reflective of the wider Dutch colonial ambitions at the time and must be understood in that context.

The United Netherland Chartered East India Company (known as VOC), formed in 1602, held the monopoly for trading east of the Cape, while its body of directors, the Heeren XVII, possessed treaty-making and defensive war-waging powers.[21] The latter were particular employed against the Portuguese, as the Dutch took issue with their proclaimed eminence over the East and therefore focused on Portuguese occupied territories in the region.[22] The prior Portuguese presence in Mauritius may have thus formed a relevant part of the attraction to the Dutch.

Crucially, the Dutch endeavour did not contain political aspirations and was conducted exclusively for commercial purposes.[23] They pursued "no idea other than that of buying cheap and selling dear",[24] an approach certainly evident in their colonization of Mauritius. There was a shortage of investment, in both material and human terms,[25] and when it became evident that their occupation was unprofitable, losses were cut unapologetically. The Dutch attempt to settle in Mauritius can be therefore characterized as one essentially lacking commitment.

The Dutch are, nevertheless, responsible for introducing sugar cane to Mauritius, the crop so significant to the island's development since, as well as installing the first African slaves. Having struggled considerably with marronage, it has been suggested that some slaves were indeed left behind after the final Dutch abandonment, who may have survived until the arrival of the French five years later.[26]

19 Addison et al, op. cit., pp. 5–10.

20 Teelock, Vijayalakshmi, *Mauritian History: From Its Beginnings to Modern Times*, 2nd Edition (Moka: Mahatma Gandhi Institute, 2009), p. 46. The complete extermination of the Dodo (the island's mascot having been unique to Mauritius) and the utter decimation of Mauritian ebony are hereby frequently cited examples.

21 Boxer, C. R., *The Dutch Seaborne Empire, 1600–1800* (History of Human Society Series; London: Hutchinson, 1965), p. 2.

22 Ibid., pp. 27–28.

23 Day, Clive, *The Dutch in Java* (Oxford in Asia, Historical Reprints; New York: Oxford UP, 1966), p. 45.

24 Ibid.

25 See Addison et al., op. cit., for a more detailed discussion.

26 See Selvon, Sydney, *A New Comprehensive History of Mauritius Volume 1: From Ancient Times to the Birth of Parliament* (Scotts Valley, CA: CreateSpace Independent Publishing Platform, 2012).

In summary, Dutch occupation effectively started various processes that would be the leading themes in the island's history for the next centuries.[27] Along with the introduction of sugar cane, cultivated under the Dutch solely for the purpose of producing rum and arrack, a need for workers to cultivate the island became established, which the was met by importing slaves as well as Batavian convicts.[28] This points to an early development of the slave trade in the region, establishing the first labour flow to this strategically important island in the Indian Ocean which was next coveted by the French.

2.4 The French

On 16 January 1715, equipped with instructions to take possession on behalf of King Louis XIV, Guillaume Dufresne d'Arsel arrived in Mauritius and renamed it "Ile de France" as directed.[29] This designation presented not only a clear announcement of ownership, but also proved indicative of the colonial ambitions for the island. Neighbouring Réunion, then known as Ile de Bourbon, had been occupied by France since the mid-17th century.[30]

It is during nearly a century under French rule that Mauritius made the transition from rough and untamed territory into a diversely populated, flourishing colony. The French Governor Mahé de Labourdonnais, who arrived in 1735, has been mainly credited with the extraordinary transformation that took place. His vision for the island included vast constructions, including the erection of the capital city Port Louis, an extensive infrastructure, experimentations with a variety of agricultural crops, and the establishment of Mauritius as a shipping hub for imports from Asia.[31] The creation of an advanced port, internal order and a steady food supply were significant milestones in the development of island, leaving Labourdonnais to be remembered as the father of the colony.[32] The workforce for his endeavours was brought predominantly from the African continent in the form of slaves, which alongside the arrival of Indian traders, marks the beginning of the multi-ethnicity now idiosyncratic of Mauritius.

Political administration closely followed the events in France despite the considerable distance between metropolis and colony. The French period is

27 *Report of the Truth and Justice Commission* (Mauritius, November 2011), pp. 59–60, available at <www.usip.org/sites/default/files/ROL/TJC_Vol1.pdf> [accessed 26 June 2022].

28 Ibid.

29 Chelin, Antoine., op. cit., p. 5. An item dated 20 September 1715 documenting Guillaume Dufresne's act of taking possession is contained in the Fonds de la Compagnie des Indes (Mauritius Archives), subseries OA 96, see Toussaint, Auguste, *Repertoire Des Archives de l'Ile de France Pendant La Régie de La Compagnie Des Indes (1715–1768)* (Mauritius: Mauritius Archives Publications, 1956).

30 The island of Réunion remains an overseas department of France to this day.

31 Mulloo, Anand, 'Isle de France under Mahé de Labourdonnais', in *Mauritius under French Administration*, ed. by S. N. Gayou (Moka: Mahatma Gandhi Institute, 1982).

32 Hollingworth, Derek, *They Came to Mauritius* (London: Oxford University Press, 1965).

distinguished by four political regimes: after the initial public administration through the French East India Company to 1767, representatives of the monarchy took over until 1790, with colonial revolutionary assemblies in charge up to 1803, which were then replaced by officers of the Napoleonic empire until British conquest in 1810.[33]

In the early days, the existence of a *Conseil Supérieur* (a principal court of justice) on the Ile de Bourbon only indicates that Mauritius was initially administered from the neighbouring island.[34] A subordinate jurisdiction existed in the form of a *Conseil Provincial* (or provincial court) in Mauritius, from which appeals were permitted to the superior court in Bourbon. This applied to civil matters and for most crimes, with an exception to slaves, in whose cases the decision of the lower court was deemed definitive and final. It was not until 1734, under Governor Labourdonnais, that a *Conseil Supérieur* was established in Mauritius, constituting then the only court of justice on the island constituted by seven judges for both civil and criminal matters, ceasing any further appeals to Bourbon with all judgments being definitive.[35]

A monopoly of Indian Ocean trade had been granted to a company, the *Compagnie des Indes Orientales*, their colonial endeavours funded by the Crown. Originally set up in 1664 by Jean Baptist Colbert, famous as the mercantilist minister of King Louis XIV, hopes for this new organization ran high, as evident from the capitalization set at 15 million *livres*.[36] Headed by 12 directors elected by the merchant community at a conference, it enjoyed considerable royal support, with the Crown subscribing to three million *livres* worth of shares immediately. A rival company, the *Compagnie d'Orient* held trading rights until 1667, but accepted an indemnity by way of 20,000 *livres* worth of shares in the new body.[37] Grand aspirations notwithstanding, the organization proved a commercial failure, mainly to due to a lack of funding. It may however be considered a political success, since it allowed the French to permanently establish themselves at Bourbon (Réunion island) and India, while also setting up a regular flow of trade.[38]

In the administration of justice in Mauritius, the *Compagnie* was highly influential, for the members of *Conseil Supérieur* "were liable to be removed at the pleasure of the directors of the East India Company in France, upon

33 Chitson, Dorish, 'Labour Laws in Mauritius during French Colonial Time', *Journal of Mauritian Studies*, 4 (2) (2009), 70–88, pp. 71–72. See Jahangeer-Chojoo et al., op. cit., for a detailed account of the administrative and constitutional development.

34 CO 415/16, Laws and Courts of Justice at Mauritius, Report by Chief Judge and Commissary of Justice George Smith, Port Louis, 30 September 1817.

35 Ibid.

36 Wellington, Donald C., *French East India Companies: A Historical Account and Record of Trade* (Lanham, MD: Hamilton Books, 2006), p. 19.

37 Ibid., p. 11.

38 Haudrere, Philippe, *La Compagnie Française Des Indes Au XVIIIe Siècle (1719–1795) – Tome 1 (Thèse pour le Doctorat d'Etat ès lettres)* (Paris: Université de Paris – Sorbonne, 1987), pp. 27–28.

whose recommendation also their successors were appointed by the king."[39] The period of company administration ceased in 1766 when a new *Conseil Supérieur* was appointed by royal edict. From 1767 onward, the court system, both in its structure and the composition of members, became increasingly more complex.[40] In terms of legislation, regulations from 1670 continued to govern criminal proceedings, while civil matters fell under the *Coutume de Paris*, local regulations and "such other Laws and ordinances, as having been made for the Kingdom in general".[41] The legal profession itself came to flourish, represented extensively by *avocats* (barristers), *procureurs* (attorneys) and *notaires* (notaries).[42]

The laws were however not applied uniformly. The population was divided into three groups, each of which had its own legal regime.[43] The regulations as set out above applied only to the white population, which in the Mauritian context was almost exclusively of French origin. Governing the conduct of slaves was the *Code Noir*, promulgated in Mauritius on 18 September 1724 as the *Lettres-Patentes* of December 1723.[44]

The *Code Noir* had been employed by France since 1685 and the *Lettres-Patentes* introduced in Bourbon and Mauritius were a slightly modified version specifically designed for the islands.[45] The Code contained provisions characteristic to the definition of slavery. Explicitly defined as chattels (Article 39: "*Voulons que les esclaves soient réputés meubles*")[46], slaves were inheritable as personal assets. They could not hold any kind of property themselves (Articles 21 and 22), and their children were born into slavery (Article 8). Crucially, slaves lacked active legal personality (for example Articles 23 and 24 stipulate that they could not be parties or witnesses in civil proceedings), but they nevertheless held legal responsibility (as for example for theft, see Articles 28 and 29) and could be prosecuted independently of their owners (Article 25).

The very existence of regulation and its attending level of judicial oversight, no matter how limited, lead early commentators to argue that the *Code Noir*

39 CO 415/16, George Smith's Report.

40 For a detailed discussion, see D'Unienville, Raymond, *L'Evolution Du Droit Civil a l'Ile Maurice (1721–1968)* (Mauritius: Temple Law Books, LexisNexis, 1994).

41 CO 415/16, George Smith's Report.

42 Domingue, P. R., 'The Historical Development of the Mixed Legal System of Mauritius during the French and British Colonial Periods', *Law, Management and Social Sciences*, 4 (2002), 61–93, p. 63.

43 Domingue, op. cit., p. 64.

44 Chelin, op. cit., p. 9.

45 Noël, Karl, *L'esclavage À l'Isle de France* (Ile Maurice) de 1715 À 1810 (Paris: Editions Two Cities, 1991), p. 55.

46 *Ordonnance ou Code Noir – Lettres Patentes En Forme d'Édit Concernant Les Esclaves Des Isles de Bourbon et de France, Décembre 1723* (Publication No. 17; Coromandel: Publication des Archives de Maurice, 2000), emphasis added.

represented a significant humanitarian achievement of the time.[47] However, practice showed that the Code was never fully observed, and slave-holding remained characterized by unfettered sadistic treatment, even if, as it is sometimes held, the situation in Mauritius may have been better than elsewhere in the French Empire.[48] Chapter 3 outlines the importance of slaves to colonial society on the island, which, as will be seen, was fundamental.

By contrast, the situation of the "coloured" population (meaning free non-whites and liberated slaves), involved an intermediate regime. Ostensibly, by virtue of the Edict of 1723, the *gens de couleur* had the same rights and privileges as the white population, but in practice they were stigmatized by their ethnicity: they were excluded from being able to exercise a legal or medical profession, have a public office or hold any kind of position of trust, and socially, black heritage denied access to the white class and their circles.[49] While in the years following the French revolution, certain resolutions were taken by the Colonial Assembly to achieve a level of political equality, in 1804 under General Decaen (the last French governor), in a return to military rule, the former restrictions were reinstated.[50]

2.5 The British

The last two decades of French rule saw Mauritius gaining importance as a base for privateering with France and Britain at war.[51] Noting the considerable commercial losses to Britain,[52] Auguste Toussaint nevertheless asserts that "the exploits of the privateers were never a serious threat to British power in the Indian Ocean."[53] Achieving control of the Cape in 1806, Britain was able to regulate the route to the Mascarenes, creating a blockade and leading an offensive that led to Bourbon's capitulation in July 1810. While the French side won the famous Battle of Grand Port during August 1810,[54] the episode left them unable to withstand a renewed attempt, and a few months later, on 3 December 1810, Mauritius capitulated.[55] The Terms of Capitulation, as discussed in Chapter 3, would prove relevant for decades to come.

47 Noël, op. cit., p. 23
48 Ibid., p. 26: "Les mauvais maîtres furent rares. Les nègres n'y furent jamais maltraités de façon systématique."
49 D'Unienville, op. cit., pp. 39–40.
50 Ibid. The Colonial Assembly was also inspired in October 1794 to abolish the slave trade, in line with revolutionary sentiments in France, which similarly was not of enduring consequence.
51 Jahangeer-Chojoo et al, op. cit., p. 9.
52 Toussaint, Auguste, *History of Mauritius* (London: Macmillan, 1977), Chapter 5.
53 Ibid., p. 58.
54 The only French naval victory to be commemorated on the Arc de Triomphe in Paris.
55 For further background history of the conquest, see Carter, M., M. S. Hall, V. Govinden, R. Ramasawmy, and E. Richon, *Kaleidoscopic Conquest, Mauritius – 1810* (Scotts Valley, CA: CRIOS, Centre for Research on Indian Ocean Societies, 2010).

2.5.1 Mauritius in the British Empire

British possession of Mauritius was confirmed through Article 8 of the 1814 Treaty of Paris,[56] which was subsequently proclaimed on the island.[57] Bourbon, in contrast, was returned to France. Sources from the period convey the impression that the capture of Mauritius was deemed an important success for the British.[58] For instance, Lieutenant Commander Henry Keating who was involved in the conquest describes the island as "a valuable Prize", for which "General Decaen did not indulge us even with a sharp fight".[59]

After the departure of the French troops (occurring not without Decaen at the point of setting sail "vent[ing] his spleen against the British Government in terms of profaness and vulgarity"[60]), the first British governor of Mauritius, Robert T. Farquhar, lost no time in requiring the French inhabitants to take the oath of allegiance.[61] Regarding its performance as a "sacred bond which can alone unite the subjects of a conquered country to its new Sovereign by its indispensable ties of fidelity",[62] he was faced for years to come with a resistance to comply, as evidenced in subsequent proclamations.[63] This is reflective of an enduringly tense relationship between the old and new colonists, investigated in detail in Chapters 3 and 4.

Dayachand Napal states that "the people of the island did not have any affection for their conquerors who had become their masters overnight at the stroke of a pen."[64] His assertion regarding the population's dislike of the new colonial rulers seems to apply particularly to the French inhabitants who harboured the hope that the Ile de France would at some point be returned to their motherland. The British however, having reintroduced the name "Mauritius" given by the Dutch, ruled until independence.

As far as the non-white inhabitants were concerned, it appears that the British takeover was initially welcomed.[65] However it soon became evident that whilst Governor Farquhar was keen to employ a "conciliatory approach" towards the

56 FO 93/33/8 France, Definitive Treaty, Signed at Paris 30 May 1814.
57 Code Farquhar No.156, 19 December 1814, reproduced in Rouillard, op. cit.
58 IOR H/MISC/701, Letters relative to the Isles of France and Bourbon, 1810–1811.
59 IOR H/MISC/701, Lieutenant Commander Henry Keating to Chairman of the Court of Directors, Port Louis, 7 December 1810.
60 IOR H/MISC/701, Governor Farquhar to Sir Barlow, Isle de France, 24 December 1810.
61 Code Farquhar No.15, 28 December 1810.
62 IOR H/MISC/701, Governor Farquhar to the Earl of Liverpool, Port Louis, 8 January 1811.
63 See Code Farquhar No.16, 31 December 1810 (exhorting the inhabitants to take the oath); Code Farquhar No. 38, 11 April 1811 (extending the period for taking the oath); Code Farquhar No.68, 7 September 1811 (appointing a Commission to investigate the persons who had failed to take the oath); Code Farquhar No.177, 14 September 1815 (setting a time limit to take the oath or to provide a security instead).
64 Napal, Dayachand, *British Mauritius, 1810–1948* (Port Louis: Hart Printing, 1984).
65 Teelock, Vijayalakshmi, *A Select Guide to Sources on Slavery in Mauritius, and the Testimony of Slaves in the Era of Sugar* (Bell Village: African Cultural Centre, 1995), p. 14–15.

French, that affability did not extend as far as the slaves, for their situation did not materially improve.[66] For them, the experience was thus one of continuity of the colonial situation where disadvantage persisted even whilst the identity of the colonizer changed.[67]

How did this French-dominated colony fit within the British Empire? The concept of a unitary British Empire has a tendency to obscure the human aspect behind it.[68] Colonial politics were influenced by several protagonists, including officials, migrants and missionaries. Control of the empire at any one time was therefore disorganized and tumultuous, and in the words of John Darwin, "to suppose that an order uttered in London was obeyed around the world by zealous proconsuls is an historical fantasy (although a popular one)."[69]

In the 19th century the British Empire consisted of three separate, but not mutually exclusive, parts: the white settlements, the territories that had been conquered or acquired during wartimes, and later, India. As such, there was not one principal section of government in charge of the Empire, but several, whose powers and responsibilities fluctuated over time according to need.[70]

The general principle was that colonies were mainly governed locally and not from London.[71] Mauritius had a governor heading a local administration installed within days of capitulation,[72] thus removing immediate responsibility from the metropolis. The Colonial Office influenced legislation only indirectly, such as through its refusal of assent to orders and proclamations.[73] The process of ratifying, amending or rejecting legislation was however perceived as a significant form of control, since "even the local governor could not be entrusted with authority to give final assent to colonial bills; and colonial laws which attempted to give him such authority were open to the strongest objections."[74] Two manners of review existed: judicial and administrative. The latter was preferred, since it allowed for

66 Ibid.
67 Osterhammel, op. cit., p. 25.
68 Darwin, John, *Unfinished Empire: The Global Expansion of Britain* (London: Penguin, 2013).
69 Ibid., p. xiii.
70 Porter, Andrew, 'Britain and the Empire in the Nineteenth Century', in *The Oxford History of the British Empire: The Nineteenth Century*, ed. by Andrew Porter (Oxford; New York : Oxford University Press, 1999), 1–28.
71 Simpson, A. W. B., *Human Rights and the End of Empire: Britain and the Genesis of the European Convention* (Oxford; New York: Oxford University Press, 2001), p. 280. For an account of how poorly equipped the Colonial Office indeed appears to have been for its role, see Cell, John W., *British Colonial Administration in the Mid-Nineteenth Century: The Policy-Making Process* (New Haven, CT; London: Yale University Press, 1970).
72 See IOR H/MISC/701, Governor Farquhar to Sir Barlow, Isle de France, 24 December 1810.
73 Simpson, op. cit., p. 283.
74 Swinfen, D. B., *Imperial Control of Colonial Legislation, 1813–65: A Study of British Policy Towards Colonial Legislative Powers* (London: Clarendon Press, 1970), p. 4.

the legislation to be examined before it came into operation. The problem posed by the former is of course that it required the law to be already in force. Most laws reviewed were already effective, however, the Royal Instructions reserved Crown assent for politically and legally sensitive bills, with the effect that they were scrutinized before passing into law.[75]

In Mauritius, the question of legislation was closely linked to the Terms of Capitulation, and in particular Article 8, which sought to preserve local laws and customs. The issue is discussed in detail in Chapter 3 of this study. From a modern perspective, Article 8 of the Capitulation can be considered as the founding aspect of the Mauritian legal system, since the Napoleonic Codes still apply and were during British rule curiously supplemented with English provisions and enforced through English procedure. It has been estimated that the modern body of law is approximately two-thirds of British origin and one-third French.[76] This has created a working legal system today which domestically is no longer considered French-British, but thoroughly Mauritian.[77]

Vijaya Teelock argues that the uniqueness of Mauritius among Britain's 19th century possessions is reflected in how it originally came to be administered "as part of an ill-assorted, disparate group", namely Ceylon, New South Wales and Van Diemen's Land.[78] Culturally different, Mauritius was considered neither part of East Africa nor South Asia, nor was it at that point a major sugar-producing colony alongside the West Indies.[79]

The latter description was about to change when in 1815 Mauritius was granted Crown Colony status, and hence on, it was able to export its sugar to Britain at a considerably preferential rate of duty.[80] This provided the impetus to grow the sugar industry as described next.

2.5.2 The role of the sugar industry

British imperial policy regarding Mauritius is inextricably linked to the sugar economy. Being the reason that required the availability of coercible labour, an understanding of the development of the industry underlies any discussion on slavery and indenture. Table 2.1 illustrates this point.

75 Ibid., p. 5.

76 See Daudet, Yves, 'L'enseignement Du Droit À Maurice', *Mauritius Law Review*, 1 (1988), 131–54.

77 Bogdan, Michael, *The Law of Mauritius and Seychelles: A Study of Two Small Mixed Legal Systems* (Lund: Juristiförlaget, 1989).

78 Teelock, Vijaya, *Bitter Sugar: Sugar and Slavery in 19th Century Mauritius* (Moka: Mahatma Gandhi Institute, 1998), p. 23.

79 Ibid.

80 Ibid., p. 42.

Table 2.1 Sugar production in imperial tons for the main British sugar-producing colonies, 1816–1860[81]

	Mauritius	*Jamaica*	*British Guiana*	*Barbados*	*Trinidad*	*St. Vincent*
1816–1820	20,874	407,626	113,962	61,982	36,103	61,948
1821–1825	55,624	353,875	159,136	59,048	41,830	61,589
1826–1830	142,500	347,106	279,780	68,264	59,881	66,727
1831–1835	167,755	329,478	272,340	85,775	77,735	50,479
1836–1840	165,138	216,423	220,947	94,715	70,408	42,274
1841–1845	173,408	165,865	162,687	79,960	76,484	31,929
1846–1850	291,610	158,005	173,390	109,428	96,454	37,366
1851–1855	435,193	126,812	222,273	158,296	118,148	35,918
1856–1860	601,137	114,943	299,070	160,435	127,187	32,088

Prima facie, a number of observations can be made from the data:

1 The initial expansion of the Mauritian sugar economy occurred at an extraordinary pace, achieving a seven-times greater output within a decade (from the period of 1816–1820 to 1826–1830).
2 The period of 1836–1840, which coincided with the abolition of slavery in 1834–1835 and the end of apprenticeships by 1838–1839, saw the West Indies suffer a significant drop in sugar production, unlike Mauritius which remained stable. (Note that despite the cumulative spike in Barbados for the same period, production more than halved from 23,679 tons in 1838 to 10,374 tons in 1840.[82])
3 By the 1840s, Mauritius had overtaken the other colonies to become the chief sugar-producing colony of the British Empire.

Certain circumstances were responsible for aiding this development.

Even prior to the emancipation of slaves, the sugar industry of the West Indies found itself in recession, having expanded during wartime and obliged to face falling prices after the peace of 1815.[83] A further nail in the coffin was when in 1825, Mauritius achieved parity in export tariffs, allowing Mauritian sugar to enter the British market with the same level of duty as imposed upon sugar from the West Indies, thus forming part of a "preferential group" (later joined by the East Indian colonies) in contrast to other producers within and outside the empire.[84]

81 Table compiled from yearly statistics contained in Deerr, Noel, *The History of Sugar* (London: Chapman and Hall, 1949), pp. 193–204. (Note: Mauritius data given in original in metric tons, here converted to imperial tons to enable clear comparison with other colonies.)
82 Deerr, op. cit., p. 194.
83 Lobdell, Richard A., 'Patterns of Investment and Sources of Credit in the British West Indian Sugar Industry, 1838–97', *Journal of Caribbean History*, 4 (1972), 31–53, p. 31.
84 Ibid., p. 39

In addition to the decline in profits, heavy indebtedness, particularly in the form of mortgages, added considerably to the distress of the West Indies.[85] Most of the mortgagees were City of London firms.[86]

With the abolition of slavery, sugar plantations were deprived of the cheap labour they required. As examined in Chapter 5, during the apprenticeship period, Mauritius had already begun to introduce indentured labourers from India to take the place of former slaves on the fields. It has been argued that indentured labour has been indeed the reason why Mauritius was able to withstand the setbacks caused in other colonies by abolition and expand its sugar economy beyond.[87] In this context, it is noteworthy that British Guiana, the second-largest recipient of indentured labour from India after Mauritius, established itself in the 1840s as the second-largest sugar producer of the British colonies, as evident from Table 2.1.

With respect to the West Indian decline, it also appears that Mauritius not only competed for the same market, but also for the same investment, as the evidence in a Select Committee Report of 1848 suggests. To the question whether excessive debt prevented sugar estates from employing the required labour, Matthew J. Higgins, a proprietor in Demerara, answered:

> I do not think that is the reason. I think the reason is, that few, if any capitalists previously unconnected with the West Indies have sent any capital out there during the last 10 years, because there was no chance of it fructifying. They preferred India and the Mauritius, where labour was less interfered with.[88]

Upon the abolition of slavery in 1834, £20 million was made available to compensate the slave-holders. Mauritius received just over £2 million. Around £17 million went to the West Indies, of which a considerable amount was used to settle the debts that had encumbered the sugar estates.[89] In such instances, the money was thus effectively returned back to London. By contrast, the early immigration of indentured labourers to Mauritius was very likely funded by the slave compensation.[90] Informally introduced from 1834 onwards, and on a large

85 *Report from the Select Committee on the Commercial State of the West India Colonies, Parliamentary Papers, 1831–32* (381), p. 18.

86 Howe, Anthony, *Free Trade and Liberal England*, 1846–1946 (Oxford: Oxford University Press, 1998), p. 53.

87 North-Coombes, M. D., 'From Slavery to Indenture: Forced Labour in the Political Economy of Mauritius 1834–1867', in *Indentured Labour in the British Empire, 1834–1920*, ed. by Kay Saunders (London: Croom Helm, 1984), p. 78.

88 *Report from the Select Committee on Sugar and Coffee Planting (8 Reports), Fourth Report, Parliamentary Papers, 1847–48* (1848), p. 101.

89 Sheridan, Richard B., 'The West India Sugar Crisis and British Slave Emancipation, 1830–1833', *Journal of Economic History*, 21 (1961), 539–51, p. 549.

90 North Coombes, op. cit., p. 87.

scale with government support beginning in 1842, contract workers from India had replaced slaves on the sugar cane fields.

The production of sugar in Mauritius remained in the hands of the white population, and in particular the French (descendants of early settlers and expatriates), who having cultivated an elite community, dominated every aspect of public life as well as the economy.[91]

Having attracted considerable British investment as a consequence of sugar industry's growing expansion, the French plantation owners were able to promote their interests in the metropolis. Thus, "British capitalists, in alliance with Franco-Mauritian planters, appointed British Members of Parliament as their political agents in London and formed pressure groups to lobby for the cause of the sugar industry with the Colonial Office."[92] Their wealth and status rested to an ability to maintain production as well as access to the British market.

As noted by Patrick Neveling, "the hierarchy that positioned the French colonisers as the subjects of British rule was to determine the patterns of struggles within the local society and economy for decades to come", and the steps to integrate Mauritian sugar production into the empire's system, including the abolition of slavery, must be understood as the actual steps of incorporating Mauritius into the dominant capitalist system of the time, namely Britain's empire.[93] Neveling's observation is congruent with an argument advanced in this study. As will become evident in subsequent chapters, the legal process of ameliorating the conditions of plantation labour, whether in the context of slavery or indentured labour, can be interpreted as repetitive steps to transfer power from the local French elite to the British imperial government.

The firm establishment of indentured labour in Mauritius, investigated in Chapter 6, coincided with a number of other socioeconomic changes within the empire. In 1846, the Sugar Duties Act was passed in Britain, effecting a gradual removal of all duties on sugar, and forcing British colonies to compete with exports from countries that still employed slavery, such as Brazil and Cuba. The financial crisis of the late 1840s, the dramatic rise of continental sugar production from beet in the 1850s, and a renewed commitment to free trade in subsequent decades, all contributed to a modification in attitudes and interests in British imperial policy in the second part of the 19th century.[94]

91 Burroughs, Peter, 'The Mauritius Rebellion of 1832 and the Abolition of British Colonial Slavery', *The Journal of Imperial and Commonwealth History*, 4 (1976), 243–65.

92 North-Coombes, op. cit., p. 89.

93 Neveling, Patrick, 'A Periodisation of Globalisation According to the Mauritian Integration into the International Sugar Commodity Chain (1825–2005)', in *Global Histories, Imperial Commodities, Local Interactions*, ed. by Jonathan Curry-Machado (London: Palgrave Macmillan, 2013).

94 Fakhri, Michael, *Sugar and the Making of International Trade Law* (Cambridge: Cambridge University Press, 2014).

2.6 Modern Mauritius

The system of labour migration under indenture largely ended with the beginning of the 20th century, reducing to negligible numbers during the first decade before completely drying up by 1920.[95] At the end of this era, the descendants of slaves found themselves in the minority.

The data contained in Table 2.2 raises an immediate question. What is the significance of the designation "General Population"? The term was introduced with the first official census to take place in Mauritius in 1846, and covered "Europeans, descendants of Europeans, and the population of mixed origin." "Indian" or "Indo-Mauritian" referred to "persons who came originally from India, Burma, Ceylon and other parts" as well as "native born Indians of unmixed extraction". "Chinese" signified simply "immigrants from China and the descendants, born in the island, of Chinese settlers".[96] These definitions, provided in a 1956 report by the Mauritius Central Statistical Office, appear puzzling, for one population group appears left out, namely former slaves, of primary Afro-Malagasy origin. An actual copy of the first 1846 census has not survived, but according to Monique Dinan, who has studied Mauritian censuses extensively, the group of "ex-apprentices" was listed only for the first two censuses, 1846 and 1851, following which former slaves were subsumed in the category of "General Population".[97] A population count published in a Mauritian newspaper in 1848 gives a clearer breakdown and is reproduced as Table 6.2 and discussed in Chapter 6 of this study. For present purposes, it should be noted that from the mid-19th century, former slaves were no longer separately identified.

The three-fold distinction (General Population, Indo-Mauritian, Chinese) remained in place until 1962, when for the first time the Indian population

Table 2.2 1921 census, by population group and gender[98]

	Male	*Female*	*Total*
General Population	49,725	54,491	**104,216**
Indo-Mauritian Population	139,150	126,374	**265,524**
Chinese Population	5,233	1,512	**6,745**
TOTAL			**376,485**

95 See the detailed numbers provided in Chapter 5.

96 Central Statistical Office, *Natality and Fertility in Mauritius, 1825–1955* (Mauritius: Central Statistical Office, 1956), p. 4.

97 Dinan, Monique, *Mauritius in the Making across the Censuses 1846–2000* (Mauritius: Nelson Mandela Centre for African Culture, Ministry of Arts & Culture, 2002), p. 8.

98 Compiled from data contained in Table 2, Central Statistical Office, *Natality and Fertility in Mauritius, 1825–1955* (Mauritius: Central Statistical Office, 1956), p. 2.

was further divided into Hindu and Muslim groupings.[99] The concept of four "communities" (Hindu, Muslim, Sino-Mauritian and General Population) subsequently became the basis for political organization following the 1972 census, which included the discredited "Best Loser" electoral system that allowed for the allocation of additional seats in parliament for underrepresented ethnicities.[100] In 2012 the UN Human Rights Committee ruled that the requirement for a declaration of ethnic and religious status by candidates running for election violated Article 25(b) of the International Covenant on Civil and Political Rights.[101]

The Mauritian census which took place in 2011 obscures the original demarcations significantly. The Housing and Population Census provides ten sets of relevant data in which the question of ethnicity is dissipated in designations which enumerate the population by reference to "language of forefathers", "language usually spoken at home" and "religion".[102]

It can thus be noted that the issue of ethnicity and identity in Mauritius continues to be a contentious one, which, it is submitted, is deeply rooted in its history. The demographic is truly unique, in that unlike other colonies (such as the West Indies or Fiji) Mauritius did not only lack an indigenous population, it maintained a significant diversity in contrast to other islands, which possess a much more homogenous population (such as the Seychelles).

The years following the end of indentured labour, 85 years after the abolition of slavery, are not very well documented, with writings on the period being very sparse indeed.[103] The epoch is however an important one, since it represents a time when all segments of Mauritian society were finally free from bondage and

99 Central Statistical Office, *1962 Population Census of Mauritius and Its Dependencies* (Mauritius: Central Statistical Office, 1962), p. 5.

100 For a brief overview, see Section 3 in Bureau of Democracy, Human Rights and Labor, 'Country Reports on Human Rights Practices for 2015: Mauritius', *US Department of State* <www.state.gov/j/drl/rls/hrrpt/humanrightsreport/index.htm?year=2015&dlid=252707> [accessed 26 June 2022].

101 See para. 15.5, Human Rights Committee Communication No. 1744/2007, 15 January 2013 (also known as *Narrain et al. v. Mauritius*, <www.opensocietyfoundations.org/sites/default/files/case-digests-human-rights-committee-105-session-20130425.pdf> [accessed 26 June 2022].

102 See Table D7, Ministry of Finance and Economic Development – Statistics Mauritius, *2011 Housing and Population Census – Republic of Mauritius*, <https://statsmauritius.govmu.org/Documents/Census_and_Surveys/HPC/2011/HPC_TR_Vol2_Demography_Yr11.pdf> [26 June 2022].

103 A little known part of Mauritian history is the British detention of 1,600 Jewish refugees at the Beau Bassin prison between 1940–1945, who having escaped persecution in Europe, were unable to enter Palestine on account of being illegal migrants. A general lack of awareness of this historical fact is not only testament to British secrecy maintained over the issue at the time, but also that the first part of the 20th century, occurring between the end of indenture and prior the independence movement, appears to be a "lost" period in Mauritian historical scholarship. For a unique account on the Jewish refugees deported to Mauritius, see Pitot, Genevieve, *The Mauritian Shekel: The Story of Jewish Detainees in Mauritius, 1940–1945* (Lanham, MD: Rowman & Littlefield, 2000).

a rough Mauritian identity began to form. The years of 1947–1948 saw important constitutional changes take place, which included a widening of the elective principle that led to the number of eligible voters increase more than six-fold.[104] Dayachand Napal has outlined the main developments during that time, which include population growth, improvements to infrastructure and an amelioration of the education system.[105] It is also a period of politicization, marked by unrest, labour riots and the birth of the party system. Party politics in their inception ran along racial lines. Notably, Indo-Mauritians came to dominate politics on the island, and an important aspect of this period is the ascent of former Indian indentured labourers in society. As pointed out by Jean Houbert, this appears to have been achieved chiefly through the acquisition of land,[106] though historian Vijaya Teelock is circumspect in regarding this as the main determinant for Indian progress and stresses that censuses of the period indicate land ownership among ex-slaves as well.[107]

During negotiations leading up to independence, an agreement was reached in 1965 between the two sides that the Chagos Archipelago, a group of small islands just south of the Maldives but territorially part of Mauritius, would be detached from the same and retained by Britain. The area since then had the designation of "British Indian Ocean Territory" (BIOT). Thus on 12 March 1968 Mauritius became an independent state, and on the same date in 1992 achieved the status of republic.

With respect to the Chagos Archipelago, Mauritius notably received £3 million in exchange, though the cession of the islands was widely understood to have been a condition for obtaining independence. Today, they are probably most well-known for accommodating a military base of the United States, situated on Diego Garcia, the biggest island of the archipelago, subject to a lease agreed by the UK. The base is reportedly comprised of "the most secretive and powerful US military facilities in the world", and has played a pivotal role in launching the invasions into Afghanistan and Iraq, and was used to threaten other nations in the region, such as Iran.[108] It is also said to host a CIA detention centre for high-profile terrorist suspects, and represents a multi-billion dollar investment in terms of logistics and personnel.[109] While the Diego Garcia military base may be of crucial

104 Mooindra Nath Varma states that following the new constitution, the number of electors rose from 11,844 to 71,569. The changes included female suffrage whilst introducing age, residence and literacy requirements, amongst other features. See Varma, Moonindra Nath, *The Making of Mauritius* (Mauritius: Editions Le Printemps, 2013), pp. 163–167, and Minogue, M. M., and S. K. Joypaul, *Notes on the Constitution of Mauritius – Occasional Paper No. 3* (Mauritius: School of Administration, University of Mauritius, 1973).

105 Napal, Dayachand, *British Mauritius, 1810–1948* (Port Louis: Hart Printing, 1984).

106 Houbert, Jean, 'Mauritius: Independence and Dependence', *The Journal of Modern African Studies*, 19 (1981), 75–105, p. 78–79.

107 Teelock, op. cit., (1999).

108 Vine, David, *Island of Shame: The Secret History of the U.S. Militarybase on Diego Garcia* (Princeton, NJ ; Woodstock: Princeton University Press, 2009), p. 2.

109 Ibid.

strategic importance to the United States, its creation followed the uprooting of an entire people: the Chagossians, an estimated 1,500 to 2,000 inhabitants, who were exiled to make place for the project. Their battle to have their rights recognized had been one of ongoing litigation. In 2012, while expressing sympathy to their plight, the European Court of Human Rights ruled their application inadmissible.[110]

On 1 April 2010, the UK declared most of the archipelago a marine protected area ("MPA"), ostensibly for conservationist reasons.[111] However revelations through WikiLeaks suggested that contrary to professed environmental concerns, the aim of declaring the MPA had been to effectively prevent the Chagossians from returning to the islands, which prompted Mauritius to commence arbitral proceedings against the UK under the UN Convention on the Law of the Sea ("UNCLOS") on 20 December 2010.[112]

Mauritius has consistently claimed sovereignty over the Chagos Archipelago, which as reiterated by its former prime minister "was excised from Mauritius prior to independence, in disregard of United Nations Resolutions 1514 and 2066 and the principles of international law".[113] The 1968 constitution of Mauritius does refer to the Chagos Islands as being part of its territory.[114] In a telling reaction to Mauritius' announcement in 2004, that it would refer the dispute to the International Court of Justice and leave the Commonwealth to do so if necessary, the UK amended its declaration under Article 36(2) of the ICJ Statute. The declaration now states that not only does the UK not accept the jurisdiction of the Court in the context of disputes with members of the Commonwealth, but also former members of the same.[115]

2.6.1 *Mauritius today*

On 18 March 2015, the Tribunal set up to adjudicate the Chagos Marine Protected Area Arbitration rendered its award.[116] With respect to Mauritius' four submissions, the Tribunal found by a majority of three to two that it had no jurisdiction in the first and second, and regarded unanimously the third as

110 Chagos Islanders v. The United Kingdom, Application No. 35622/04, ECHR 460 (2012).

111 Rincon, Paul, 'UK Sets up Chagos Islands Marine Reserve', *BBC News* <http://news.bbc.co.uk/1/hi/8599125.stm> [accessed 26 June 2022].

112 Prows, Peter, 'Mauritius Brings UNCLOS Arbitration Against The United Kingdom Over The Chagos Archipelago', *ASIL Insights*, 15 (8) (2011).

113 Permanent Mission of the Republic of Mauritius to the United Nations, *Statement by Dr The Hon Navinchandra Ramgoolam, GCSK, FRCP, Prime Minister, Sixty-Sixth session of the United Nations General Assembly, 24 September 2011* (New York: United Nations), p. 7.

114 See Chapter XI, Article 111.

115 'Declarations Recognizing the Jurisdiction of the Court as Compulsory – United Kingdom of Great Britain and Northern Ireland', *International Court of Justice* <www.icj-cij.org/en/declarations/gb> [accessed 26 June 2022].

116 *The Republic of Mauritius v. United Kingdom of Great Britain and Northern Ireland* <https://pca-cpa.org/en/cases/11/> [accessed 26 June 2022].

non-contentious. But crucially, it ruled unanimously in favour of Mauritius regarding its fourth submission. It found that Britain's undertakings from 1965 (as repeated several times over the next decades) regarding certain rights as retained by Mauritius over the Chagos Archipelago were legally binding, and accordingly, Britain had breached its obligations under UNCLOS. Notably however, the Tribunal did not find improper purpose in the declaration of the MPA based on the evidence before it and declined to comment on the issue further.[117]

It should be noted that despite the muted outcome, it is a victory that cannot be underestimated. The ruling has been widely celebrated in the Mauritian media, not at least due to the powerful opinions issued by the two dissenting Judges James Kateka and Rüdiger Wolfrum, who lament the indeed missed opportunity by the Tribunal to address the fundamental issue of sovereignty over the Chagos Archipelago. Having been achieved by a previous island colony against its former colonizers, the challenge presented a power imbalance likened to David and Goliath, validating Mauritius now as an equal member in the international community. The true and full import of the decision is as yet unclear. In February 2022, as part of an expedition to the archipelago, the Mauritian Ambassador to the UN raised the Mauritian flag on the Peros Banhos atoll, in what was reported to be a formal challenge to Britain's ownership claims. A spokesperson for the UK Foreign Office is quoted to have said that "Mauritius has never held sovereignty over the territory and the UK does not recognise its claim."[118]

2.7 Conclusion

The history of Mauritius, as has been seen, is not solely Mauritian history. Its major political and legal developments were, and continue to be, closely linked to that of the powerful nations at any given time. The evolution of its diverse people from colonial influence to a free nation occurred in fairly recent history. Mauritius therefore presents a unique setting in which to examine the impact political and legal changes had on identities individually and collectively.

117 Para. 543.

118 Bowcott, Owen and Bruno Rinvolucri, 'Mauritius Formally Challenges Britain's Ownership of Chagos Islands', *The Guardian* <www.theguardian.com/world/2022/feb/14/mauritius-formally-challenges-britains-ownership-of-chagos-islands> [accessed 14 February 2022].

Part I

Slavery

3 The abolition of the slave trade

3.1 Introduction: slavery and the slave trade

Slaves were the first workforce brought to cultivate and transform Mauritius. Their labour was of paramount importance to the very existence of colonial society on the island. Eventually, in the production of sugar and thus wealth-creation of the white ruling class, the availability of their labour was deemed essential. Unsurprisingly therefore, the abolition of first the slave trade and then slavery itself was resisted vehemently. While these changes affected colonies throughout the British Empire, the peculiarities of the local context caused in Mauritius an aggravated response.

The aim of this chapter is to achieve an understanding of how the initial changes brought by the British affected the prevailing system of labour, and how this in turn affected societal composition. The issue of the slave trade presents the earliest clash between the former and new colonists on the island and is therefore the first event to be examined. An analysis of the legal mechanics in effecting the ban provides insight into the matters underlying colonial rivalries. The prohibition on slave trading highlights a number of jurisdictional conflicts as defined in Chapter 1, on both a metropolitan and local level, which set the tone for relations on the island. To this end, a brief overview of the Abolition of Slave Trade Act is provided and Mauritian slavery is put into its wider context before the application of the Act is discussed. Hereby a discussion of the Terms of Capitulation becomes necessary since these guaranteed protection of the local French laws, which up until British takeover included the legality of the trade. The remainder of the chapter addresses enforcement of the ban, practical and judicial, before concluding in an overall assessment of the period.

3.2 Developments towards abolition

Abolitionist sentiments in Britain had been rising and falling during the late 18th and early 19th century. A small yet noteworthy step towards abolition of the slave trade had already been made in 1788, when "Dolben's Act" was passed seeking to limit the number of slaves that could be carried on a vessel according to its

DOI: 10.4324/9781003313366-4

tonnage.[1] While the Act further required the presence of surgeons on board and a record to be kept of illnesses and deaths, it has not been clearly established whether the statute led indeed to a decrease of mortality during the voyages, as had been its purpose.[2]

It was during a "second wave", as Robin Blackburn describes it, that following several failed bills in parliament, the Slave Trade Abolition Act was finally passed in 1807 (hereafter the "1807 Act").[3] The endeavour had been successful arguably because it had focused exclusively on the trade, "explicitly disavowing any intention of pressing for slave emancipation in the British colonies."[4] The ban was expected to result in an amelioration of conditions since further supply of slaves would be limited to natural reproduction,[5] though this hope amongst abolitionists did not materialize.

Following the enactment, Britain made campaigning against the Atlantic slave trade a central plank of its diplomatic efforts. The policy allowed the British Empire to assume a position of moral authority against those states which continued to allow their vessels to carry out the traffic.[6] Following the Peace of Vienna in 1815, the European maritime powers passed a succession of abolition Acts, "often unwillingly . . . under diplomatic pressure from Great Britain".[7] The achievement of an international ban was a milestone that was reached towards the end of the century, at the Brussels Conference in 1890.[8] The process was thus a prolonged one, though not, as Jean Allain points out, for the lack of a multilateral agreement. Difficulties arose due to the legal doctrine of freedom of the seas (*mare liberum*), which meant that the slave trade could only be tackled via the indirect right permitting ships to be visited, but not searched by forces policing the ban.[9] Further concessions were evidently deemed too intrusive. However, where nations entered into treaties with Britain curtailing the slave trade, the Royal Navy was commonly granted authority to search and seize foreign vessels. This provided Britain with a legal justification for intercepting and harassing the merchant fleet of other powers.[10] Thus whilst operating under the guise of a compassionate cause, the British obtained other gains from policing the ban,

1 'An Act to regulate, for a limited Time, the shipping and carrying Slaves in British Vessels from the Coast of Africa', 28 Geo III, c. 54, 11 July 1788.
2 Morgan, Kenneth, *Slavery and the British Empire: From Africa to America* (Oxford: Oxford University Press, 2007), p. 160.
3 'An Act for the Abolition of the Slave Trade', 47 Geo III, c. 36, 25 March 1807.
4 Blackburn, Robin, *The Overthrow of Colonial Slavery, 1776–1848* (London: Verso, 1988), p. 322.
5 Ibid.
6 Allain, Jean, 'The Nineteenth Century Law of the Sea and the British Abolition of the Slave Trade', *British Yearbook of International Law*, 78 (2008), 342–88, p. 346.
7 Curtin, Philip, *The Atlantic Slave Trade – A Census* (Madison, WI: The University of Wisconsin Press, 1969), p. 231.
8 Ibid., p. 342.
9 Employing the French concept of a "*droit de visite*", see ibid.
10 Ibid., p. 321.

particularly when considering the fate of the captured cargo, the so-called "Prize slaves", as discussed in the Mauritian context below.

3.3 Slavery in Mauritius

3.3.1 The Indian Ocean

Situated in the southwest Indian Ocean, the slave trade in Mauritius was not part of the Atlantic paradigm, the primary model in the academic literature on slavery.[11] In the Americas, plantation slavery predominantly involved the removal of persons from western Africa, through what has become known as a "triangular trade", describing the route from Europe to Africa, to the Americas, and back.[12]

By contrast, the context of the Indian Ocean slave trade was more complex, with the traffic being "multidirectional".[13] Dating back 4,000 years, here the slave trade involved both overland and maritime passages that carried slaves from eastern Africa, India and the Arab states far across the region. Referred to by Gwyn Campbell as the "Indian Ocean World" (IOW) and said to cover "the entire area from the Cape to Cairo to Calcutta to Canton and beyond",[14] the region was part of an extensive system of labour migration, trade and capital flows,[15] "the first 'global' economy" through the establishment of a lasting network which connected "Africa to China, and all points in between."[16]

Slave-holding around the IOW took various forms, such as debt bondage and other types of servitude.[17] It was the ascent of the sugar economy in

11 For a classic account of the Atlantic slave trade, which also includes a review of the early literature, see Curtin, Philip, *The Atlantic Slave Trade – A Census* (Madison, WI: The University of Wisconsin Press, 1969). A very detailed treatment of the subject in provided by Black, Jeremy, ed., *The Atlantic Slave Trade*, I–IV vols (Aldershot: Ashgate Publishing, 2006), with each of the four volumes dedicated to a specific century, from the 17th to the 19th.

12 Also referred to as the "Middle Passage".

13 Campbell, Gwyn, 'Introduction: Slavery and Other Forms of Unfree Labour in the Indian Ocean World', in *The Structure of Slavery in Indian Ocean Africa and Asia*, ed. by Gwyn Campbell (Studies in Slave and Post-Slave Societies and Cultures; London: Frank Cass, 2004), p. ix.

14 Ibid., p. viii.

15 Harms, Robert W., 'Introduction: Indian Ocean Slavery in the Age of Abolition', in *Indian Ocean Slavery in the Age of Abolition*, ed. by Robert W. Harms, Bernard K. Freamon, and David W. Blight (New Haven, CT: Yale University Press, 2013), p. 2.

16 Campbell, Gwyn, 'Servitude and the Changing Face of the Demand for Labor in the Indian Ocean World, c. 1800–1900', in *Indian Ocean Slavery in the Age of Abolition*, ed. by Robert W. Harms, Bernard K. Freamon and David W. Blight (New Haven, CT: Yale University Press, 2013), p. 24.

17 For a collection of essays which discuss labour and debt in region, covering along Mauritius several other localities, including East Africa, the Arabian Gulf, India and China, see Campbell, Gwyn, and Alessandro Stanziani, eds., *Bonded Labour and Debt in the Indian Ocean World* (Financial History; London: Pickering & Chatto, 2013).

Mauritius and Réunion which brought the plantation system to the region.[18] The Mascarene islands presented the exception in the Indian Ocean by employing chattel slavery in a practice which mirrored the structure prevalent in the Americas.[19]

A further observation must be made with reference to the various sections of the Indian Ocean. It is important to note that while Britain dominated the northern part, including the Arab Gulf and the Red Sea,[20] the southwestern aspect, where Mauritius is located, was in fact controlled by the French.[21] This is of notable relevance because the persistence of the slave trade after abolition is at least partially a consequence of the island's geographical location, and more specifically, the French influence in the region, which resonated more with the Franco-Mauritian oligarchy than orders from the imperial government in Britain. The issues raised in this section will be revisited in an evaluation of the realities faced in enforcing the ban in Mauritius at 3.5 below.

3.3.2 Slavery during French colonization

As discussed in Chapter 2, slavery in Mauritius dates back to Dutch occupation, but became a significant component of the French period of colonization. Historical studies indicate that a wide array of ethnicities existed among slaves, including Mozambican, Malagasy and Indian.[22] It has been noted that "racial and ethnic diversity [was] the most distinctive feature of Mauritius slavery."[23]

Table 3.1 indicates that slaves formed by far the largest group of inhabitants during the late 18th and early 19th century.

18 Harms, op. cit., p. 2.
19 Campbell (2004), op. cit., p. x.
20 Crouzet, Guillemette, 'Chapter 16: "A Slave Trade Jurisdiction" – Attempts against the Slave Trade and the Making of a Space of Law (Arabo-Persian Gulf, Indian Ocean, Red Sea, circa 1820–1900)', in *Legal Histories of the British Empire: Laws, Engagements and Legacies*, ed. by Shaunnagh Dorsett and John McLaren (Abingdon; New York, NY: Routledge, 2014).
21 Teelock, Vijayalakshmi, *Mauritian History: From Its Beginnings to Modern Times*, 2nd Edition (Moka: Mahatma Gandhi Institute, 2009), p. 104.
22 Allen, Richard B., 'The Mascarene Slave-Trade and Labour Migration in the Indian Ocean during the Eighteenth and Nineteenth Centuries', in *The Structure of Slavery in Indian Ocean Africa and Asia*, ed. by Gwyn Campbell (Studies in Slave and Post-Slave Societies and Cultures; London: Frank Cass, 2004), pp. 35–36. Note that many other ethnicities were present and that this simplified categorization is academic. The Truth and Justice Commission has launched various initiatives to achieve a greater understanding of slaves' origins, still deemed insufficient, to enable descendants to trace their cultural heritage, see TJC Report, op. cit., p. 81.
23 Barker, A. J., *Slavery and Antislavery in Mauritius, 1810–33: The Conflict between Economic Expansion and Humanitarian Reform under British Rule* (Basingstoke: Macmillan, 1996, p. 13.

Table 3.1 Early censuses of Mauritius[24]

	Whites	*Free People of Colour*	*Slaves*	*Total*
1766	1,998	500	18,100	20,598
1788	4,457	2,456	37,915	44,828
1797	6,237	3,703	49,080	59,020
1807	7,194	7,366	60,509	75,069

Harold Adolphe, former archivist of Mauritius, provides the following explanations:[25]

- The "Whites" came from French provinces or possessions, and very rarely, other European countries (though Adolphe does not specify which countries, and in what quantity they had arrived, indicating a negligible amount).
- The "Slaves" had been imported from Africa, Madagascar and India.
- The "Free People" (in records interchangeably called "*Libres*" or "*Gens de Couleur*") were composed of locally manumissioned slaves and other free-born non-white inhabitants, predominantly of Indian origin.

In an appraisal of the economic situation of Mauritius during French rule, Megan Vaughan observes: "for the free inhabitants of the Ile de France, by far the most valuable commodity they possessed was that of slaves and by far the most important trade was that which ensured them a regular supply of this commodity."[26] She explains that without slaves, subsistence depended on long-distance shipping, capital invested in land would lay dormant, and the colony as a whole could not have been maintained. "To exist as a free person on Ile de France depended utterly on the possession of unfree persons – those who possessed none (and there were some throughout the 18th Century) were reduced to vagrancy."[27]

24 Reproduced from Adolphe, Harold, *Les Archives Démographique de L'ile Maurice: Registres Paroissiaux et D'état Civil (1721–1810)* (Mauritius: Mauritius Archives Publications, 1966), p. 6. The template of enumerating only three classes (Whites, Free Coloured, Slaves) was later perpetuated under the British. Robert Kuczynski suggests that the Mauritian context until abolition in fact requires distinction of eight classes of people (not identifiable in ordinary censuses), namely: "(1) Whites, excluding King's Troops and Resident Strangers; (2) Free Coloured; (3) Slaves (privately owned); (4) King's Troops; (5) Resident Strangers; (6) Government Slaves; (7) Apprentices; (8) Indian Convicts", see Kuczynski, Robert R., *Demographic Survey of the British Colonial Empire. Volume II: South Africa High Commission Territories, East Africa, Mauritius and Seychelles* (Oxford: Oxford University Press, 1949), p. 762.

25 Adolphe, op. cit., pp. 5–6.

26 Vaughan, Megan, 'The Character of the Market: Social Identities in Colonial Economies', *Oxford Development Studies*, 24 (1996), 61–77, p. 66.

27 Ibid.

3.4 Application of the 1807 Act

By the beginning of the 19th century, French colonial life on the island was settled and well-established.[28] It remains difficult to appraise what the precise living conditions were, for some commentators, such as Allister Macmillan in his extensive historical study, paint the picture of a thriving colonial society,[29] which however contrasts sharply with more contemporary observations highlighting squalid conditions and significant poverty.[30] What is undisputed is that every aspect of public life was firmly in French hands, as supported and sustained by their slaves, and as legal historian Tony Angelo observes: "In 1810, Mauritius had a strong legal culture, and the colony had considerable self-confidence."[31] It is in this context that British conquest must be understood.

The slave trade was a matter that immediately brought itself to the attention of the first British governor, Robert T. Farquhar, whose correspondence highlights how reliant life in Mauritius was on slavery. Notably, while Britain had abolished the slave trade, France by that point had not, and would actually in 1814 (through the Treaty of Paris) be given a further five years to do so.[32] Governor Farquhar's exchange with the Earl of Liverpool[33] on the subject two months after the takeover is revealing, for he makes a reasoned argument for the disapplication of the Slave Trade Act to Mauritius. Several paragraphs of his now-famous letter have been subject to criticism, not only in modern scholarship but by contemporary commentators as well.[34] The focus here is on the section that concerns the validity of the 1807 Slave Trade Act, which merits direct quotation:[35]

> I believe it has been generally agreed, that a British Act of Parliament does not extend to a colony, unless that colony be specially mentioned, either by name or general inclusive words; and that an Act made previously to the acquisition of a colony, and which therefore it could not be in the contemplation

28 For a description of the different aspects of Mauritian life during that period (e.g., commercial, cultural, ecclesiastical), see Macmillan, ***Mauritius Illustrated***, op. cit.

29 Ibid.

30 See for example IOR H/MISC/701, Governor Farquhar to the Earl of Liverpool, Port Louis, 8 January 1811, or CO 172/38, 'Three years' administration of Mauritius' by Edward Byam, 1822.

31 Angelo, Tony, 'Mauritius: Capitulation, Consolidation, Creation', in *A Study of Mixed Legal Systems: Endangered, Entrenched or Blended*, ed. by Sue Farran, Esin Örücü, and Seán Patrick Donlan (Farnham: Ashgate, 2014), 117–38, p. 133.

32 'Additional Articles, Article I', see FO 93/33/8 France, Definitive Treaty, Signed at Paris 30 May 1814

33 Robert Jenkinson, Earl of Liverpool, Secretary of State for War and the Colonies from 1 November 1809 to 11 June 1812, see Appendix A in Panton, Kenneth J., *Historical Dictionary of the British Empire* (London: Rowman & Littlefield, 2015).

34 The Anti-Slavery Reporter of November 1828, discussed below.

35 Governor Farquhar to the Earl of Liverpool, Port Louis, 15 February 1811, *PP 1826 (295) Papers and Communications Relative to the Slave Trade at the Mauritius and Bourbon, and the Seychelles, from the time of their capture to the present time: 1811–1817*, pp. 6–7.

> of the legislature to bind at the time of passing the Act, will not, generally speaking, bind the colony acquired subsequently to the making of the Act.
>
> Besides those general positions, my instructions were to grant these islands, on capitulation, their laws, customs and usages; they have been granted in express terms by the capitulations. Those laws, customs and usages recognise not only slavery, but the Slave Trade; without that trade, or some other substitute or remedy, these colonies promise shortly to be annihilated; and the inhabitants are likely to be rendered desperate, if the supply of slaves be refused them.

Governor Farquhar wraps up the point by stating that he understands the slave trade as remaining sanctioned to an extent in Trinidad or other places in the West Indies.

Further, while claiming that he would seek to ameliorate the position of the slaves, he believes that any "any sudden alteration, or an ill-timed display of sympathy, might be attended with the worst effects", since there seemingly persisted a view in Mauritius "that the arrival of the English was to be the signal of emancipation, and the release of the slave from all obligation towards his master."

The return despatch, dated two months later, saw the governor being severely admonished for his interpretation of the application of the Act, declared "entirely misinformed" regarding the continuation of the slave trade in other colonies, and receiving alongside the reply a copy of the Slave Trade Act, with instructions to carefully study it.[36] It seems unlikely that Farquhar expected to receive the scathing response he did. Marina Carter and others claim, however, that the above exchange allowed him to delay promulgation of the Act.[37] In that line of argument, his stance would amount to little more than a brief stalling of the ban. It is submitted that the governor's objective went further than that. But whatever Farquhar's intentions, a number of conclusions may be drawn from the communication.

There are two possible readings of Farquhar's first paragraph, on what he deemed to be "generally agreed". The most obvious interpretation is taking it to mean that since Mauritius was not a British colony in 1807, having only become a possession in 1810, the Act did not apply to the island. Prima facie, there appears a certain plausibility to the argument which will be considered shortly. Another interpretation is an implicit assertion that, since Mauritius had not been "in the contemplation of the legislature", *had* it been a British possession at the time of the passing of the Act, parliament is likely to have made certain allowances, warranting subsequent exemption. This line of reasoning is supported by Farquhar's representations in the second paragraph, where he underlines the absolute necessity of the slave trade for the viability of the colony that is otherwise risking,

36 Earl of Liverpool to Governor Farquhar, 2 May 1811, ibid., pp. 7–8.

37 Carter, M., V. Govinden, and S. Peerthum, *The Last Slaves: Liberated Africans in 19th Century Mauritius* (Mauritius: CRIOS, Centre for Research on Indian Ocean Societies, 2003), p. 7.

he claims, "annihilation". Cognizant of the island's need, Farquhar presupposes parliament to not have had legislated against it.

While this second reading of the governor's argument (possibly lost on the Earl of Liverpool) had no basis in law, it is nevertheless quite cogent, given its focus upon the imperial interest: the survival of the colony. This, no doubt, would have been quite a significant concern in London even if arguably, making an exception in case of Mauritius would have been damaging to Britain's self-projected humanitarian image and to its efforts in achieving international cooperation in effecting the ban. Either way, it was evident that the Earl was not amenable to entertain any notion of the continued legality of the slave trade in Mauritius:[38]

> I cannot sufficiently express my surprise that you should have supposed it possible that when the Parliament of the United Kingdom had thought proper, upon general principles, to abolish the Slave Trade with respect to all the ancient colonies and established settlements of Great Britain, it could have been in their contemplation that this trade should be suffered to exist with respect to those islands or foreign possessions, which the fortune of war might place under His Majesty's dominion.

A close reading of the wording employed in the 1807 Act does indeed reveal that its intended application was wide and oriented towards the future.[39]

The constitutional position as articulated by the Earl was codified with the adoption of the Colonial Laws Validity Act ("CLV Act") by the British Parliament.[40] Under the CLV Act, a legal continuation of the slave trade in Mauritius would have probably been void for "repugnancy",[41] as it would have presented a direct contradiction to the 1807 ban. The CLV Act however did not pass until 1865, and while it may reflect how Parliament intended its imperial laws to apply, it cannot be relied on for the situation in Mauritius in 1810.

What then, of Farquhar's argument against the retrospective application of the 1807 Act to an island conquered three years subsequently? In the absence of clear statutory guidance at the time, did the Earl's answer have a legal basis?

38 Earl of Liverpool to Governor Farquhar, cited above.

39 See for example Section 4: "And be it further enacted, that if any Subject or Inhabitant . . . not being in the Dominion, Possession, or Occupation of His Majesty, who shall, **at any Time from and after the Day aforesaid** [the day of coming into force] have been unlawfully carried away or removed from Africa, or from any . . . Territory . . . contrary to any of the Prohibitions or Provisions in this Act contained, . . . may be seized and prosecuted, as forfeited to His Majesty" (emphasis added).

40 'An Act to remove Doubts as to the Validity of Colonial Laws', 28 & 29 Vict, c. 63, 29 June 1865.

41 See Section 2: "Any Colonial Law which is or shall be in any respect repugnant to the Provisions of any Act of Parliament extending to the Colony to which such Law may relate, . . . shall be read subject to such Act, . . . and shall, to the Extent of such Repugnancy, . . . be and remain absolutely void and inoperative."

This inquiry questions the very source of law in a newly acquired territory. An examination of the jurisprudential underpinning of the idea of conquest is hereby instructive. According to Halleck's 19th-century treatise on international law, the laws which remain valid "do not derive any force from the will of the conquered, for the person capable of having and expressing a will – the body politic, or law-making power of the conquered – is extinguished by conquest." The laws which continue to operate do so on the presumption that "the new political sovereign has adopted and continued them as a matter of convenience." As a consequence, "whatever is in conflict with or directly opposed to, such expressions of his will, we cannot assume to have been adopted by his tacit consent."[42] Thus, if under 19th-century international law, a new sovereign's power was deemed not only to project into the future, but extend into the past as well, the legality of the slave trade in Mauritius would have ceased upon conquest, because the 1807 Act would at that point be deemed effective, since the French slave trade laws, which are in contradiction to it, cannot be presumed to have been adopted by the British parliament.

It is the preservation of the French laws which thus becomes an issue. While the Earl of Liverpool denounced Farquhar's logic regarding the Slave Trade Act emphatically, Farquhar's second argument regarding the Terms of Capitulation was not at all addressed in the Earl's reply. If the inhabitants of Mauritius had been granted the protection of their French laws, would that not encompass the legality of the French slave trade?

3.4.1 Legal effect of the Terms of Capitulation

Before considering the ramifications of the 1810 Terms of Capitulation between France and Britain concerning Mauritius, it should be helpful to illuminate the concept of capitulations more generally. Historically, the term "capitulation" was used to describe two different kinds of instrument. On the one hand, capitulations were understood to be treaties which granted certain powers and privileges to the nationals of one of the parties whilst residing in the territory of the other – a system of consular jurisdiction that, in the context of the Ottoman Empire was referred to as the "capitulatory system".[43] A second usage was to be found in the military context, in which the capitulation was a localized act to be legally distinguished from surrender.[44] As it was later described, a capitulation was to be understood as "a mutual agreement

42 Baker, Sherston Sir, *Halleck's International Law – Rules Regulating the Intercourse of States in Peace and War, Volume II*, 3rd Edition (London: Kegan Paul, Trench, Trübner & Co. Ltd, 1893), p. 488.

43 For a discussion of this type of capitulation, see Özsu, Umut, 'Ottoman Empire', in *The Oxford Handbook of the History of International Law*, ed. by Bardo Fassbender et al. (Oxford: Oxford University Press, 2014).

44 Dedijer, Vladimir, 'Legal Character of the Capitulation of Norwegian Armed Forces On June 10, 1940', *Nordic Journal of International Law*, 30 (1) (1960): 39–51.

on the future surrender" of one of the parties, surrender being the obligation that is "the essential content of an agreement on capitulation".[45] As such, an agreement on capitulation can be reached with or without conditions, conditional capitulation offering more advantageous terms than straightforward surrender.[46] This modern definition is very close to 19th-century definitions of the concept.[47]

Examining the Terms of Capitulation between France and Britain in Mauritius, it is apparent that they took indeed the form of an agreement, with British stipulations being followed by French "Answers", meaning confirmations of the aforesaid, with the wording revealing varying degrees of assent.[48] The most crucial item, and notably the only one reiterated verbatim in response, is Article 8: "The inhabitants shall preserve their Religion, Laws and Customs."

This concession appears to be rather broad and extensive. International legal doctrine ordinarily restricts terms of capitulation as binding only on the troops under the command of the officer concluding the agreement. Lassa Oppenheim, in his treatise on International Law, states:

> Capitulations are military conventions only and exclusively; they must not, therefore, contain arrangements other than those of a local and military character concerning the surrendering forces, places, or ships. If they do contain such arrangements, the latter are not valid, unless they are ratified by the political authorities of both belligerents.[49]

Similarly, in Halleck's 19th-century rules on the intercourse of states, it is stated that the power to enter into a capitulation is implied in the office of the commander in charge, and any agreements "not coming within his implied powers would be null and void, unless special authority to that effect had been given to him, or his acts should subsequently receive the sanction of his government."[50]

45 Ibid., p. 41.

46 Ibid.

47 See § 10 on Capitulations in Baker, Sherston Sir, *Halleck's International Law – Rules Regulating the Intercourse of States in Peace and War, Volume II*, 3rd Edition (London: Kegan Paul, Trench, Trübner & Co. Ltd, 1893), p. 319.

48 Capitulation (Code Farquhar No.1), 3 December 1810, reproduced (in both English and French) in Rouillard, John, ed., *A Collection of the Laws of Mauritius and Its Dependencies. Volume III: 3rd December 1810–16th November 1831* (Mauritius: Published by the Authority of the Government, 1866) <http://catalog.hathitrust.org/Record/011570339> [accessed 26 June 2022].

49 Oppenheim, Lassa, *International Law: A Treatise. War and Neutrality*, 2nd Edition (London: Longmans, Green and Co., 1912), p. 285.

50 Baker, Sherston Sir, *Halleck's International Law – Rules Regulating the Intercourse of States in Peace and War, Volume II*, 3rd Edition (London: Kegan Paul, Trench, Trübner & Co. Ltd, 1893), p. 320.

In the case of Mauritius, the wide-ranging concession of Article 8 was clearly granted purposefully by the British side, evident not only from Governor Farquhar's statement in his letter above, but also corroborated by an account of Admiral Bertie, who as a party to the negotiations confirmed: "His Majesty's Instructions . . . have been the rule and guide of the occasion".[51]

Concluded on 3 December 1810, the Capitulation was subsequently proclaimed on the island two days later.[52] As mentioned in Chapter 2, Mauritius was officially ceded to Britain through Article 8 of the Treaty of Paris in 1814. However, commentators have correctly pointed out that the Treaty makes no allusion made to the Terms of Capitulation or the proclamation of 1810.[53] While the conclusion of the Paris Treaty too, was subsequently proclaimed in Mauritius,[54] Justice Wood Renton argues that since it was never confirmed by imperial statute, the "maintenance of French law in Mauritius depends solely on the Capitulation, the Proclamation of December 5, 1810, and the rule . . . that the law of a conquered or ceded Colony at the time of conquest or cession remains in force till it has been altered by competent legislative authority."[55] Though not cited by Renton, the "rule" he refers to actually derives from the 1774 case of *Campbell v. Hall*.[56]

3.4.2 *Campbell v. Hall*

The material facts of the case turned on the legality of British duties imposed in lieu of French duties at the island of Grenada, which had been acquired by Britain through conquest from France. Not dissimilar to Mauritius, Grenada capitulated subject to the provision that it "should continue to be governed by its present laws until His Majesty's further pleasure be known."[57] Lord Mansfield, who delivered the judgment, was one of the government's most influential people on

51 IOR H/MISC/701, Admiral Bertie to Lord Minto, Port Louis, 12 December 1810.

52 Code Farquhar No. 2, reproduced in Rouillard, op. cit.

53 Renton, Justice Wood, 'French Law within the British Empire', *Journal of the Society of Comparative Legislation*, 10 (2), 250–60, pp. 105–106; see also Toussaint, op. cit., p. 59

54 Code Farquhar No.156, 19 December 1814, reproduced in Rouillard, op. cit.

55 Renton, op. cit., p. 106. The implications of the above have continued to attract comment in the context of ascertaining which specific laws were in force in Mauritius at what time; see Angelo, Tony, 'Mauritius: Capitulation, Consolidation, Creation', op. cit. above, and Twomey, Mathilda, 'The Parts That Make A Whole? The Mixity of the Laws of Seychelles', in *Mixed Legal Systems, East and West*, ed. by Vernon Valentine Palmer, Mohamed Y. Mattar, and Anna Koppel (Farnham: Ashgate, 2015), pp. 55–74. From a modern perspective, the Supreme Court of Mauritius confirmed in 1902 that it considers the French laws as having been validly preserved at Capitulation, the wording of the 1814 Treaty of Paris notwithstanding, see the case of *Colonial Government v. Widow Laborde and Others* (1902) MR 19.

56 *Campbell v. Hall* [1774] 1 COWP 204. See also *Calvin's Case* [1608] 7 Coke Report 1a, 77 ER 377 for an early ruling on the application of English law subsequent to conquest.

57 Ibid., p. 205.

colonial affairs in the Upper House and took the opportunity to provide a decision of lasting relevance to the imperial context.[58]

The most significant pronouncement for present purposes was that "the laws of a conquered country continue in force until they are altered by the conqueror."[59] Further, no privilege existed for the Englishman as against the locals, who, receiving the Crown's protection, emerged as British subjects. While the articles of capitulation "are sacred and inviolable according to their true intent and meaning", a conquered country became a dominion of the Crown and was consequentially placed under the authority of the British parliament.[60]

It is thus evident that Article 8 of the Capitulation was not a concession unique to Mauritius. British imperial practice allowed for retention of local laws upon conquest, though it is the absence of any limitation or caveat to that grant (as for example placed in the Grenadian capitulation described above) which appears surprising in the Mauritian Capitulation. However, Lauren Benton explains that while colonialism set the stage for legal pluralism, individual approaches varied.[61] In all instances "strategic decisions" regarding the type of legal control to be imposed were made, yet while sometimes this involved "aggressive attempts to impose legal systems intact", frequently, there "were conscious efforts to retain elements of existing institutions and limit legal change as a way of sustaining social order."[62] This appears to have also been the case in Mauritius. Broadly allowing the French oligarchy to keep their laws and customs ensured their continued superior position on the island, possibly allowing the takeover to be more peaceful than it otherwise could have been. The concession may also be taken to indicate from the beginning the absence of an intention to anglicize Mauritius. The British, indeed, did not settle on the island in significant numbers.

With respect to the application of the 1807 Slave Trade Act in Mauritius after conquest, the decision of *Campbell v. Hall* makes it clear that while the terms of the Capitulation were to be honoured and French laws continued, this would be subject to the authority of the British parliament. As such, laws which were inconsistent with Acts passed by the legislature could no longer apply.[63] While this did not affect the laws to slave-holding per se, as far as the sale and purchase of slaves was concerned, the legality of the French slave trade remained of

58 Ward, John Manning, *Colonial Self-Government: The British Experience, 1759–1856* (Cambridge Commonwealth Series; London and Basingstoke: Macmillan, 1976), p. 11.

59 *Campbell v. Hall*, above, 209.

60 Ibid., 208

61 Benton, Lauren, *Law and Colonial Cultures: Legal Regimes in World History, 1400–1900* (Cambridge; New York, NY: Cambridge University Press, 2001), p. 2.

62 Ibid.

63 See also the commentary in *Halsbury's Laws of England*, Volume 13 (2009), para. 867: 'Continuance of former law in conquered or ceded colonies'.

no substantive relevance to Mauritius. Therefore, contrary to common historical assessment, the Slave Trade Act of 1807 took effect upon conquest, irrespective of the Crown or parliament actively altering the local law, whether through proclamation or otherwise.[64]

3.5 Enforcement of the ban in practice

The 1807 Act specifically prohibited "all manners of dealing or trading" in African slaves, imposing a penalty of £100 per slave on contravention of the ban.[65] Further, it stipulated that any slave unlawfully carried would be forfeited to the king,[66] and could be taken as prize of war and be enlisted into Crown service at land or sea, or bound as an apprentice for a period not exceeding 14 years.[67] The legislation of 1807 was subsequently superseded by a similar Act in 1824,[68] extended in 1843[69] and consolidated again in 1873.[70]

The provisions of the 1807 Act were eventually promulgated in Mauritius in January 1813,[71] through legislation that declared the carrying-out of the slave trade a felony.[72] The concept of trading in slaves had been framed in very broad terms, effectively applying to any person resident in the British Empire who purported to

> deal or trade in, purchase, sell, barter, or transfer, or contract or agree for the dealing or trading in, purchasing, selling, bartering, or transferring of any Slave or Slaves, or any Person or Persons intended to be sold, transferred, used, or dealt with as a Slave or Slaves contrary to the Prohibitions of [the 1807] Act.[73]

Successful enforcement however remained elusive in subsequent decades.

64 In 1835, the case of *Jephson v. Riera* confirmed that such alteration could occur through proclamation, Order in Council, Letters patent or Charter under the Great Seal; or alternatively through the British or local legislature, see *Jephson v. Riera* [1835] III KNAPP, 130.
65 Section II.
66 Section IV.
67 Section VII.
68 'An Act to amend and consolidate the Laws relating to the Abolition of the Slave Trade', Geo IV, c. 113, 24 June 1824.
69 'An Act for the more effectual Suppression of the Slave Trade', Vict., c. 98, 24 August 1843.
70 'An Act for consolidating with Amendments the Acts for carrying into effect Treaties for the more effectual Suppression of the Slave Trade, and for other purposes connected with the Slave Trade', 36 & 37 Vict., ch. 88, 5 August 1873.
71 Code Farquhar No. 112, (undated), which gives an incorrect citation for this updated version of the Act: 'An Act for rendering more effectual an Act made in the Forty Seventh Year of His Majesty's Reign, intituled, An Act for the Abolition of the Slave Trade', 51 Geo, c.13, 14 May 1811.
72 Ibid., Section I. The legislation has commonly been called the Slave Felony Act.
73 Section I of the 1807 Abolition of Slavery Act, cited above.

Assessing the precise dimensions in which the slave trade continued unofficially in and around Mauritius is difficult, since by definition it became clandestine. Slave-holders were required from an early stage to provide returns on the number of slaves for tax purposes,[74] as well as keeping registers of births and deaths,[75] yet the statistics available are considered unreliable.[76] This is not surprising as slave-holders would have had little incentive to submit accurate records given their undoubted desire to avoid taxation and prevent any detection of the illicit importation of slaves. Nevertheless, the numbers that are available are striking. Proprietors' returns and the tax collectors' rolls indicate a slave population of 53,060 and 61,918 respectively for the year 1811, yet in 1818, the latter indicates a slave population of 80,019, with no number from proprietors' returns given.[77] While the 1818 figure includes slaves the French were allowed to import from Madagascar following conquest, historians suspect the trade continued to an extensive degree.[78] In the most detailed piece of research on this subject to date, Richard Allen provides several estimates and sets the number of illegally introduced slaves to Mauritius and the Seychelles in the period from 1811 to 1827 at a projected 52,550.[79]

Historical records, whether statistics or otherwise, are very inconsistent,[80] and given the politically charged context must be read while taking into account the circumstances and possible intentions of the source.[81] What can be said, however, is that the ban on the trade in slaves would have put in place a set of incentives, on the part of the plantation owners, to pursue a series of strategies for its avoidance, and had the potential to put the local administration and the French oligarchy at odds with one another.

74 First British census order through Code Farquhar No. 21, 24 January 1811.

75 First required under Code Farquhar No. 82, 4 February 1812.

76 Kuczynski, Robert R., *Demographic Survey of the British Colonial Empire. Volume II: South Africa High Commission Territories, East Africa, Mauritius and Seychelles* (Oxford: Oxford University Press, 1949), p. 762. See also CO 415/19 *Report of the Commissioners of Eastern Enquiry in Mauritius 1826–1828*, Statistical Returns, p. 3 'Statement of Population of Mauritius in 1825', which contains the following observation: "The birth and deaths among the slave population as contained in the above return must be considered as very incorrect – the owners having hitherto been very irregular in making their declarations."

77 CO 415/6 *Report of the Commissioners of Eastern Enquiry in Mauritius 1826–1828*, 'Return of the Slave Population of the Isle of France', A.130.

78 See e.g. Nwulia, op. cit., p. 46.

79 Allen, Richard B., 'Licentious and Unbridled Proceedings: The Illegal Slave Trade to Mauritius and the Seychelles during the Early Nineteenth Century', *Journal of African History*, 42 (2001), 91–116, p. 100. Note that in presenting statistics, Allen fails to distinguish between unavailable records and the return being nil.

80 Kuczynski, op. cit., notes: "The statistics [for the period 1811–1834] are difficult to interpret since different figures appear in different documents and since none of the statistics are all-inclusive", p. 762.

81 See the discussion on Governor Farquhar below.

3.5.1 Prize slaves

The treatment of captured slaves from trade vessels around Mauritius belied the avowed benevolent sentiments behind the ambition to abolish the slave trade. Captured slaves were not freed but retained at Port Louis, the capital. Usually described in records as "Prize Negroes", other popular designations are "Liberated Africans" and "Apprentices", though some historians prefer the term "Recaptives" to more accurately describe their subsequent fate.[82] Pursuant to section VII of the 1807 Act, as extended[83] and confirmed[84] in 1808 and 1817 respectively, Prize slaves were possessions of the British Crown and could be enlisted or bound as apprentices.

An examination of a document governing such service agreements provides interesting insight as to how this operated in practice.[85] Designed as a standard form to be filled out and titled an "Indenture of Two Parts", between the Collector of Customs and the person taking on the slave, the document was to be executed in the style of a deed, in the presence of a witness. The provisions stipulated that the named "Negroe" would be "put, placed and bound" as "an Apprentice" for a term of years to be fixed, to be instructed in trade to be specified, "or as the case may be . . . other useful employments thereto relating, according to the usage and customs of this Colony". Further, "said Negroe" was expected to "faithfully serve", according to his or her "power, wits and abilities", and "honestly and obediently in all things shall behave [him or her]-self". The other party was held to "promise and covenant to and with His Majesty, His Heirs and Successors" that the slave would be "diligently and faithfully" instructed in the trade, provided with "sufficient and comfortable food, clothing, and other necessaries" and not treated "with hardship or severity".

Evidently, to prevent further slave-trading, the document also stipulated that the recaptive was not to be assigned to another person, or sent to another colony, "without previous Licence", as well as having "from time to time, as often as . . . shall be required by the said Collector" to be produced "for inspection and examination" at a "Return" where "a full, true and just account of the state of health, of employment and treatment" was to be rendered. A Penal Sum "being double the value of the said Negroe" would be incurred if he or she was sold on as a slave, and under the threat of forfeiture, "all the covenants" contained in the document were to be "duly and faithfully" performed.

The provisions of the contract reveal the contradictory attitudes prevailing at the time, which is arguably the result of the slave trade having had been

82 Carter, M., V. Govinden, and S. Peerthum, *The Last Slaves: Liberated Africans in 19th Century Mauritius* (Mauritius: CRIOS, Centre for Research on Indian Ocean Societies, 2003).
83 CO 854/1 Order in Council, 16 March 1808.
84 CO 854/1 Prince Regent's Order in Council, 11 July 1817.
85 CO 415/11, B No. 7, *Commissioners of Eastern Enquiry Report* 'Returns of Documents relating to Prize Negroes', which contains a printed copy of such a contract.

abolished, but not slavery itself. Slaves captured were not specified as such (the document consistently uses the term "Negroe"), yet under the legislation they were considered as belonging to the Crown. The hypocrisy inherent in designating them as "Prize" upon the interception of their illegal transportation is difficult to reconcile with the ostensibly humanitarian aims of banning the slave trade. Further, the recaptive is not a party to the agreement, which takes place between the Collector of Customs and the new "employer", which thus affirms his or her status as chattel, the mere object of a contract, effectively reduced to an item being loaned out. Notably, this so-called "indenture", while purporting to govern the conditions of an "Apprentice" supposedly bound for the purposes of being instructed in a "trade", makes no mention to remuneration of any kind. Instead, the "employer" is expected to maintain the apprentice, which is more akin to the manner in which slaves were kept. The issue of wages was only addressed when slavery itself was abolished and recaptives became workers alongside emancipated slaves, who acquired the legal status of what was equally called an "apprenticeship",[86] discussed in the next chapter. It is thus evident that the recaptive, whilst not officially designated a slave, was kept in de facto slavery. Extraordinarily, he or she entered that slavery not upon sale or transfer to a private owner, but at the point of being rescued and "freed" from the slave traders.

It has been pointed out that Prize slaves in Mauritius were frequently treated worse than their counterparts,[87] despite the apparent guarantees that were to be found in the indenture agreement as outlined above. But given that unlike "actual" slaves they were not considered personal property and did not present an investment to their keeper, this lack of care towards loaned workers is not entirely surprising.

The data contained in Table 3.2, taken from the report of the Commissioners of Eastern Inquiry into the slave trade,[88] certainly indicates that recaptives were not accorded the kind of humane treatment that the legislation envisaged. As the numbers show, during a period of 14 years, nearly 26 per cent of "apprentices" loaned out had either died since their apprenticeship or were unaccounted for, and only 0.2 per cent had achieved freedom or return to their country of origin.

86 Post-emancipation apprenticeship is discussed in Chapter 4. The work by Marina Carter et al., *The Last Slaves*, op. cit., addresses the history of recaptives in Mauritius and remains unique in its scope. Unfortunately, the subject is treated uniformly and there is a failure to clearly distinguish between the periods before and after emancipation. However, a consideration of the legal status of slaves in general is essential to an effective appraisal of British policy regarding Prize slaves in particular.

87 Banton, Mandy, 'The "Taint of Slavery"', in *Slavery, Diplomacy and Empire: Britain and the Suppression of the Slave Trade, 1807–1975*, ed. by Keith Hamilton and Patrick Salmon (Brighton: Sussex Academic Press, 2009), pp. 143–164.

88 The Inquiry Report is discussed in more detail below.

Table 3.2 Apprenticed Prize slaves in Mauritius between 1813 and 1827[89]

2,419		*Total apprenticed out*
2		Condemned but not yet apprenticed out
2,421		**Total**
		of which
Male	***Female***	
459	133	Died since apprenticeship
2	9	Servitude has expired
22	8	Missing or unaccounted for
3	2	Restored as free or permitted to return to their country
638		Total
1,783		**Remaining (on 31st August 1827)**

In practice, recaptives had one particularly important function in Mauritius – they helped alleviate the lack of available labourers that had resulted from the ban on the trade in slaves. In this context, however, Barker observes that in the period from 1813 to 1826, the employers of Prize slaves were mostly British not French – the main beneficiaries being "military and government officials, including the Chief Judge, George Smith".[90] Governor Farquhar himself was in fact "the second most prolific hirer" having received over a period 47 apprentices in total, a number exceeded only by Irish-born Charles Telfair (a notable inhabitant of the island and supposed slave-cause advocate) with 59 apprentices.[91] When viewed in the broader context of British-French antagonism, one can understand this as a small-scale initiative on the part of the British administration to wrest political and economic control of the Islands away from the French oligarchy. In taking control of the supply of labour the British administration was effectively presented with two opportunities: The first being to dry out the supply of labour to French plantation owners and hence make them ever more dependent upon the munificence or generosity of the British administration, and the second being to use such labour for the establishment of rival economic endeavours that might ultimately undermine the French control over the economy of the island. This latter opportunity, however, was never fully to be seized in part at least because of a continued policy of conciliation on the part of the British governor Farquhar.

89 Table compiled from data in CO 167/141 Report on the Slave Trade. Miscellaneous Returns: No. 19 Return of the number of Prize Negroes, captured condemned and apprenticed at Mauritius from 1813 to 1827.

90 Barker, op. cit., pp. 41–42.

91 Rather ominously, out of these 59, 27 had died during service, see Barker, ibid.

3.5.2 Political sympathies

The interval between the abolition of the slave trade and the abolition of slavery presents a complex period in Mauritian history, for it was influenced by a number of factors: the attitude of the local British administration, Franco-Mauritian interests and British imperial policy.

The lack of success in eradicating the slave trade is invariably tied up with an appraisal of Robert T. Farquhar himself, the first British governor of the island. Farquhar held that position twice, initially from 1810 to 1817, and again from 1820 to 1823. Modern historians ignore a brief interval in 1811, when Farquhar was removed from his post and made governor of neighbouring Bourbon, with Major-General Henry Warde taking his place for three months.[92] This is surprising, for research revealed that this brief period, though otherwise unremarkable, witnessed a highly memorable event: the designation "Island of Mauritius" appears for the first time publicly in a proclamation dated 30 April 1811 signed by Governor Warde, in substitution to the hitherto used name "Ile de France".[93] The alteration no doubt irked the French inhabitants, and it is perhaps characteristic that it was not Farquhar who effected the change in name, as their appeasement was a major feature of his administration.

Scholars are divided in their evaluation of Farquhar's policies, with some more pronounced in their criticism of the governor's role than others.[94] To be sure, the challenge he faced in governing the island was complex and cannot be underestimated. In assuming the governorship, Farquhar found himself in midst of a multitude of political, economic and jurisdictional conflicts. The situation in Mauritius required not only mediation between the divergent concerns of old and new colonists over the question of slavery, but also consolidation of incongruous imperial interests, which on the one side endeavoured to support and promote the economic development of the island and on the other side implementation of the Slave Trade Act. Imperial ambitions were at odds because the position of the slaves was markedly different in each context. Economically, slaves presented nothing more but an anonymous mass of labour that enabled the existence of French colonial society. Yet with the abolition of the slave trade, the hitherto deemed passive workforce acquired an identity through the introduction of accountability and control over slave-holding. Confronted with this disparity, it is

92 Code Farquhar No. 35, 8 April 1811. Governor Farquhar was reinstated on 15 July 1811, see Code Farquhar No. 56.

93 Code Farquhar No.44, 30 April 1811.

94 Compare for example the strict interpretation in Nwulia, Moses D. E., *The History of Slavery in Mauritius and the Seychelles, 1810–1875* (Rutherford, NJ; London: Fairleigh Dickenson University Press; Associated University Presses, 1981) and Barker, A. J., *Slavery and Anti-slavery in Mauritius, 1810–33: The Conflict between Economic Expansion and Humanitarian Reform under British Rule* (Basingstoke: Macmillan, 1996) with the moderate assessment of Teelock, Vijaya, *Bitter Sugar: Sugar and Slavery in 19th Century Mauritius* (Moka, Mauritius: Mahatma Gandhi Institute, 1998) and Allen, Richard B., *Slaves, Freedmen and Indentured Laborers in Colonial Mauritius* (Cambridge: Cambridge University Press, 2006).

clear Governor Farquhar made a choice to prioritize one over the other, even if not openly admitting doing so.

Six years after conquest, a proclamation confirmed that the "Letters Patent of 1723" (the *Code Noir*)[95] remained in force with respect to the slave population,[96] demonstrating the absence of any material progress as far as slavery conditions were concerned. Notably, during Farquhar's tenure, legislation from Britain aside, no ordinances for the improvement of slave conditions were passed. A survey of the early ordinances in fact reveals repeated extensions granted by Farquhar to the French slave-holders to comply with the legal requirements of slave registration.[97] However it was not before the mid-1820s that the British Colonial Office became aware of the extent of the governor's sympathies with the slave-holders[98], imperial attention having been focused primarily on the West Indies up to that time.[99]

In 1826 Thomas Fowell Buxton, William Wilberforce's successor as anti-slavery spokesperson in Parliament, presented extensive information to the House of Commons on the enormous scale of the continued trade in slaves in Mauritius, the unannounced revelations taking place in Farquhar's presence no less.[100] The by-then-former governor's administration was subsequently put under scrutiny in a series of articles published in Zachary Macaulay's *Anti-Slavery Reporter* in 1828 and 1829.[101] Not only was the absence of any protective measures towards slaves highlighted, but also Farquhar's obvious sympathies towards the French inhabitants, which contrasted sharply with his disregard for the conditions of the former. Farquhar defended himself vigorously against the accusations, without however addressing the substantive issues of his indictment.[102] In correspondence with the Colonial Department, the former governor similarly refuted the allegations raised in the *Reporter*, speaking of "numerous regulations" which he had supposedly enacted for the benefit of slaves, without however providing concrete details.[103] His disdain for being held to account in this fashion is evident in the passage where he states: "It surely is not expected from me, at this time of day, neither do I consider it consistent with my own dignity, to attempt to wade in detail

95 The *Code Noir* in Mauritius is discussed in Chapter 2.

96 Code Farquhar No. 217, 6 November 1816.

97 See for instance Code Farquhar No. 178, 13 September 1815 and Code Farquhar No. 189, 7 December 1815.

98 Barker, op. cit., p. 24.

99 Burroughs, Peter, 'The Mauritius Rebellion of 1832 and the Abolition of British Colonial Slavery', *The Journal of Imperial and Commonwealth History*, 4 (1976), 243–65.

100 Parliamentary Debates, New Series, Volume 15, 20 March 1826–33 May 1826, May 9, p. 1014.

101 'Anti-Slavery Reporter', November 1828 (No. 42); January 1829 (No. 44); July 1829 (No. 50)

102 Ibid., No. 50.

103 PP XXV 1829 *(337) Copies of any Correspondence which has passed between Sir Robert Farquhar and the Colonial Department, upon the subject of certain Charges contained in a Publication, intituled, "The Anti-Slavery Reporter, No.42"*, pp. 3–7 (97–101).

through the mass of impure matter contained in the pamphlet in question".[104] Defending himself, he resorted back to his disputed interpretation of the effects of the anti-slavery legislation in Mauritius: "The sneering and insolent remarks on the tenderness of my early friendship for the slave trade, referring to a time when the abolition Acts were not known at the Mauritius, and were not *law there*, though the spirit of them was acted upon my order, and upon my sole responsibility, merits little or no observation from me".[105]

As established above, his assertion regarding the application of the Slave Trade Act was incorrect, and Farquhar must be taken to have knowingly made this misrepresentation to the Colonial Department. While he possibly could plead ignorance regarding its validity for the early days after conquest, within a few months he had been enlightened by Lord Liverpool's dispatch. In the same memorable exchange just shortly after British takeover, Farquhar had stated the number of slaves to be 60,000,[106] yet now being questioned, 18 years later, he mentions General Decaen, the last French governor, who had left a handwritten note which set the number of slaves at the time of surrender at "upwards of 80,000". Farquhar explains that the tax collectors' roll return only accounted for 60,000 since the difference consisted of "the aged and the children incapable of work, for whom they were unwilling to pay."[107] The implied assertion that in 1810 Mauritius was home to 20,000 elderly and infant slaves, who were being maintained by French colonists (themselves amounting to less than 8,000 people), despite being useless to them, is incredulous. Farquhar also stretches the truth in claiming that "there was no law at Mauritius requiring a registration of slaves . . . except [for] the regulation which was made upon the spot for fiscal purposes" until the relevant British order in council of 1814.[108] Despite these numerous deceptions, it does not appear that Farquhar was further questioned on the matter.

In the same year that the former governor had to face the *Anti-Slavery Reporter* allegations, a report on the extent of the slave trade in Mauritius was published. From 1826 to 1828, the Commissioners of Eastern Inquiry[109] had visited Mauritius to investigate the slave-trading allegations.[110] Given that no slaves were interviewed by the Commissioners, their legal status barring them from testifying

104 Ibid., 3 February 1829, p. 5 (99).
105 Ibid., emphasis in original, p. 7 (101).
106 Governor Farquhar to the Earl of Liverpool, Port Louis, 15 February 1811, cited above, p. 6.
107 PP XXV 1829 (337) above, p. 4 (98).
108 Registration of slaves required by law dates back to an Act dated 9 April 1753, when Mauritius was under the administration of the French East India Company, see Kuczynski, op. cit., p. 707.
109 Frequently spelled as Commissioners of Eastern Enquiry and abbreviated "CEE".
110 Their report remains the largest and most comprehensive record of slave-holding in Mauritius during the early period, held at the British National Archives, CO 415 and CO 167 series.

on oath,[111] the final report must be regarded as fundamentally incomplete. Nevertheless, in 1829 the findings confirmed that the slave trade had continued on the island to a significant extent. Farquhar's response, "after perusing it with great attention", was to describe the Commissioners' report as "the most inconclusive, vague, incoherent and frivolous rhapsody that was ever produced in the shape of a public document".[112]

3.5.3 Aspiration and reality

Farquhar's evident sympathies and resistance to being held accountable notwithstanding, it cannot be denied that a combination of facts rendered Mauritius particularly liable to a persistence in the slave trade.

In first instance, the island indeed required a supply of labour to sustain continued colonization, a matter that Farquhar sought to address. The colony's requirement for workers was an inescapable fact. Having indicated the need for an alternative to the slave trade,[113] Farquhar requested in 1814 that convicts from India be sent to Mauritius as labourers.[114] His letter reveals his exasperation that the slave trade had not been allowed to continue in Mauritius, lamenting "the Blank which must be occasioned in our labouring population by the operation of the Slave Trade Abolition Acts", stating further that "the abolition was expected, and gradual, in all the British possessions, and . . . here it was unexpected, sudden, and final".[115] He explained that the need to borrow slaves from inhabitants as *corvées* for necessary public works such as road repairs were a regular, but to slave-holders unwelcome imposition. Research into the early proclamations indeed demonstrates that the call for *corvées* became a fixture.[116] Requesting initially 1,500 to 2,000 convicts, after being informed that a like number of such condemned prisoners did not exist, Farquhar asked for 500, balanced equally in the sexes. Since the nature of the sentence did not extend to women, in the end he had to be satisfied with approximately 236 male convict labourers, who after much care and consideration finally arrived in Mauritius in 1815.[117] Notably, contrary to

111 An enduring shortcoming and sign of entrenched oppression, see Barker, op. cit., p. 23.

112 *PP 1829 (335) Copy of a Letter addressed by Sir Robert T. Farquhar to the Secretary of State, dated 10th June 1829, upon the Report made by the Commissioners of Eastern Inquiry on the Slave Trade at the Mauritius*, p. 3 (137).

113 See the letter to Lord Liverpool of 15 February 1811, quoted above.

114 IOR/F/4/534/12853 Correspondence with Governor Farquhar relative to the measure of supplying the Island of Mauritius with Convicts sentenced to transportation for Life.

115 Ibid., Governor Farquhar to the Earl of Moira, 29 December 1814.

116 See for example, Code Farquhar No. 89, 5 May 1812; Code Farquhar No. 93, June 1812; Code Farquhar 127, 24 May 1813; Code Farquhar 183, 2 November 1815.

117 IOR/F/4/534/12853 Letters dated 29 December 1814 and 23 May 1815. Clare Anderson has produced several items on convict labour in Mauritius, see for example, Anderson, Clare, *Convicts in the Indian Ocean: Transportation from South Asia to Mauritius, 1815–53*

the declaration that convicts were to be employed on public works only, by May 1817 the governor had assigned nearly a third of them privately to work in the fields or as domestic servants.[118]

The most decisive influence in the continuation of the slave trade seems to have been the geographical proximity of Mauritius to eastern Africa. In this context it must be remembered that the nearby island of Bourbon was returned to France at the 1814 Treaty of Paris, where the trade thus continued to be legal for a considerable period.[119] Farquhar highlighted the issue in private correspondence over ten years after conquest when describing "the temptation" as "almost irresistible to the Planter, who regards his patrimony as dwindling to nothing, from the effects of abolition", thus claiming that "it is difficult to prevent occasional infractions of the Laws against the Slave Trade, more especially whilst the Island of Bourbon, within our horizon, and seen from our shores, is so rapidly advancing in prosperity".[120] He therefore underlined the need to eradicate the trade at the "source".[121]

Governor Farquhar certainly pursued policies conceived to terminate the trade, by seeking diplomatic cooperation from the rulers in proximate regions engaged in trafficking, such as Madagascar, Zanzibar, Quiloa and Muscat, and offering trade advantages in return.[122] However, these endeavours have also been interpreted as designed primarily to further British influence in the region.[123] As observed by Barker, "a charitable view would recognize the validity of Farquhar's attempt to cut off the slave trade at its sources, rather than risking alienation of the French plantocracy by strict measures within Mauritius".[124] Analysis however renders the governor's intentions questionable, and raises doubts about "not only the wisdom and efficiency, but also the honesty of his administration."[125]

It is perhaps surprising that in the Mauritian context, having experienced a persisting slave traffic, the 1807 Act was not sought to be circumvented by

(Basingstoke: Macmillan, 1999); and Anderson, Clare, *Legible Bodies: Race, Criminality and Colonialism in South Asia* (Oxford: Berg, 2004).

118 Anderson, Clare, 'The Bel Ombre Rebellion: Indian Convicts in Mauritius, 1815–535', in *Abolition and its aftermath in Indian Ocean Africa and Asia*, ed. by Gwyn Campbell (Milton Park: Routledge, 2005), pp. 50–65, p. 51.

119 See Chapter 2. France abolished the slave trade in 1817, but the ban was not enforced until 1826.

120 Add MS 41265 Clarkson Papers, Volume V, Governor Farquhar to the Marquis of Hastings, 14 July 1821.

121 Ibid.

122 Ibid., Governor Farquhar to the Imaum of Muscat, Port Louis, 10 May 1821; Governor Farquhar to the Marquis of Hastings, Port Louis, 11 May 1821. Note that Zanzibar and Quiloa (modern Kilwa, Tanzania) fell under the government of Muscat.

123 Allen, 'Licentious and Unbridled Proceedings', op. cit., p. 112.

124 Barker, op. cit., p. 25.

125 Ibid.

establishing other types of labour systems common around the Indian Ocean. As mentioned at 3.3.1 above, the Indian Ocean World (IOW) knew many types of bonded labour, of which chattel slavery was just one. Others included agrestic servitude, pawnship and debt bondage.[126] The last in particular was very common in region, with persons entering in this type of servitude often voluntarily to as a way of ensuring their survival during harsh periods. With the added costs of maintaining the worker, the debt could increase dramatically and "servitude could become permanent, even hereditary, at which point there was little to distinguish debt bondage from slavery."[127] Since this type of servitude was prevalent in the countries of southern Asia, it arguably presented an avenue that could have been employed to sidestep the provisions of the 1807 Act. While this would have still violated the spirit of the legislation, it specifically outlawed only "the *African* Slave Trade",[128] and not, for example, "Asian debt bondage". Had that kind of servile labour been sought, the argument, doctrinally at least, would have been stronger than Farquhar's lines of reasoning which tried to justify the continued slave trade. It is outside the ambit of this study to fully investigate the question why Mauritius, as part of the IOW, only experienced slavery, a small measure of convict labour (as noted above) and indentured labour on a grand scale (as investigated in Part II), in the absence of other bonded labour systems. It does however pose an interesting query for further research.

3.6 Judicial enforcement

Expenditure on the suppression of the slave trade by the local administration was generally small, well below 5 per cent of total expenses, peaking only in 1822 and 1827 to reach nearly 12 and 10 per cent respectively.[129] This did not aid judicial enforcement of the ban, which, perhaps unsurprisingly, proved exceedingly difficult. In 1817, Chief Judge and Commissary of Justice of Mauritius George Smith admitted to the "mortifying reflection" that "in no one instance have we yet been able to bring any person liable to a charge of felony, under the Slave Trade Felony Act, to justice", citing escapes from seizure or custody and jury acquittal as the reasons.[130]

Despite the suspected high-volume slave traffic, condemnations and prosecutions were exceedingly low, as Table 3.3 shows.

126 Campbell, Gwyn, 'Servitude and the Changing Face of the Demand for Labor in the Indian Ocean World, c.1800–1900', in *Indian Ocean Slavery in the Age of Abolition*, ed. by Robert W. Harms, Bernard K. Freamon and David W. Blight (New Haven, CT: Yale University Press, 2013), p. 28.

127 Ibid.

128 Stated in section I, II, VII and XI of the 1807 Act; emphasis in the original legislation.

129 As calculated by Allen based on several sources, op. cit., p. 108.

130 George Smith to Governor Farquhar, Port Louis, 6 September 1817, Parliamentary Papers 1926 (295), p. 131.

Table 3.3 Slave trade returns, following British conquest until 1827[131]

	Captured Slaves and Vessels			*Cases of alleged breach of the Slave Trade Abolition Laws*		
	Vessels captured and condemned	*Slaves condemned*	*Slaves seized on shore*	*Court of First Instance*	*Court of Vice-Admiralty*	
					Prosecutions entered	*Persons condemned*
1811	–	–	–	–	–	–
1812	1	373	Nil	–	–	–
1813	4	622	Nil	1	–	–
1814	1	104	63	10	–	–
1815	10	1000	1	3	6	1
1816	7	368	9	–	7	1
1817	9	743	24	–	14	4
1818	9	361	216	1	25	1
1819	4	153	73	–	16	9
1820	Nil	72	77	–	6	1
1821	1	507	57	–	4	2
1822	Nil	2	2	–	1	Nil
1823	–	–	–	1	–	–
1824	–	–	–	–	–	–
1825	2	295	6	–	6	1
1826	–	–	–	–	–	–
1827	–	12	12	–	5	3

Farquhar's role in the context of the slave trade remained controversial throughout the period, for in the same year he had to maintain his position emphatically against the Earl of Liverpool's successor, Earl Bathurst.[132] The Earl had raised the issue of Farquhar's character in the failure to enforce the abolition laws.[133] Farquhar defended his efforts passionately and cited the difficulties in containing the trade when he was restricted in his ability to do so.[134] Slave trade vessels in practice were not seizeable beyond "a hundred paces from the Sea side", and liability

131 Compiled from CO 167/141 Report on the Slave Trade. Miscellaneous Returns: No. 18 Return of Vessels & Negroes captured at Sea, and Negroes seized on Shore and condemned in the Vice Admiralty Court at the Cape of Good Hope, and the Colonial and Vice Admiralty Courts at Mauritius from 1808 to 1827; No. 20 Return of all Cases of alleged breach of the Slave Trade Abolition Laws brought before the Court of First Instance from 1810 to 1823; No. 21 Return of all Cases of alleged Breach of the Slave Trade Abolition Laws brought before the Court of Vice Admiralty at Mauritius from the 2nd of September 1815 to the 6th of September 1827. Note that where the records provide no entries for a particular year, a blank has been logged as distinct from the number being "nil".

132 Henry Bathurst, Earl Bathurst, Secretary of State for War and the Colonies from 11 June 1812 to 30 April 1827, see Panton, op. cit.

133 Earl Bathurst to Governor Farquhar, 1 April 1817, Parliamentary Papers 1826 (295), pp. 118–119.

134 Governor Farquhar to Earl Bathurst, 11 October 1817, ibid., pp. 121–123.

of the captain was avoided by the frequent use of "nominal captains", with the real captain travelling as a member of the crew, which was not accountable.[135] After being condemned, a vessel would be sold at auction, invariably to its former owner.[136] The last practice was a courtesy that the French inhabitants customarily extended to each other, a kind of protectionism that also seems is evident in the jury acquittals indicated by Judge Smith.

Congruent with the overarching argument advanced in this study, Lauren Benton argues that the abolition of the slave trade across the empire "reflected and reinforced pressures to strengthen imperial legal authority."[137] According to her, in the broader project of consolidating legal order, the ban acted as a form of control by the imperial state. "For abolitionists, imperial officials, and some reforming colonial elites, the goal of creating an effective ban on the slave was logically tied to the objective of reining in slave owners' prerogatives".[138] An examination of the practical aspects of the slave trade ban in Mauritius appears to support this line of argument. However, an analysis of individual cases also demonstrates that while imperial control may have been increasing, the British administration was passing up opportunities to strengthen its authority locally.

Farquhar's successors, especially those who took over in the interim period between his two tenures, demonstrated a different approach, notably Major-General Gage John Hall (from November 1817 to December 1818) and Major-General Ralph Darling (from February 1819 to July 1820).[139] They preferred to submit certain cases concerning the violation of the slave trade laws to the Privy Council in London, an overview of which may illustrate the attitudes of the French inhabitants and the British on the matter.

One of these is the case of Monneron.[140] In 1818, Jacques Aristide Monneron, a young man less than 20 years of age, found himself arrested on the felony of slave trafficking, following the inception of two young boys, who he had sent with a letter to his mother informing her of his "troubles" with the British, requesting her to shelter his slaves. As a consequence of that letter, British Forces attended at the estate of Madame Monneron, where they discovered a temporary building that housed a large number of evidently newly imported slaves. New slaves were said to be "very easy" to identify, from their condition (often suffering from "the itch", i.e., small pox), their demeanour (a fragile mental state, evident from

135 Add MS 41265 *Clarkson Papers Volume V*, Governor Farquhar to Sir Alexander Johnston, Mauritius, 18 February 1822.

136 Ibid.

137 Benton, Lauren, 'Abolition and Imperial Law, 1790–1820', *The Journal of Imperial and Commonwealth History*, 39 (2011), 355–74, p. 355.

138 Ibid., p. 368.

139 The short tenure of Colonel John Dalrymple (from December 1818 to February 1819) may be disregarded.

140 PC 1/4177 *Papers relative to five persons sent from the Isle of France charged with having violated the laws for the Abolition of the Slave Trade*, Monneron v. R (1818).

being easily startled) and most obviously perhaps, their inability to converse in French.[141]

Special slave trade jurisdiction rested with the local Vice-Admiralty Court,[142] and the chief judge as well as the governor were Commissaries of the Court.[143] A right to appeal to the Privy Council had been established early in the island, though appeals were primarily made to the governor.[144] As such, Governor Hall could have intervened in Monneron's case, but he declined to act and recommended the matter be referred to London.[145] From the case papers it can be deduced that while the evidence, which included unsworn slave testimony, had been heard by the Privy Council, after 12 months imprisonment on indictment, Monneron was sent back to Mauritius. His lawyer claimed that "the Bill of Indictment preferred against him was thrown out by the Grand Jury from which it may be considered that the charge against him was ill founded."[146] Monneron originally sought to bring a suit against General Hall for the expenses incurred and detriment suffered by him and his family as a consequence of having been sent for trial to England.[147] A letter from Lord Bathurst implies that General Hall, by then no longer governor and faced with Monneron's suit, effected the latter's return to Mauritius for trial.[148] Monneron subsequently dropped the action in favour of a simple request for compensation in form of a grant of an allowance,[149] which appears to have been denied.

The proceedings of Monneron's case appear futile and unnecessarily circular. There existed however definite reasoning behind such referrals to the Privy Council, as elucidated by Governor Darling in the context of another case passed to London the same year.[150] Admitting to "being fully aware of the inconvenience

141 Ibid., the Information of Charles Mackenzie Campbell, Lieutenant in the Bourbon Regiment.
142 As affirmed in 1820 following certain opposition to its standing, see CO 167/57 *Slave Trade – Admiralty Court*, Vice-Admiralty notice issued by Judge George Smith, 28 December 1820.
143 Code Farquhar No.185, 1 February 1815.
144 Code Farquhar No.14, 28 December 1810.
145 PC 1/4177 Lieutenant Campbell to the Earl of Bathurst, Spithead, 15 January 1819.
146 Ibid., Letter from Mr Cookney, on the Subject of the Memorial of Jacques Aristide Monneron, praying Compensation for Losses and Expenses incurred in consequence of the Charge of Felony for trafficking in Slaves at the Isle of France, 11 November 1819.
147 Citing a nonexistent proclamation of 11 November 1815, which supposedly authorizes the deputy governor to hear such trials in the colony, see PC 1/4177 Memorial of Mr Jacques Aristide Monneron, praying compensation for the losses and Injuries he has sustained from having been brought from the Isle of France on a charge of illegally trafficking in Slaves, 22 April 1819.
148 PC 1/4177 Letter from Earl Bathurst to the Lord Prudent requesting to be informed whether the Evidence adduced in the Examinations before the Privy Council was of such a nature as to justify General Hall in sending home Mr Monneron for Trial on a charge of Felony, 11 March 1819.
149 PC 1/4177 Memorial of Mr Jacques Aristide Monneron, above, 22 April 1819.
150 PC 1/4177 Case of Pepin, Odierre and others (1819).

which must be occasioned by sending these people to England", he nevertheless deemed it "a matter of indispensable necessity". According to Darling,

> were these people, or in fact any others, concerned in the slave trade, to be brought to trial here, they would to a certainty be acquitted, which such a result would at once prove the impotence of the Government, or the insufficiencies of the Laws, and serve to give fresh life and vigour to a system which can only be suppressed by extraordinary exactions.[151]

Darling's contemplations are evidently plausible, and the practice appears to serve as a means by which imperial control could be consolidated through restricting the rights of slave-holders. By transferring the issue of judicial enforcement to London however, the local administration missed the opportunity to reinforce British rule locally. If the court system, dominated by French influence as it was, proved ill-equipped to give effect to British policy and legislation aimed at abolishing the slave trade, the situation provided obvious incentive for a reform of the judicature. Reconstruction was however forgone in favour of keeping the status quo, while drawing authority from the metropolis. If, in the process, imperial control was enhanced, it came at the cost of a weakening of the local administration.

3.7 Conclusion

As has been observed, the early period of British occupation of Mauritius was fundamentally influenced by the problems inherent in enforcing the abolition of the slave trade. An enduring point of contention between new and old colonists for decades, the issue became directly linked to the establishment of British authority on the French-dominated island. The position of Governor Farquhar exemplifies the tensions and contradictions inherent in Britain's colonial project. On a macro level, the legal ban on the slave trade itself was, neither in its conception nor in practice, exclusively adopted for altruistic purposes, as evidenced through the invasive power granted to the British navy and the notion of Prize slaves. On a micro level, the prohibition operated contrary to the established economic interests of its new colony. As a consequence, the abolition of the slave trade in Mauritius was an abolition in theory only and continued around the island for a long time unabated. Farquhar's sympathetic stance towards slave-holders may or may not be considered as legitimate, as he was certainly faced with very real difficulties to enforce the ban and occupied the unenviable position of enforcing British policy while not alienating the French ruling class and ensuring the commercial viability of the colony. His particular style of administration was briefly interrupted by Hall and Darling, whose governorships took a different

151 PC 1/4177 Governor Major-General Darling to the Earl of Bathurst, Mauritius, 27 July 1819.

tone. However, while they sought to implement metropolitan policy more stringently, they did so in a way that failed to strengthen the colonial government locally. Implementing an effective administration in the context of the slave trade provided a potential avenue for the British to strongly assert their authority in Mauritius, but none of the governors appear to have found it feasible to do so. In the process, the population of Mauritius swelled with illegally imported slaves, and the lives of those who survived the journey, and of those who did not, were inevitably left unaccounted for.

With Farquhar's final departure after his second tenure, the slavery question confronting the governors of Mauritius became more pressing, for not only did slave-holding become more important due to an expansion of the sugar industry, but amelioration and ultimately abolition were British policies to be implemented among a very hostile French population.

4 The abolition of slavery

4.1 Introduction

This chapter considers the period prior to the abolition of slavery in Mauritius. The years leading up to this event witnessed a hardening of positions between the French inhabitants and the British administration, and was marked by ineffective amelioration policies which eventually culminated in the legal abolition of a system that had been part of the colonial project in Mauritius from the very beginning. In a continuation of the approach taken by the first British governor, Farquhar's successors preferred to adopt a placatory policy towards the local French elite, yet the latter continued their resistance to directives from Britain. The result was growing tensions between the metropolitan government and the local British administration, which to a significant degree sympathized with the ruling class. These frictions (between Britain and its own local government, and the latter with the resident oligarchy) only eased with the arrival of indentured labourers, the first phase of which occurred simultaneous to the "apprenticeship" term of emancipated slaves.

The concurrence of post-abolition apprenticeship and early indenture is a significant one. In Mauritius, the impact of emancipation cannot be evaluated without considering the large-scale introduction of indentured labour from the Indian subcontinent, since the presence of the new workers changed the dynamics on the island fundamentally. For this reason, emancipated apprenticeship is discussed alongside the first phase of indentured labour in Chapter 5. This gives opportunity in this chapter to focus on the Franco-Mauritian elite, for whom, as will be seen, the abolition of slavery came at an inopportune time.

It should be noted that an evaluation of the severity of Mauritian slavery is not an aim within the ambit of this work. Research suggests that the experience of slavery generally varied with time and location. Inevitably, assessments into its harshness are frequently hampered by the limited availability of sources. The concern here is to attend to the underlying dynamics of slavery as a system of labour.

Having already considered the importance of slavery to Mauritian colonial society and the Indian Ocean context in Chapter 3, the backdrop of amelioration and pending abolition in this chapter serves to illuminate the position of the Franco-Mauritian plantation owners, and their relationship with the slaves

DOI: 10.4324/9781003313366-5

and the British colonial government. First, the concept of slavery will be examined to provide the context for a discussion of the 1833 Abolition Act. In the section that follows, the actual management of slavery in Mauritius is examined, and how its importance increased rather than diminished in the decade preceding abolition.

4.2 The notion of slavery

Slavery has been part of social organization for a very long time, yet a full and clear definition of the concept remains elusive. As indicated previously, slavery is often associated with other types of servitude. These have been touched upon already and will be revisited in the context of indentured labour in Part II of this study. Despite such frequent comparisons, made in academic and non-academic literature alike, the pursuit of categorizing systems of labour as "continuations" or "forms" of slavery is, as discussed in Chapter 1, of limited value. There are without doubt numerous working arrangements to be found throughout history and up to modern times which could be deemed as having been "akin" to slavery. Nevertheless, the specificity of slavery and its distinction from other related phenomena is important for purposes of understanding its dynamics.

To this end, Herman Nieboer attempted a definition in his seminal work.[1] For Nieboer, at its most basic, "a slave is one who is not free." He concedes that "no man is literally free" for as long as he is a participant in society, yet "freemen, at any rate, are relatively free". Evidently, this exposition is far from satisfactory. To further clarify, Nieboer enumerates three conditions a slave is subjected to. Firstly, slaves are subject to a master's free exercise of power, by virtue of being the latter's "property" or "possession"; secondly, a slave does not hold any political rights, for "socially he is despised"; and thirdly, he performs compulsory labour, though Nieboer admits that all compulsory labour is not slavery.

It is submitted that out of Nieboer's three conditions, only one holds permanence. The third stipulation, compulsory labour, may appear as he himself admits in a variety of settings that are not slavery. Equally, the absence of political powers or social status, Nieboer's second aspect, is also not truly determinative of slavehood. As discussed in Chapter 2, the *gens de couleur* (free people of colour) in Mauritius lacked the ability to exercise civic rights or hold public offices, but this did not render them slaves. Therefore only the first condition, that of being considered another person's property, can be taken as the key component of the practice of slavery. In the absence of a commonly accepted definition, this basic delineation amounts to the fundamental determinant. It is the existence of property rights in a person which is fundamental to slavery

1 Nieboer, H. J., *Slavery as an Industrial System*, 2nd Edition (The Hague: Martinus Nijhoff, 1910).

in a strictly legal sense.[2] Within the context of 19th-century plantation labour as discussed here, one attribute is indisputable: the slave is deemed chattel.

It has been stated that globally, all peoples have at one time or another been involved in slavery, either as slaves or owners of them.[3] Historians commonly trace ancient slavery back to the Greek and Roman eras, both of which knew different slave systems.[4] From a jurisprudential point of view, Roman law is noteworthy for encompassing two opposed notions. On the one hand, it contained the first legal framework which regulated slavery, but on the other, it admitted that the practice was contrary to natural law, since nature postulates the equality of man.[5] Thus, as per Roman jurist Domitius Ulpian, "the introduction of slavery . . . lead to the benefit of manumission", for without slavery, there is no need for liberation.[6] The possibility of freedom then, however remote, is a necessary aspect of the concept of slavery.

Within the context of English law, in 1772 Lord Mansfield famously declared in the Sommersett case the state of slavery to be "so odious, that nothing can be suffered to support it, but positive law."[7] Contrary to popular perception, the case did not declare slavery as illegal under English law, nor did it effect emancipation. It was a decision decided on its own facts, limited to the issue of removing a slave from Britain against his will.[8] Nevertheless, it was an important decision, not at least for its public denouncement of slavery at time when the institution supported Britain's imperial endeavour in colonies around the world. Such early sentiments in the judiciary notwithstanding, considerable time elapsed between the Slave Trade Abolition Act of 1807 and the passing of the Act which abolished slavery itself.

The long-anticipated Abolition of Slavery Act of 1833[9] however did not bring about unfettered freedom, but took effect by turning slaves over the

2 For a discussion on this subject, see Engerman, Stanley L., 'The Rise, Persistence, and Slow Decline of Legal Slavery', in *The Legal Understanding of Slavery: From the Historical to the Contemporary*, ed. by Jean Allain (Oxford: Oxford University Press, 2012).

3 Eltis, David, and Stanley L. Engerman, 'Dependence, Servility, and Coerced Labor in Time and Space', in *The Cambridge World History of Slavery: Volume 3, AD 1420-AD 1804*, ed. by David Eltis and Stanley L. Engerman (New York: Cambridge University Press, 2011), p. 2.

4 McKeown, Niall, 'Greek and Roman Slavery', in *The Routledge History of Slavery*, ed. by Gad Heuman and Trevor Burnard (London: Routledge, 2012).

5 Honoré, Antony, 'The Nature of Slavery', in *The Legal Understanding of Slavery: From the Historical to the Contemporary*, ed. by Jean Allain (Oxford: Oxford University Press, 2012), p. 9.

6 Ibid.

7 *The Case of James Sommersett, a Negro, on Habeus Corpus*, King's Bench, 12 George III, 1771–72. Howell's State Trials, Vol. 20, cols 1–6, 79–82 (1816), p. 82.

8 Notably, James Sommersett had converted to Christianity during his sojourn in Britain, which may have played some role in swaying the court to decide against his forcible removal.

9 'An Act for the Abolition of Slavery throughout the British Colonies; for promoting the Industry of the manumitted Slaves; and for compensating the Persons hitherto entitled to the Services of such Slaves', 3 & 4 Will IV, c. 73, 28 August 1833.

age of six into "apprenticed Labourers".[10] This delay to full liberation was not solely intended as an advantage to slave-holders but also reflected the attitude of leading abolitionists, who, like famous spokesperson William Wilberforce, favoured a gradual approach and regarded emancipation as a necessarily prolonged process.[11]

The Act principally made a two-fold distinction among apprentices: "praedials" and "non-praedials". The former were further distinguished as being either "attached to soil" or not so attached, effectively creating three types of apprentices.[12] The main difference was that praedials, meaning agricultural labourers, would serve a slightly longer apprenticeship period than non-praedials.[13]

Importantly, the 1833 Act was not to apply to the entirety of the British Empire, effectively abolishing slavery only in the West Indies, the Cape of Good Hope and Mauritius.[14] Having received Royal Assent on 28 August 1833, commencement of the Act itself was also incremental, taking effect in the West Indies on 1 August 1834, four months later at the Cape, and notably, coming into force in Mauritius last, namely six months later, on 1 February 1835.[15]

Among the reasons which facilitated the passing of the 1833 Act at that particular point in time was arguably the diminishing relevance of the West Indies as producers of sugar for Britain.[16] Eric Williams' study, which since its publication has attracted supporters and critics alike,[17] argued that behind the abolition of the slave trade was in fact the desire to curb sugar production, because it was no longer commercially worthwhile.[18] This suggestion grates against the humanitarian image Britain preferred to promote at the time. Broader imperial policy considerations aside, reported disquietude among missionaries administering to slaves labouring on sugar plantations together with frequent revolts, particularly in Jamaica, acted as repeated impetus to the many attempts of passing the bill in Parliament.[19] Public opinion played hereby a significant role. It is probably no coincidence that the Act was finally approved by a reconstructed

10 Section I.
11 See Morgan, Kenneth, ***Slavery and the British Empire: From Africa to America*** (Oxford: Oxford University Press, 2007), Chapter 8.
12 Section IV.
13 Sections V and VI.
14 India was crucially left out. Section LXIV makes the following exemptions: "nothing in this Act contained doth or shall extend to any of the Territories in the Possession of the East India Company, or to the Island of Ceylon, or to the Island of Saint Helena".
15 Section LXV.
16 Discussed in Chapter 2.
17 See an interesting discussion of Williams work in Fryer, Peter, ***Black People in the British Empire*** (London: Pluto Classic, 1988).
18 Williams, Eric Eustace, ***Capitalism & Slavery*** (Chapel Hill, NC: University of North Carolina Press, 1994).
19 See Blackburn, op. cit., Chapter 11.

legislature, post the Reform Act of 1832.[20] Symbolical of the more general mood to address social inequalities, a greater platform was accorded to voices criticizing the entitlement of aristocrats and the wealthy. Robin Blackburn states that during the election of 1832, demands for slave emancipation became linked to criticism of the privileged class which held colonial interests and possessed significant political influence. Slave emancipation thus became a convenient instrument to carry out an "assault" on the oligarchy.[21] This observation, if true for the British ruling class, applies doubly in the case of Mauritius, where the local oligarchy was cognizably French rather than British. The latter's superior standing on the island being closely linked to slavery however led them to react with an aggressive vehemence.

4.3 Slavery by the French under British Rule

4.3.1 Retention of slaves

As discussed in the previous chapter, any records relating to the quantity of slaves residing on the island are considered unreliable given that the slave trade became illegal, but it is understood to have been extensive. An early census three years prior to British conquest indicates that in 1807 there were already over 60,500 slaves on the island,[22] and based on historical evidence, numbers may have had actually reached 80,000 when France capitulated,[23] though this is not certain. A return provided and signed by Governor Farquhar gives only three entries on the slave population for the first decade post British takeover, as reproduced in Table 4.1.

Table 4.1 Slave population, 1812–1822[24]

Year	*Number of slaves*
1814	78,102
1815	87,352
1819	80,185

20 'An Act to amend the representation of the people in England and Wales', 2 & 3 Will IV, c. 45, 7 June 1832.
21 Blackburn, op. cit., p. 454.
22 See Table 3.1, Early censuses in Mauritius, contained in Chapter 3.
23 See Governor Farquhar's statement on a handwritten note supposedly left by General Decaen, PP XXV 1829 *(337) Copies of any Correspondence which has passed between Sir Robert Farquhar and the Colonial Department, upon the subject of certain Charges contained in a Publication, intituled, "The Anti-Slavery Reporter, No.42"*, discussed in Chapter 3.
24 Compiled from 'A Return of the Population in each year, from 1812 inclusive to March 1822', 22 July 1822, Governor Sir R. T. Farquhar to the Earl of Bathurst, Port Louis, Mauritius, 7 November 1822, Enclosure No.7, contained in *PP 1823 (89) Slave population*, above, p. 127.

Table 4.2 Manumissions, 1 January 1808–22 July 1822[25]

	Male	*Female*
1808	9	34
1809	16	27
1810	6	17
1811	62	78
1812	117	164
1813	95	144
1814	96	141
1815	14	14
1816	25	27
1817	42	55
1818	46	71
1819	40	67
1820	39	49
1821	60	112
1822	14	23
	681	**1,023**
Total	**1,704**	

In tandem with the inconsistent slave numbers, whether gleaned from registration entries or the tax collectors' roll, data on manumissions also varies by source.[26] For the sake of continuity, the numbers for Table 4.2 have been calculated from another return also originally provided and signed by Governor Farquhar.

These numbers should be regarded as illustrative only, since counts subsequent to the legal abolition of the slave trade cannot be relied upon with confidence. They do however indicate a very low level of manumission in a colony with a significant slave presence. It is evident that 1,704 manumissions over a 15-year period is a meagre amount for a slave population anywhere between 60,000 to 80,000. It should be noted that Farquhar's data does not fit well with a later return, made by the Acting Registrar of Slaves in 1830, who gives the number of slaves counted in 1826 as 69,472, and in 1830 as 66,183. The latter excludes

25 Compiled from 'Return of all Manumissions effected by Purchase, Bequest or Otherwise', 22 July 1822, Governor Sir R. T. Farquhar to the Earl of Bathurst, Port Louis, Mauritius, 7 November 1822, Enclosure No.3, contained in *PP 1823 (89) Slave population. Papers and returns, presented pursuant to address, relating to the slave population of Dominica, Grenada, St. Vincent, Barbados, Antigua, Tobago, Demerara, Berbice, St. Christopher, Trinidad, and Mauritius*, p. 125.

26 See the discussion in Kuczynski, Robert R., *Demographic Survey of the British Colonial Empire. Volume II: South Africa High Commission Territories, East Africa, Mauritius and Seychelles* (Oxford: Oxford University Press, 1949), pp. 762–763. A multi-volume set of statistics exists, complied by Baron Antoine d'Unienville, the Franco-Mauritan archivist, and submitted to Governor Cole in 1825, available at the Public Records Office, CO 172/39–42. However, the numbers he provides are at odds, sometimes significantly, with the data in the Blue Books.

1,164 manumissions effected from 16 October 1826 until 31 December 1829, a number which contrasts dispiritingly with 6,475 slave deaths recorded during the same period.[27]

The rules relating to manumission were certainly onerous, as an analysis of Ordinance No. 21 of 1827 demonstrates.[28] The title of the ordinance stated its purpose clearly: to modify and consolidate all previous rules regarding emancipation by establishing through "a fixed Regulation, and in one and the same ordinance, all that regards such Emancipation". Article I stated unequivocally that no slave should be emancipated without the permission of the governor and must be sought via a petition, and such petition was to include the motives for emancipation. If permission was granted, the petitioner was obliged to fulfil a series of "formalities".

In the first instance, three consecutive weekly advertisements in the Mauritius Gazette outlining certain details regarding master and slave were required, the purpose being "the prevention of any Emancipation prejudicial to the right of Creditors or to public order". Further, "all Persons are to notify, to the Procureur General, the Grounds of opposition which, to their knowledge, may exist against the intended Emancipations".[29] The three advertisements had to be certified by a declaration of the Government Printers, and together with a Certificate of the *Procureur Général* that no oppositions to the intended Emancipation existed, in the eight days following the final advertisement, "the Master shall make known, in writing, to His Honour the Chief Judge and Commissary of Justice, the means he purposes placing at the disposal of the Slave he wishes to emancipate".[30] The reason for such provision was to avoid the emancipated slave becoming "a burden to the Colony". Should the chief judge, upon the report of the *Procureur Général*, deem the means sufficient, the "Master shall assure the property, in the same, to the Person emancipated by notarial Act." A further requirement was the obligation for the slave-holder to make a payment of £5 into the "*Caisse de Bienfaisance*" (which may be understood as a type of benevolence fund), the sum of which was to be "applied to the wants of the Poor."[31]

After these steps had been satisfied, a second petition to the governor was required to obtain confirmation of the emancipation. The petition had to be accompanied with: (1) the certificate confirming the three advertisements in the Gazette; (2) the certificate of the *Procureur Général* confirming that no opposition to emancipation existed; (3) the decision of the chief justice regarding the means of subsistence; (4) a copy of the notarial Act granting the means of subsistence to the emancipated person; (5) the receipt showing the payment to the

27 "Mauritius: Statement, showing the Number of Slaves Recensed, Slave Registry Office, Port Louis, 11 May 1830, contained in *PP 1831–32 (333) Mauritius slave registration* . . ., p. 80.
28 CO 171/3, Ordinance No. 21 as published in the Mauritius Gazette, 3 February 1827.
29 Article II, ibid.
30 Article III, ibid.
31 Ibid.

Caisse de Bienfaisance had been made.[32] Confirmation of Emancipation was then delivered and registered free of charge.[33]

These formalities undoubtedly represented veritable hurdles, particularly given the obligation for slave holders to pay £5 for each emancipated slave and the fact that anyone could register an opposition with the *Procureur*. In these circumstances, it is surprising that any slaves at all achieved manumission through this procedure.

Emancipation by marriage appears to have been slightly easier.[34] While Ordinance No. 21 did not prohibit marriage between whites and slaves explicitly, Article VIII envisaged the potential marriage of a slave as only taking place to either a former slave or a free person of colour. In either instance, emancipation of the enslaved partner was said to take place "de jure". The £5 payment to the charitable fund was not required, however confirmation of the three advertisements, the absence of any opposition and a certificate from the Chief Commissary of the Police verifying the means of subsistence of the free partner to the proposed marriage were required to obtain confirmation of the Emancipation.

From the data and the regulations, it thus transpires that the slave-holders of Mauritius did not easily relinquish their slaves. A clear picture of the reason for this emerges when the development of the sugar industry of the period is investigated.

4.3.2 An incentive for slavery: the sugar industry

In 1825 a decided impetus for the cultivation of sugar was created with the equalization of Mauritian tariffs with those of West Indies,[35] the result of a sustained appeal by local planters during the two preceding years.[36] The measure has been described in a parliamentary report as "so efficacious and so prompt in its result, that within six years from that date, the supply from Mauritius was increased six-fold."[37] It was thus the equal access granted to the British sugar market that provided the incentive to a large-scale retention of slaves for plantation owners in Mauritius, in a development that baffled officials at the Colonial Department in London.[38]

32 Article V, ibid.
33 Article VI, ibid.
34 Article VIII, ibid.
35 'An Act to extend to the Island of Mauritius the Duties and Regulations which relate to the British Islands in the West Indies', 6 Geo IV, c. 76, 27 June 1825.
36 CO 415/12, see 'The Petition of Your Majesty's loyal and faithful Subjects, Planters at the Island of Mauritius', and E. No. 22, Letter from the Secretary to the Committee of the Privy Council, relative to admitting the Produce of Mauritius into England on the same duties as paid on West India Produce, 4 June 1824.
37 *PP 1889 [C.8706] Customs Tariffs of the United Kingdom from 1800 to 1897*, p. 209 (213).
38 Discussed below at 4.5.

How could have the importance of slavery have increased in the aftermath of the abolition of the slave trade? As noted in Chapter 2, the existence of slavery had been part of the colonial project in Mauritius from the earliest point. Unlike in the United States, where slavery was preceded by an indenture system,[39] the colonists in Mauritius employed slavery first, and only resorted to indentured labour after its abolition by imperial law. The question "What causes slavery?" must be modified in the Mauritian context to: "What caused the retention of slavery?"

Following his extensive ethnological research on slavery as an industrial system, Nieboer identified several factors necessary for the existence of slavery and grouped them into *internal* and *external causes.*[40] The former may be properly described as "motive forces", covering aspects that provide the incentive for slave-keeping, whereas the latter are better defined as conditions, such as the opportunity to obtain slaves in the first place. According to Nieboer, both categories are required: if one type of cause is totally absent, slavery will not exist.[41]

The "most important result" of his research appears to be the observation that the incidence of slavery is related to "the division . . . of all peoples of the earth, into peopled with open and closed resources." For, he was to explain "the principal internal cause which prevents the rise of slavery, or where slavery exists, tends to make it disappear, is the dependence of subsistence upon closed resources."[42] Nieboer claims, as a consequence, that it is the availability of limitless resources which would motivate a slave-holder to increase his number of slaves in order to augment his income accordingly, whereas "a man who owns a limited capital, or a limited quantity of land, can only employ a limited number of labourers".[43]

Nieboer's ideas were later reframed by Evsey Domar, who proposed a hypothesis which correlated the availability of free land with the existence of serfdom or slavery.[44] Domar's formula however is highly unreliable, since in its clearest statement, it completely disregards factors such as politics, capital and management.[45] By his own admission, "the presence of this exogenous political variable seriously weakens the effectiveness of my model",[46] which in essence renders it unworkable.

The case of Mauritius demonstrates that the political element can prove decisive. Had it not been for the 1825 tariff equalization, it is unlikely that sugar production would have developed in the manner it did. The dramatic increase

39 Finkelman, Paul, 'Slavery in the United States', in *The Legal Understanding of Slavery: From the Historical to the Contemporary*, ed. by Jean Allain (Oxford: Oxford University Press, 2012), p. 107.
40 Nieboer, op. cit., p. 417.
41 Ibid.
42 Ibid., p. 418.
43 Ibid.
44 Domar, Evsey D., 'The Causes of Slavery or Serfdom: A Hypothesis', *The Journal of Economic History*, 30 (1970), 18–32.
45 Ibid., p. 21.
46 Ibid.

Table 4.3 Sugar mills imported to be erected in Mauritius, 1824–1828[47]

Year	*Number*
1824	4
1825	1
1826	4
1827	48
1828	46

in the erection of sugar mills during the latter part of the 1820s suggests that heightened production was indeed the result of the 1825 adjustment in duties payable on exporting sugar to Britain, as Table 4.3 indicates.

Further records indicate the extent to which that the sugar industry had expanded. With only about 9,000 *arpent* under sugar cane cultivation in the period from 1812 to 1820, by the next decade, 1821 to 1830, this number had nearly tripled, to 26,000 *arpent*.[48]

Nieboer's requirements regarding internal and external causes for slavery must thus be qualified. In the Mauritian context, the motivating force for the expansion of slavery was not, as he stipulates, internal, but external: tariff equalization. His argument regarding "closed resources" as a discouragement for slave-keeping equally proves not applicable: at a territorial size of just over 2,000 square kilometres, natural resources in Mauritius were certainly finite. An argument can be made that during the early decades, much land was still unused, however this does not negate the clear limits to potential growth. Additionally, Mauritius was not a wealthy colony. In an early dispatch, Governor Farquhar stated that "nothing could be more deplorable than the state of poverty and wretchedness to which this colony was reduced previously to its surrender to His Majesty. . . . We found all the inhabitants involved in debt bordering on a state of general bankruptcy."[49]

The decision to focus on sugar cultivation did not improve the situation the governor described. On the contrary, it made Mauritius highly dependent on the British market for income and returns of investment which, "with deep

47 CO 172/43 Returns of the Receipts and Expenditure of the Mauritius Government in each Year from the Capture of the Island in 1810 to the end of 1828: Sugar Mills imported for the purpose of being erected in the Colony.

48 BL X.319/4471, *Mauritius and its Sugar Industry*, p. 21. By 1840, following the introduction of indentured labour, this would increase to 40,000 *arpent*. Note: An "*arpent*" is an ancient French unit, still popularly used in Mauritius. The size of a standard French *arpent*, which alternatively may denote a length or an area, varied, but Richard Allen's research fixes one *arpent* in 19th-century Mauritius at 1.403 acres, or 5,678 square metres, see Allen, Richard B., *Slaves, Freedmen and Indentured Laborers in Colonial Mauritius* (Cambridge: Cambridge University Press, 2006).

49 IOR/H/701 *(1810–1811) Capture of Mauritius and Reunion*, Governor Farquhar to the Earl of Liverpool, Mauritius, 8 January 1811.

indebtedness and personal resources stretched to the utmost", rendered the economic situation on the island precarious indeed, as any profits were yet to materialize.[50] Additionally, the emphasis on sugar cane came at the expense of other crops, such as coffee or spices, and was carried on to such an extent that Mauritius, previously almost self-sufficient, came to be dependent on imports for essential food supplies.[51] Research revealed that 1828 was the year in which, for the first time since British conquest, revenue exceeded the government expenditures (fixed military and civil).[52] In effect, Mauritius had been administered at a loss for nearly two decades. It was in this environment of a finally improved economic standing, and heavy reliance on future profits, that plantation owners were to implement amelioration policies regarding slave-holding.

4.4 The prelude to abolition: amelioration

The idea of "amelioration" implies gradations in the severity of slavery, the determination of which may appear useful for the purpose of hypothetical discussion, but in reality can lead to a certain degree of incoherence. An illustration of this problematic approach is the assessment of American black slavery by Robert Fogel and Stanley Engerman.[53] The scholars present an image of slavery which is at variance with the more common perceptions of the institution. For instance, on the question of nutrition, despite admitting that "surviving plantation records are not complete enough to permit determination of the average amounts of each of the foods purchased for slaves",[54] available census data showing the range of foods available was sufficient for the scholars to assert that "the belief that the typical slave was poorly fed is without foundation in fact."[55] Equally, the results of their research led Fogel and Engerman to conclude that medical care was adequate in the circumstances,[56] and that sexual exploitation of female slaves did not exceed what was experienced by white women at the same time.[57] The scholars subscribe to the notion that the existence of a legal right to the full submission of the slave did not imply exercise of the same.[58] Such an assessment is problematic, for it not only imposes an external standard on a highly subjective experience, but leaves the existence of the institution

50 Burroughs, Peter, 'The Mauritius Rebellion of 1832 and the Abolition of British Colonial Slavery', *The Journal of Imperial and Commonwealth History*, 4 (1976), 243–65, p. 248.
51 Ibid.
52 With a surplus of just over £5,252, see CO 172/43 above, Return of the Amount of Revenue and Expenditure of the Colony of Mauritius in each Year from 1810 to 1826 (extended).
53 Fogel, Robert, and Stanley L. Engerman, *Time on the Cross – The Economics of American Negro Slavery* (New York: Norton, 1995).
54 Ibid., p. 111.
55 Ibid., p. 109.
56 Ibid., p. 117.
57 Ibid., pp. 130–135.
58 Ibid., p. 133.

unquestioned and can even amount, with its apologist undertones, to a justification of slave-holding practices.

It is precisely the notion that gradations in harshness exist which drove the idea of an "improved" slavery. The fallacy of the concept however became apparent in its practical implementation. Moses Nwulia and Vijaya Teelock both emphasize the absurdity of the idea of amelioration in the context of slavery. "The policy of 'amelioration' was based on a very limited conception of slavery and the needs of the slave", states Nwulia. "There can be no such thing as 'enlightened' slavery any more than there is an 'improved' hell".[59] Teelock for her part refutes the notion of "mild slavery", and of the mildness of Mauritian slavery in particular,[60] denouncing it as a "myth" popularized in the 19th century as a consequence of the island's climate and fertile soil, as well as a humanitarian image French planters sought to promote of themselves, leading to the assumption amongst contemporary commentators that labour conditions were not cruel, or at least not as cruel as in the West Indies.[61] Amelioration was nevertheless a British policy pursued for a significant period of time, though as will be seen, one that was largely ineffective in Mauritius.

4.4.1 The implementation of British policies

In May 1823 the House of Commons adopted several resolutions for ameliorating slavery conditions which were communicated by Lord Bathurst to Governor Cole[62] (Farquhar's immediate successor) shortly afterwards.[63] These included, amongst other things, that there should be an absolute prohibition on the flogging of female slaves. The example serves to gauge Cole's attitude with respect to ameliorative measures. His stance has been described as "cynical"[64] by Nwulia in light of the fact that the governor took more than three years following Lord Bathurst's instructions to issue a circular which advised to limit the flogging of females to "extraordinary cases".[65]

The governor's attitude is actually better described as one of contempt and indifference, for not only was Cole's act late and devoid of legal force, the

59 Nwulia, Moses D. E., *The History of Slavery in Mauritius and the Seychelles, 1810–1875* (Rutherford, NJ: London: Fairleigh Dickenson University Press; Associated University Presses, 1981), p. 89.

60 See Chapter 2 of this study, and the account by Noël, Karl, *L'esclavage À l'Isle de France (Ile Maurice) de 1715 À 1810* (Paris: Editions Two Cities, 1991).

61 Teelock, Vijaya, *Bitter Sugar: Sugar and Slavery in 19th Century Mauritius* (Moka: Mahatma Gandhi Institute, 1998), p. 8.

62 Sir Lowry Cole, Governor of Mauritius from 1823 to 1828.

63 CO 415/4, Earl Bathurst to Sir Cole, 28 May 1823.

64 Nwulia, op. cit., p. 91.

65 Cole to the Commandants and District Civil Commissaries, Port Louis, 15 December 1826, in *PP 1828 (526) Slaves in Mauritius. Return to an order of the Honourable House of Commons*, pp. 32–33.

language he used pandered to the planters' interests, lacking conviction or clear intent. He stated:[66]

> It must, in fact, be admitted, that the weakness of their sex and public decency would seem to require, that Negro-women should undergo the lash only in extraordinary cases, and with the concurrence of the local authority. Do not irons, the stocks, imprisonment, offer sufficient means of punishing a Negro-woman, whose condition, besides being almost always precarious, requires great care? Avail yourselves, Gentlemen, of your influence with your fellow-country men, to prevail upon them to give up, of their own accord, the use of flogging in respect to female Slaves.

Governor Cole's actual view on the matter, however, is revealed in a dispatch to Lord Bathurst composed merely days later:[67]

> From the great numerical disproportion which exists between the male and the female slaves of this colony, a very general promiscuous intercourse prevails, which naturally debases the latter; and in many instances their conduct in every respect is fully as bad as that of the worst of the male slaves; therefore although I admit that the abolishing of corporal punishment, in the cases of female slaves, is highly desirable, yet I conceive that bad consequences might result from its immediate prohibition.

Cole's administration, in general terms, showed remarkably little commitment to the slave cause and, like that of Farquhar before him, attended more to the needs or interests of the French plantocracy. This is particularly evident in Ordinance No. 20 of 1826, which regulated the use of chains and fetters on slaves.[68] Adopted on the same day as Ordinance No. 19, which granted yet another extension to the deadline by which slave returns had to be supplied,[69] the chain ordinance gave sanction to a cruel system of punishment, and arguably widened it. As stated in the ordinance's preamble, Article 37 of the *Lettres Patent* of 1723 (i.e., the *Code Noir*) already allowed the use of chains for punishment, but did not specify their weight, an oversight this ordinance ostensibly sought to rectify.[70]

Ordinance No. 20 prescribed that for a single slave over the age of 15, the chain was not to exceed 6 pounds including the collar, or 9 pounds where two

66 Ibid.

67 Sir Cole to Earl Bathurst, Mauritius, 24 December 1826, in *PP 1829 (333) Papers explanation of the measures adopted by His Majesty's government, for the melioration of the condition of the slave population in His Majesty's possessions in the West Indies, on the continent of South America, and at the Mauritius.*

68 CO 171/2, Mauritius Gazette No. 89, 16 December 1826.

69 Ibid., 13 December 1826.

70 Ibid.: "and it being necessary to good order that the same should be fixed, in an invariable manner, by some Regulation."

male slaves were chained together. For slaves under the age of 15, whether male or female, the weight was not to exceed 3 pounds when chained singly, or 5 pounds when two were joined together. Male and female slaves were not to be chained together in any instance. Crucially, despite these prescribed measures, slave-holders were able to apply to the Chief Commissary of the Police or the Civil Commissaries, "and provided they are of opinion the Slaves shall have merited it", the authorities could augment the burden and "fix themselves the weight of the Chains and the duration of the increase of the Punishment." Further, the ordinance decreed that foot fetters or "the Iron Ring" was not to be used except on males over 15 years and should not exceed 3 lbs. While ordinarily the application of both types of punishment at the same time was not allowed, authorization as described above could be sought in order to do so. Finally, the collar "with three branches" was forbidden to be used, thereby impliedly restricting collars to two branches.[71]

Contravention of the law, whether by "the Proprietor, the Overseer, Superintendent or Holder of Slaves under whatsoever Title", would attract a penalty, not exceeding 10 pounds sterling and not less than 40 shillings on the first offence, and no more than 20 pounds and not less than 10 pounds on the second. In practice, this "ameliorative" measure did not do much to deter slave-holders. It effectively confirmed their rights to use chain and fetters, and with the laxity of the rules, Governor Cole furthermore conveyed the impression that ameliorative measures could be adjusted to suit slave-holders, which amounted to "a subtle defiance of authority that the grateful planters did not fail to notice."[72] A similarly covert subversion of instructions from Britain occurred in the context of the prohibition of Sunday work, already banned by the *Code Noir*, but left at the discretion of the planters "when circumstances require it", as outlined in another of Cole's Circulars which allowed slave-holders to circumvent the regulations with relative ease.[73] Governor Cole's main measures thus did not aid the conditions of slaves, and they may have arguably acted to worsen them since the local French planters knew that at least the local British administration was on their side and would not seriously interfere with their slave-holding practices.

Cole's successor, Governor Colville,[74] came to preside over the island at a period of heightened sensibilities. Following the publication of the report of the Commissioners of Eastern Inquiry, Mauritian slavery was firmly on the radar of the British metropolis. In May 1829, Sir George Murray[75] informed Colville that

71 The "branches" were prongs which protruded on the outside of the collar, significantly restricting the movement of persons wearing it, including the ability to lie down. Having to wear such a collar also served as a mark for misconduct.

72 Nwulia, op. cit., p. 93.

73 Sir Cole's Circular to the Commandants and District Civil Commissaries, 3 August 1826, *in PP 1828 (526)*, above, p. 30.

74 Sir Charles Colville, Governor of Mauritius from 1828 to 1833.

75 Secretary of State for War and the Colonies from 30 May 1828 to 22 November 1830, see Panton, op. cit.

the king would not confirm the chain ordinance, expressing surprise and concern at the enactment, as well as regret that Cole had not abolished the use of chains and fetters altogether, noting that in the West Indies their use "had been very generally, if not universally, prohibited under severe penalties."[76] Having received specimens from the Commissioners of Inquiry,[77] Murray observed that "they appear, in reality, to be nothing less than instruments of torture."[78] This sentiment was repeated by Viscount Goderich[79] almost three years later, reiterating Murray's words and declaring that those chains from Mauritius "remain in this office a visible and irrefragable argument in favour of that change in the law", which Murray directed Colville to enact.[80] Colville's failure to do so over a prolonged period is reflective of the similar approach he took to his predecessor in governing the island.

On the recommendation of the Commissioners of Inquiry, a new, and as far as the plantation owners were concerned, decidedly more intrusive, ameliorative measure was taken: the creation of the office of a Protector of Slaves. Previously, the duties of protector and guardian of slaves fell on the *Procureur Général*, an arrangement deriving originally from the Mauritian *Code Noir*, and maintained and confirmed by an ordinance issued by Governor Cole in 1827.[81]

Ordinance No. 43 of 1829[82] created a separate of office of Protector of Slaves, a post held for the entire duration of its existence, until the abolition of slavery, by R.M. Thomas, an official sent from Britain. Thomas' understanding of his role is articulated in his preliminary notes prefacing his first report, where he recounts events which occurred shortly after his arrival in Mauritius:[83] After having announced his intention to visit the different districts, Thomas found himself confronted with a delegation of concerned planters, whom he placated by explaining that

> although it would be his duty to protect the slaves from any oppression or injury to which their unfortunate situation might expose them, and in all cases to obtain for them strict justice, yet it was not intended that

76 Sir Murray to Sir Colville, Downing Street, 8 May 1829, in *PP 1829 (333)*, above, p. 101.
77 Transmitted alongside a detailed description, see CO 415/3, Descriptive List of Irons used by the Inhabitants of Mauritius in confining or punishing their Slaves, Mauritius, 25 June 1828.
78 Sir Murray to Sir Colville, above.
79 Federick Robinson, Viscount Goderich, Secretary of State for War and the Colonies from 30 April 1827 to 3 September 1827 and 22 November 1830 to 3 April 1833, see Panton op. cit.
80 Viscount Goderich to Sir Colville, 15 January 1832, in *PP 1831–1832 (733)*, above, p. 395.
81 1 September 1827, Ordinance for the Government and Protection of Slaves in the Mauritius, in *PP 1829 (338) Slaves, Mauritius. Return to an address of the Honourable the House of Commons*, pp. 3–16.
82 CO 171/4, Mauritius Gazette, 7 February 1829.
83 Protector of Slaves Reports, Part VI – Mauritius, in PP 1830–1831 (262).

> he should defend their cause, right or wrong; on the contrary, it would be his special care to impress upon their minds, that the measure of protection afforded to them would be proportionate to their good conduct, industry and obedience to their masters.[84]

These words as well as their subsequent implementation have led Thomas to be described as a "disciplinarian" rather than a "protector" of slaves.[85]

An examination of the complaints contained in Thomas' first report, and how these were dealt with, does indeed question the very name of his office, as Table 4.4 indicates.

Notably, unlike in cases where a complaint was outright "dismissed", if a grievance had been declared "unfounded", the slave in question suffered severe punishment. For the period at hand, such a penalty was waived in only two instances at the request of the slave-holder.

A set of examples has been selected below to illustrate the risk as well as the futility that existed in addressing the so-called "Protector of Slaves":

> Complaint No. 19 involved a slave named Zephirin and seven others, the grievance in question being an insufficiency of food. The resolution was as follows: "This complaint being proved to be entirely false and malicious, the Protector, to mark his displeasure at this attempt to impose upon him, directed each of the individuals complaining to receive 30 stripes of the cat-o'nine-tails on the habitation of their master, and in the presence of their comrades."[86]
>
> Complaint No. 21, regarding a slave named Cupidon, who similarly reported an insufficiency of food as well as severe punishment, is summarized thus: "Cupidon, who was sent to the civil hospital died there on

Table 4.4 Protector of slaves report, 20 March–24 June 1829[87]

Number of complaints	*How disposed of by the Protector of Slave*
23	Deemed alternatively "false", "groundless", "frivolous" or otherwise unfounded
7	Dismissed
4	Resolved by proprietor promising better treatment
1	Fined
8	Referred for prosecution
43	**Total**

84 Ibid., p. 4.
85 Nwulia, op. cit., 112.
86 PP 1830–1831 (262), p. 11.
87 Compiled from 'Abstract Statement of Complaints preferred to the Protector and Guardian of Slaves, from the 20th March to the 24th June 1829', in PP 1830–1831 (262), pp. 10–14.

the 26th April; not from any punishment inflicted upon his person, but (according to the opinion of the medical officer in charge of that establishment) from a depraved habit of body, paralysis, and other constitutional causes."[88] Further details on the case indicate that upon receiving notice of Cupidon's death, Protector Thomas simply informed the slave-holder that he had passed away, and "thus terminated the investigation of the matter."[89]

Complaint No. 35 concerned a slave named Rosalie, who objected to being ill-treated and over-worked for her constitution. "Rosalie's complaint of ill treatment being unfounded, but her state of health somewhat delicate, she was returned to her master under a promise of giving her medical assistance and careful treatment, and of not employing her in any work until she shall be recovered."[90]

The last example in particular demonstrates that the Protector was disinclined to make an official finding against slave-holders despite evidence that would justify such a finding, and even while seeking to hold in favour of a slave. As the case of Zephirin shows, by having the slave punished in front of his comrades, Protector Thomas also sought to make public examples which communicated how he perceived his role, effectively discouraging slaves from approaching him. Since the majority of complaints led to even more maltreatment in the form of punishment, Thomas made his stance on the slave cause very clear. Cupidon's case shows that even where the death of a slave evidently appears to have been caused by the owner, the Protector did not regard it as necessary to make a referral for prosecution, possibly concluding that with the complainant's death, "protection" was no longer required.

Despite Thomas' obvious sympathy with slave-holders, their cooperation with the Protector's Office remained limited. As time went on, Thomas repeatedly noted in his observations how difficult his role was, how little regard the *Procureur Général* paid to this referrals, and how the list of those defaulting to comply with the regulations regarding punishment records and other slave returns kept ever growing.[91]

For the slave-holders in Mauritius, British ameliorative measures amounted in practice to not much more than an inconvenience to be circumvented. The metropolitan government, largely due to the failures of British administrators locally, did not succeed in positively impacting conditions of slave-keeping in Mauritius. Recent research reinforces the impression that slave-holders were largely unimpressed by British measures. Examining succession and bankruptcy sales via

88 Ibid.
89 Ibid., p. 26.
90 Ibid., p. 13.
91 CO 172/28, Protector of Slaves Report of the Colony of Mauritius, June 1831, see General Observations.

public auction as evidenced through notarial acts, the work of Shirley Chenny, Pascal St-Amour and Désiré Vencatachellum appears to suggest that the abolition of slavery was not expected during the mid- to late 1820s. Observing steady prices in slave sales, the scholars reason that had emancipation been expected, slave prices would have decreased.[92] In this context, it is perhaps unsurprising that intensification of ameliorative measures lead to a planter rebellion in Mauritius.

4.5 The resident planter

The image of the "absentee" plantation owner commonly associated with other sugar colonies such as the West Indies does not apply in the case of Mauritius, where the majority of planters were locals of French descent, and the number of British settlers remained negligible. That is not to say that Britain did not have an interest in the Mauritian sugar industry. The 1825 tariff equalization had affected the island's economy permanently. The rapid rise of Mauritius from minor colony to a major sugar producer would, over the years, attract considerable British investment providing the local planters with avenues to lobby the metropolitan government for the sugar cause via their London stakeholders.[93] Locally however, sugar plantations remained firmly in Franco-Mauritian hands throughout the decades. Their power did not derive from the size of their social group: Governor Farquhar's returns show that the white inhabitants remained significantly in the minority, as is evident from Table 4.5.

These numbers were explicitly stated not to include the British troops stationed at Mauritius at the time, which research indicates numbered their highest in 1813 with 4,210, and then slowly decreased over the years, being at their lowest in 1825 with 1,131, only to increase again over the following decade to

Table 4.5 White population, 1812–1822[94]

Year	*White population*
1814	7,076
1816	7,231
1819	8,036

92 Chenny, Shirley, Pascal St-Amour and Désiré Vencatachellum, 'Slave Prices from Succession and Bankruptcy Sales in Mauritius, 1825–1827', *Explorations in Economic History*, 40 (2003), 419–442.

93 Discussed in Chapter 2, see especially North-Coombes, M. D., 'From Slavery to Indenture: Forced Labour in the Political Economy of Mauritius 1834–1867', in *Indentured labour in the British Empire, 1834–1920*, ed. by Kay Saunders (London: Croom Helm, 1984).

94 Compiled from 'A Return of the Population in each year, from 1812 inclusive to March 1822', 22 July 1822, Governor Sir R. T. Farquhar to the Earl of Bathurst, Port Louis, Mauritius, 7 November 1822, Enclosure No. 7, contained in *PP 1823 (89) Slave population*, above, p. 127.

Table 4.6 Population of Mauritius in 1825[95]

Whites	*Coloured*	*Slaves*	*Total*
8,178	14,133	61,187	83,498

reach another, albeit lower, peak in 1833 (the year the Abolition of Slavery Act was passed), with 2,228.[96]

A count in 1825, see Table 4.6, indicates that the white population remained fairly constant.

The 19th-century planter class in the Americas has been described as having enjoyed a lifestyle similar to European nobility, a result of the power they held over the lives of slaves as well as the extensive political influence accrued by virtue of their wealth.[97] From historical accounts it appears that the French planters in Mauritius benefitted from a similar setting,[98] and through intermarriage were well-connected to important figures in public life. It was the existence of this locally bred, resident group of planters which accounts for a different dynamic between the colony and the metropolitan government than witnessed in other sugar colonies. As explained in Chapter 2, the French maintained their power through the legal profession, with judges and lawyers acting as guardians to an archaic legal system, which (preserved through the Terms of Capitulation) acted as an counterbalance to the lack of direct governmental power. The French oligarchy had demanded an elected assembly, but to its dismay was denied.[99] Instead, in August 1825 Governor Cole established a "legislative council" with himself as president, and only four other members: the Chief (and Commissary of) Justice, the Chief Secretary to Government, the officer second in command and one further official of the local British establishment.[100]

Peter Burroughs states that by 1830, since sugar exports amounted to 85 per cent of the colony's income, a dramatic increase from 29 per cent in 1823. Consequentially, falling sugar prices at the turn of the decade lead to "hypersensitivity" among the planters to any imperial interference with slavery conditions.[101] Meanwhile, the substantial growth of the Mauritian sugar

95 Compiled from CO 415/19 *Report of the Commissioners of Eastern Enquiry in Mauritius 1826–1828*, Statistical Returns, P. 3 'Statement of Population of Mauritius in 1825'.

96 Selected from data reproduced in Kuczynski, Robert R., *Demographic Survey of the British Colonial Empire. Volume II: South Africa High Commission Territories, East Africa, Mauritius and Seychelles* (Oxford: Oxford University Press, 1949), p. 765.

97 Burnard, Trevor, 'The Planter Class', in *The Routledge History of Slavery*, ed. by Gad Heuman and Trevor Burnard (London: Routledge, 2012), pp. 187–203, p. 188.

98 See for example Macmillan, Allister, *Mauritius Illustrated: Historical and Descriptive, Commercial and Industrial, Facts, Figures and Resources* (New Delhi: Asian Educational Services, 2010).

99 See Burroughs, op. cit., p. 245–247.

100 CO 170/1 Mauritius Minutes of Council, Transcript of Minutes 17 August 1825.

101 Burroughs, op. cit., p. 248.

industry caused profound concern at the Colonial Department in London. Viscount Goderich's communication to Governor Colville in 1831 is very revealing, stating that such an expansion had been neither anticipated nor welcomed. The relevant passage highlights important issues and is therefore transcribed here fully:[102]

> Had such a result been foreseen it may be doubted whether Parliament would have been induced to equalize the duties. But it was alleged at that time upon the highest local authority that the extension of Sugar cultivation in Mauritius under any circumstances could be but very inconsiderable in as much as physical obstacles placed insurmountable limits to it. In reliance probably upon such assurances Parliament passed the bill and I must now advert to the effects as connected with the interests of the Slave Population which have followed from the unexpected impulse which was thus given to the growth of Sugar. It has been very frequently alleged and upon grounds which do not appear to be easily confuted, that the extent to which Sugar is cultivated in the different Sugar Colonies is generally speaking a not inaccurate index of the rate of mortality amongst the Slaves. In the Colonies where the soil is most prolific and where Sugar is most abundantly grown it is found by the returns of the Slave Population that the deaths far exceed the births and that the numbers of the Slaves are consequently in a course of rapid diminution, whereas their numbers in the Bahamas where no Sugar is grown are in a course of constant increase. It has been very forcibly represented on this and other grounds, that the labour required for the cultivation of Sugar is much more severe than any other species of labour in which Slaves are employed. It is also well known that where little or no sugar is grown, the value of the Slaves to their owners is trivial.

Goderich went on to state that where slaves are not retained for sugar cultivation, they enjoy a level of independence that allows for an easy transition from slavery to "a state, if not legal at least of practical enfranchisement". He believed therefore that the effect of the increase in sugar cultivation to be "adverse to the health and wellbeing of the Slaves", while at the same time serving "greatly to diminish their prospect of being able to liberate themselves by self purchase".

A number of important conclusions can be derived from the Viscount's dispatch. Firstly, Goderich states emphatically that had the drastic expansion in sugar cultivation been anticipated, Mauritian tariffs would not have been equalized to match those of the West Indies. Where he refers to the "highest local authority" at that time who made assurances to the limits of any possible growth, this appears to be an allusion to Governor Cole who held office from 1823 to 1828, and who was incidentally responsible for the unsatisfactory implementation of the amelioration directives, discussed above. Crucially, Goderich links

102 CO 168/16, Viscount Goderich to Governor Colville, Downing Street, 27 July 1831.

large-scale sugar cultivation directly with poor slavery conditions, evidenced through high mortality, and further, with a decreased likelihood for slaves to achieve self-emancipation.

Thus, in an ironic, unexpected twist, instead of improving the conditions of the colony as a whole by allowing preferential access to the British market alongside the West Indies, the 1825 equalization of sugar tariffs worsened the lot of the Mauritian slaves. It gave planters a strong impetus to further ignore the ban on the slave trade and worked to actually stimulate the illegal import of slaves. It also made the local plantocracy less amenable to amelioration policies from Britain. Already loathing the "foreign" occupation, any interference with their holding of slaves, the possession of which had suddenly become much more valuable and important, would naturally be rejected. Local "discontent" with regard to slave regulations had been reported in 1831, though in the absence of any further instructions from the British administration in Mauritius, was thought to have passed "without bad consequence."[103]

Nevertheless, the British imperial government realized action with respect to the situation in Mauritius had to be taken. In 1832, John Jeremie, having just terminated his position as president of the royal court of St. Lucia and conversant in the languages and laws of both England and France, was appointed to the newly fused role of *Procureur Général* and advocate-general in Mauritius. He was being sent by Britain to cooperate with the Protector of Slaves and enforce the amelioration policies, and the announcement caused considerable disquiet among slave-holders.[104] In an act of extraordinary defiance, on the day of his arrival, the entire public life came to a standstill, with the majority of public buildings in the capital Port Louis remaining closed. This "general strike" gripped the island for nearly two months, after which Jeremie was ordered to leave by Governor Colville, who in the face of the anarchy displayed by the French saw no other choice.[105] Unsurprisingly, Colville was shortly after removed from his post. He was replaced by Sir William Nicolay,[106] who carried on his shoulders the expectation that British authority would be re-established. In his later recollections, Jeremie claims that ammunition had been smuggled into Mauritius by the white population in the years prior to his arrival, and that a pamphlet circulated during his stay threatening the use of violence.[107]

103 IOR/F/4/1402 Board's Collections, 55506 Extract of Political Letter from Fort William, 15 December 1831.

104 Burrroughs, op. cit., p. 255.

105 Ibid., p. 256.

106 Sir William Nicolay, Governor of Mauritius from 1833 to 1840, see Macmillan, Allister, *Mauritius Illustrated: Historical and Descriptive, Commercial and Industrial, Facts, Figures and Resources* (New Delhi: Asian Educational Services, 2010).

107 Jeremie, Sir John, and John Reddie, *Recent Events at Mauritius* (London: Hatchard and Son; J. & A. Arch, 1835), pp. 5–7, available through Google Books at <https://books.google.co.uk>.

Burroughs argues that the unrest in Mauritius, which within the context of the wider British Empire could amount to no more than a "storm in a teacup", nevertheless acted to precipitate abolition generally, by demonstrating the futility of amelioration efforts and thus forcing the only available alternative: the outright end of slavery.[108] Whether the events in Mauritius may have had such a profound impact on imperial policy is open to debate. A more definite conclusion is that the French ruling class in its small and remote Indian Ocean possession was a serious concern to the metropolitan government,[109] a fact which is also reflected in the compensation Franco-Mauritian slave-holders received post abolition.

4.5.1 Compensation

In "The Wealth of Nations", Adam Smith makes the observation that the condition of slaves is arguably better under an arbitrary government than under a free one, for under the latter, there is less likelihood of interference with private property.[110] It is the idea that abolishing slavery was fundamentally an interference with the private property of slave-holders that drove the idea of compensation.

In his work on the issue of post-emancipation compensation, Nicholas Draper sets out that for slave-holders, indemnity was an integral part of the debate when the end of slavery was being considered, whereas several abolitionists sought to keep the question of emancipation separate from any remuneration slave-holders may or may not receive.[111] Underlying the question of whether compensation ought to have been paid is, as Draper observes, the fraught issue of "property in men".[112] This has been briefly touched upon at the beginning of this chapter. A recurrent theme is also the observation that it was not slaves who were being considered for remuneration.[113] If not as "compensation" for having been kept in slavery, the British taxpayers' money could have been used, at least, in part, to endow them with the means to begin life outside of bondage. However, the question whether compensation ought or ought not to have been paid is arguably a moral one. For present purposes, it shall suffice to observe that the British Parliament did vote to indemnify the slave-holders.[114] A fund of £20 million was

108 Burroughs, op. cit., p. 262.

109 Due to the impending abolition of slavery, a 1833 proposal to overhaul the Mauritian judicial system by introducing a Charter was shelved, possibly to avoid any further aggravation of the French oligarchy at that particular moment in time. See CO 168/18, Goderich to Attorney General, Downing Street, 12 March 1833.

110 Smith, Adam, *An Inquiry into the Nature and Causes of the Wealth of Nations*, ed. by Edwin Cannan, 5th Edition (London: Methuen & Co., 1904), Book IV, Chapter 7.

111 Draper, Nicholas, *The Price of Emancipation: Slave-Ownership, Compensation and British Society at the End of Slavery* (Cambridge: Cambridge University Press, 2009), p. 75.

112 Ibid., pp. 76–85.

113 Ibid.

114 'An Act to carry into further Execution the Provisions of an Act passed in the Third and Fourth Years of His present Majesty, for compensating Owners of Slaves upon the Aboltion of Slavery', 5 & 6 Gulielmi, c. XLV, 31 August 1835. For the Act and its General Rules,

set aside by the government, out of which the planters in Mauritius received approximately £2.1 million[115] for 68,613 slaves registered.[116]

Not much information is available on the compensation process in Mauritius. Unfortunately, Draper too excluded Mauritius from his seminal research because of the "different cultural and national backgrounds of the slave-owners".[117] Incidentally, as set out in Chapter 2, Franco-Mauritians were subjects of the Crown, and it is unlikely that had they been not considered as such, compensation would have been paid. With respect to practical aspects in the process, the history of a British company founded in Mauritius shortly after conquest provides some interesting details.[118] Augustus Muir notes that the Mauritian planters themselves had valued their slaves at about £4 million, about double what they eventually received. Compensation was paid in debentures,[119] and James Blyth, who had arrived in Mauritius in 1830 to extend the family business, saw an immense opportunity. Muir observes that "these debentures were payable in Whitehall, and their collection in London on behalf of the Mauritian slave-owners was lucrative." By requesting sufficient funds from his brothers in London, Blyth ensured his company had enough hard currency early on, a foresight which in time placed him ahead of competitors and his firm was able to negotiate a large number of the debentures.[120]

The French plantation owners in Mauritius were thus included in the bounty the British government decided to extend upon the abolition of slavery. Their generous remuneration was largely the result of the efforts of Adrien d'Epinay, a wealthy planter of the time, who spent two years in London lobbying for the Franco-Mauritian interest.[121] The success of d'Epinay's efforts underline that it was their economic standing and not actual political power which presented the true source of their influence in the political sphere.[122] This evidently held true in London with the metropolitan establishment as much as it did in Mauritius in regard to the local British administration.

---

see PC 1/4444. In 2013 University College London, launched a website identifying individual compensation claims made by or on behalf of former slave-holders. See <www.ucl.ac.uk/lbs/project/> [accessed 26 June 2022]. The database continues to expand as further research is conducted.

115 NDO 4/26, Compensation Awards under Slavery Abolition Acts, litigated and uncontested claims, including interest.

116 Kuczynski, op. cit., p. 764.

117 Draper, op. cit., p. 6.

118 Muir, Augustus, *Blyth, Greene, Jourdain & Company Limited 1810–1860* (London: Newman Neame, 1961).

119 A type of bond, secured primarily by the creditworthiness of the issuer.

120 By 1836, James Blyth had made a profit of £25,000. In competition with the French planter-controlled *Banque de Maurice*, Blyth cofounded in 1838 the Mauritius Commercial Bank, see ibid., pp. 14–15. The bank, having retained its name, remains one of the dominant financial institutions on the island and in the region to this day.

121 Salverda, Tijo, *Franco-Mauritian Elite: Power and Anxiety in the Face of Change* (New York: Berghahn Books, 2015), p. 40.

122 Ibid.

Even after abolition, planters still expected slavery to be re-established. In the event, they had to look elsewhere for labour. After the compulsory period of "apprenticeship", the fully emancipated slave did not return to the plantations even for a wage in Mauritius. The reasons for this are closely connected to the arrival of a new type of worker, who even before the apprenticeship period came to an end, began to take the slave's place on the plantations: the Indian indentured labourer.

4.6 Conclusion

The discussion in this chapter has demonstrated the importance of slavery in Mauritius just prior to abolition. The institution had already been considered essential for maintenance of the colony well before British conquest, and was recognized as such by the first British administrators, as discussed in Chapter 3 in context with the abolition of the slave trade. The equalization of sugar tariffs in 1825 lead to an unexpected expansion of the industry, increasing the importance of slave retention even further. Hereby, the finite resources of Mauritius did not act as a deterrent, confounding traditional conceptualizations on investment and slave-keeping.

The amelioration period in Mauritius is characterized by one issue in particular: persistent conflict between the local British administration and the metropolitan government. The desire of the British officials to give priority to the concerns of the Franco-Mauritian slave-holders created repeated tensions in their own relationship to the Colonial Department. After general amelioration policies failed, Britain sought to intensify its efforts in this respect, since slavery conditions were considered grave as a direct result of large-scale sugar cultivation. The legal measure designed to enhance the island's economic situation ultimately undermined all other regulatory efforts to improve the living conditions of the largest segment of Mauritian society, the slaves. Both the tariff equalization and the compensation provided post abolition benefitted one group: the white ruling class.

Part II

Indentured labour

5 Informal indenture and apprenticeships

5.1 Introduction

The arrival of indentured labourers from India indicates the second large-scale importation of workers brought to Mauritius in support of the colonial project, and an important piece in the "assembly process" of what would eventually lead to the composition of Mauritian society as it is known today. The official date for the commencement of this wave of immigration is commonly stated as 1834, the year the Abolition of Slavery Act came into force in the West Indies and the Cape. In Mauritius, the Act came into force on 1 February 1835, marking the legal end of slavery on the island. While experiments with bringing workers from India had taken place earlier, the impending abolition of slavery provided the impetus for a broader, more concerted effort in ensuring that the demand for inexpensive, coercible labour required by a still-expanding sugar industry would be met.

In the Mauritian context, it is important to understand that indentured labour was introduced within the context of slavery and more importantly, by reference to its structure. The fact that the abolition of slavery and the large-scale introduction of indentured labour occurred simultaneously means that the period of apprenticeship of former slaves and the acclimatization period of indentured labourers took place at the same time, thus presenting a phase of adaptation for both. How the two labour regimes worked in relation to each other is discussed in this chapter.

The sugar industry was driving the political economy of the island. This steady development caused the metropolis to be considerably more attentive to its Indian Ocean possession, as discussed previously. While the first two decades of British colonization had been predominantly defined by the regime of slavery issue which had proven divisive, with the island's rise as an important sugar-producer, economic considerations had moved to the forefront. Relations between the colony and the imperial government changed, not at least due to British investment now being defended by lobbyists at Whitehall. Additionally, the introduction of indentured labourers not only re-configured existing legal structures locally and within the imperial relationship between Britain and Mauritius, but also brought a further stakeholder to the political mix: the government of India.

DOI: 10.4324/9781003313366-7

This chapter deals specifically with the "first phase" of indentured labour in Mauritius, which here refers to the period in the aftermath of the abolition of slavery, but before indenture immigration to the island became formalized. These early years, which saw indenture being organized on a private basis, tend to be ignored in accounts of Mauritian indentured labour, with academic emphasis placed predominantly on the state-regulated scheme that took place from 1842 onwards.[1] In this study, the formal, "second phase" of indentured immigration is discussed separately in Chapter 6. It is submitted that a thorough understanding of early immigration is necessary for a comprehensive analysis of the latter period, because the subsequent structures of immigration developed in response to the failures of the informal system. Exclusive focus on the latter period masks the serious shortcomings that accompanied the indenture experience as a whole, and neglects the fact that the new labour regime was not a static, once-conceived arrangement, but rather an evolving process.

Further, the period in question is of fundamental importance in the colonial narrative of Mauritius, since for the first time in the island's history, all inhabitants were nominally free. It thus changed the footing on which the colonial project would be undertaken. British colonization, which first brought the slave trade to an end (Chapter 3), and then slavery itself (Chapter 4), came to oversee the final part in the "assembly process" of Mauritian society by allowing large-scale indentured immigration.

Before addressing the issues of early indenture and post-emancipation apprenticeship, this chapter will first situate the events at Mauritius in the wider context of colonial labour migration more generally. This chapter aims to address how the transition from slavery to indentured labour took place legally and culturally. An examination of the local politics of the early 1830s is then followed by an analysis of the legal frameworks for indentured labour and apprenticeships in Mauritius. The nature of coercion in the new labour regime, particularly in the context of recruitment, is examined before concluding with a study of cultural issues which were relevant for Indian emigration and pertinent in identity formation on the island.

5.2 Colonial labour migration: the case of the "coolie"

The concept of contract labour or indenture was part of British colonial history for a long time, and not limited to the context of 19th-century sugar plantations. As observed by David Northrup, estimates suggest that during the 17th and 18th centuries more than half of European migration to the British Americas took place under indenture.[2] Unlike their later Asian and African counter-

1 See for example Engerman, Stanley L., 'Contract Labor, Sugar, and Technology in the Nineteenth Century', *The Journal of Economic History*, 43 (1983), 635–59, who for his assessment on the severity of contract labour conditions generally focuses almost exclusively on the second part of the 19th century.

2 Northrup, David, *Indentured Labor in the Age of Imperialism, 1834–1922* (Studies in Comparative World History; Cambridge: Cambridge University Press, 1995), p. 4.

parts however, European labourers under indenture travelled predominantly to the temperate climates of the northern United States, as part of developments which encouraged white settlements in the New World.[3] However, while certain similarities may be drawn, particularly as far as the motivations for entering into indenture are concerned,[4] the experience of European labourers bore little resemblance to what the "coolies"[5] (which is how Asian indentured labourers of the 19th century came to be known) encountered. Occurring in the aftermath of emancipation, Indian indentured labour is inextricably linked to the context of slavery. The vast majority of such workers, an estimated two-thirds, came from India, and the single largest recipient of these migrants was indeed Mauritius[6] (see Table 5.1).

Until the mid- to late 1870s, Mauritius received the most Indian labourers. Beyond that period, the largest number went to the British West Indies, notably

Table 5.1 Destinations of indentured migrants from India, 1831–1920[7]

Total	*1,336,030*
Mauritius	455,187
British Guiana	238,861
Natal	152,932
Trinidad	149,623
French Caribbean	79,089
Reunion	74,854
Fiji	61,015
East Africa	39,437
Jamaica	38,595
Dutch Guiana	34,503
Other British West Indian islands	11,152

3 Ibid., p. 9.
4 Ibid., p. 10.
5 The term "coolie", though considered derogatory to some extent, is one which appears frequently in scholarship. Its origin is unclear, but possibly derived from native Indian languages. In the context of this thesis, "indentured labourer" is preferred. Recently, ethnic writers have sought to reclaim the designation under the concept of "coolitude", see Bahadur, Gaiutra, *Coolie Woman: The Odyssey of Indenture* (Chicago: University of Chicago Press, 2014), and Carter, Marina, and Khal Torabully, *Coolitude: An Anthology of the Indian Labour Diaspora* (London: Anthem Press, 2002), discussed in Chapter 1 of this thesis. For a discussion of the genealogy of the term "coolie", see Tinker, Hugh, *A New System of Slavery: Export of Indian Labour Overseas, 1830–1920*, 2nd Edition (London: Hansib Publications, 1993), pp. 41–42, and also Knight, G. Roger, 'The Language of Colonial Power: The Sugar Industry's "Coolies" in Colonial Java', in *White and Deadly: Sugar and Colonialism*, ed. by Bill Ashcroft, Roger Knight and Pal Ahluwalia (New York, NY: Nova Science Publishers, 1999), pp. 68–74.
6 Engerman, op. cit., p. 644.
7 Compiled from data in Northrup, David, *Indentured Labor in the Age of Imperialism, 1834–1922*, Studies in Comparative World History (Cambridge: Cambridge University Press, 1995), pp. 156–157.

British Guiana.[8] Then, during the first two decades of the 20th century, the largest number of indentured migrants were destined for East and South Africa.[9] Indian indenture largely ended by the mid-1920s. In Mauritius, the number of arrivals began to taper off considerably from the turn of the century onwards, with no arrivals at all recorded after 1910–1911, until the final batches of 1923–1925, a period during which just under 1,400 emigrants arrived at the island.[10]

Indentured labour, on occasion also referred to as indentured servitude, is traditionally considered a type of "unfree labour", alongside other historical systems of organizing work, including slavery and serfdom.[11] However, the dichotomy of "free" and "unfree" labour itself is problematic, and as a binary not universally accepted.[12] The issue of how a system of labour may be determined as "free" or not will be considered in Chapter 6, which contains an analysis of state-regulated indentured labour as it occurred in Mauritius from 1842 onwards. For current purposes, it will serve the discussion to conceptually distinguish indentured labour from other regimes traditionally deemed not free, such as debt bondage and serfdom. In theory, indentured labour was limited to a fixed-time period, under a contractual agreement. Payments to the worker were considered a wage. In contrast, debt bondage "was a form of servitude based upon an initial agreement to borrow funds and continued until the time, if ever, the debt was repaid."[13] Either indentured labour or debt bondage is conceptually quite remote from the notion of serfdom. Serfs, while predominantly agricultural workers like indentured labourers, were, unlike the latter, subject to a feudal agreement which involved allegiance to a "lord". Historically, serfdom occurred as a way of social organization in many rural areas of Western Europe and Russia during medieval times, and operated to provide a level of protection for the peasantry in return for their services.[14]

8 As evident from "Table IV, British India", in Ferenczi, Imre, and Walter F. Willcox, *International Migrations: Volume I – Statistics* (New York: National Bureau of Economic Research, 1929), pp. 904–905.
9 Northrup, op. cit., Figure 5.1., p. 107.
10 Ferenczi and Walter, op. cit., p. 905.
11 See Steinfeld, Robert J., *Coercion, Contract, and Free Labor in the Nineteenth Century* (Cambridge; New York, NY: Cambridge University Press, 2001), p. 4.
12 For a selection of contributions on the divide, see Brass, Tom, and Marcel van der Linden, eds., *Free and Unfree Labour: The Debate Continues* (International and Comparative Social History, 5; Bern; New York: Peter Lang, 1997).
13 Eltis, David, and Stanley L. Engerman, 'Dependence, Servility, and Coerced Labor in Time and Space', in *The Cambridge World History of Slavery: Volume 3, AD 1420-AD 1804*, ed. by David Eltis and Stanley L. Engerman (New York: Cambridge University Press, 2011), p. 5.
14 See Eltis and Stanley, ibid. Peter Boomgaard has applied the term "serf" also to a category of workers of "a status between that of a slave and that of a debt bondman" in 18th century Java, see Boomgaard, Peter, 'Human Capital, Slavery and Low Rates of Economic and Population Growth in Indonesia, 1600–1910', in *The Structure of Slavery in Indian Ocean Africa and Asia*, ed. by Gwyn Campbell, Studies in Slave and Post-Slave Societies and Cultures (London: Frank Cass, 2004), p. 87.

Returning to a conceptualization of indentured labour, the question whether the regime was indeed no more than "a new system of slavery", as the title of Hugh Tinker's seminal work famously declared,[15] continues to divide academics.[16] Indeed, Suzanne Miers posits this query as central to the work of researchers, rivalled only by the question whether indentured labour presented an escape from poverty for those seeking a better life.[17] Miers makes this claim after listing the various attributes and purposes of slavery. As part of her argument, she states that "no definition of slavery can be separated from the definition of its antithesis – freedom."[18] Cognizant of the vast complexities involved in any attempt to define "freedom", she arrives at the notion that "the term, therefore, may be taken to designate the norm in any society, and hence is culturally defined, but within certain limits."[19]

The structure of Miers' argument reveals the limitations inherent in framing a discussion on indentured labour by reference to slavery, even as it seeks to advocate such an approach. As highlighted in the previous chapter, slavery itself lacks a commonly accepted definition, the very attribute which renders it so susceptible to be applied to diverse contexts. Miers' demarcation cited above, that freedom would connote whatever is the "norm" in any given society, simply raises further questions. How would the "norm" of freedom be determined? By which markers? How does the argument apply to a society such as it existed in 19th-century Mauritius, where slaves significantly outnumbered the free population (whether white or *gens de couleur*), and accordingly, it was slavehood which arguably constituted the "norm"?

It is submitted that the perennial query, whether indentured labour amounted to no more than a new system of slavery, is fundamentally misguided, and its pursuit as a consequence hampered by methodological shortcomings. As indicated in the introductory chapter, most scholars make the assessment one way or the other by focusing on a narrow aspect, such as legal status, working conditions or the quality of the transport across sea. The fallacy of using an approach which takes slavery as the yard stick by which to make evaluations lies in the fact that it is becomes fundamentally limited by its own parameters. As pointed out by Amit Kumar Mishra, direct comparisons to slavery fail to allow for an appraisal of all

15 Tinker, op. cit.

16 Clare Anderson has produced a paper which seeks to transcendent this frame of analysis by demonstrating that within India at the time, the recruitment for indentured labour was less associated with slavery and more with penal transportation. While convict labour occurred on a significantly lower scale than indentured labour, the connection was easily made due to cultural issues relevant to Indian recruitment, also discussed in this thesis below at 5.6.1. See Anderson, Clare, 'Convicts and Coolies: Rethinking Indentured Labour in the Nineteenth Century', *Slavery & Abolition*, 30 (2009), 93–109.

17 Miers, Suzanne, 'Slavery: A Question of Definition', in *The Structure of Slavery in Indian Ocean Africa and Asia*, ed. by Gwyn Campbell (Studies in Slave and Post-Slave Societies and Cultures; London: Frank Cass, 2004), pp. 1–16.

18 Ibid., p. 2.

19 Ibid.

variables relevant to the indentured labour experience.[20] Applying this methodology, the discovery of any aspect denoting an "improvement" upon the conditions experienced under slavery leads to the conclusion that indenture was not a continuation of the previous system, or conversely, through the detection of a similar level of barbarity, that indeed it was.

The approach offered in this thesis presents a departure from the traditional model. Focusing on legal processes, the question it seeks to answer is not whether indentured labour was better or worse than slavery, but rather how indentured labour redistributed power in Mauritius. As Engerman notes, the ability to exploit both labour and land depended to a large degree on legislation that regulated the flow of labour as well as the controls placed locally, but "what remains to be discovered . . . is how much of the politics as distinct from the economics of the matter determined the outcome." Focusing attention in this direction rather than towards an evaluation of indentured labour by reference to the institution of slavery, one can grasp more clearly the broader social implications of abolition and the political and economic dynamics that were unleashed in its aftermath.

5.3 Indian indentured labour in Mauritius

5.3.1 Local politics

The person in charge of the British administration in Mauritius during the transition from slavery to indentured labour was Governor Nicolay.[21] A member of the military, of the rank of lieutenant colonel, he previously held governorships at Dominica, Antigua and St. Kitts and Nevis, before arriving in Mauritius in January 1833.[22]

The new governor reportedly disembarked on the island with great apprehension, due to the events in Mauritius which had accompanied the news of the abolition of slavery, discussed in the previous chapter. He was however able to assume his position peacefully and one of his first acts was to dismiss the Vice-President of the Court of Appeal, J.M. Virieux, as well as Colonel Draper, the Collector of Customs, and Adrien d'Epinay, in his capacity as a member of the Legislative Council.[23] Their removal paved the way for the return of John Jeremie, who after his unceremonious ejection the previous year, was finally able to

20 Mishra, Amit Kumar, 'Indian Indentured Labourers in Mauritius: Reassessing the "New System of Slavery" vs. Free Labour Debate', *Studies in History*, 25 (2009), 229–251.

21 Sir William Nicolay, governor of Mauritius from 1833 to 1840, see Macmillan, Allister, *Mauritius Illustrated: Historical and Descriptive, Commercial and Industrial, Facts, Figures and Resources* (New Delhi: Asian Educational Services, 2010).

22 Napal, Dayachand, *British Mauritius, 1810–1948* (Port Louis, Mauritius: Hart Printing, 1984), p. 23.

23 Macmillan, Allister, *Mauritius Illustrated: Historical and Descriptive, Commercial and Industrial, Facts, Figures and Resources* (New Delhi: Asian Educational Services, 2010 (reprint)), p. 50.

take up his position as *Procureur Général* on the island. Unfortunately, Jeremie's tenure appears to have been chiefly concerned with the pursuit of a personal vendetta against the local establishment, which in the end led to his dismissal after only a short time in office. The governorship of Nicolay remained otherwise quiet and largely uneventful as far as disturbances on the island were concerned.[24] Emancipation was effected peacefully on 1 February 1835,[25] though as already indicated, slaves were not actually free but bound as apprentices for a further number of years. Their anticipated freedom however motivated planters to find a substitute workforce quickly, to sustain the sugar monoculture that had been cultivated for over a decade.

5.3.2 *First arrivals*

As noted above, scholarly assessments of Indian indentured labour tend to focus predominantly on state-regulated emigration post-1842, neglecting the period in the immediate aftermath of slave emancipation, which saw private importation taking place on an informal basis. The second phase however saw a modified version of immigration that built upon the experience of the first phase, and therefore must be placed in relation to it.

In Mauritius, the Indian presence can actually be traced back to Dutch occupation, where Indians were to be found among both slaves and free people in a society that never exceeded a few hundred.[26] Another significant component of the workforce were also, as previously discussed, Indian convicts first introduced under Governor Farquhar in 1815.[27] The first arrival of individual workers from India at the initiative of the French planters is commonly placed between 1820 and 1830. A random sample from the MGI Archives[28] indicates the embarkation of workers from various Indian provinces in 1826.[29] Detailed records of the outcome of these early experiments with Indian labour do not appear to have been made,[30] but given the subsequent large-scale expansion it may be assumed to have been satisfactory to the local planters.

With the abolition of slavery already effective in the other colonies, the latter part of 1834 saw the arrival of Indian indentured labourers under a private, yet

24 Ibid., p. 51.

25 Nicolay to Spring Rice, Mauritius, 3 February 1835, in *PP 1835 (278-I) (278-II) Papers presented to Parliament, by His Majesty's command, in explanation of the measures adopted by His Majesty's government, for giving effect to the Act for the abolition of slavery throughout the British colonies. Part II. Jamaica–(continued), Barbados, British Guiana, and Mauritius, 1833–1835.*

26 Deerpalsingh, S., J. Ng Foong Kwong, V. Govinden and V. Teelock, *Labour Immigrants in Mauritius – A Pictoral Recollection* (Mauritius: Mahatma Gandhi Institute, 2001), p. 6.

27 Discussed in Chapter 3.

28 The policy of the Mahatma Gandhi Institute in Mauritius regarding access to the immigration records held at their archives is discussed in Chapter 1.

29 Deerpalsingh et al., op. cit., p. 22.

30 Ly-Tio-Fane Pineo, Huguette, *Lured Away: The Life History of Indian Cane Workers in Mauritius* (Moka: Mahatma Gandhi Institute, 1984), p. 15.

organized, importation scheme. Records show that in September 1834, 36 Indians signed five-year contracts with a representative of Hunter Arbuthnot & Co. of Mauritius, in front of the chief magistrate at the police office in Calcutta, and arrived at the island on 2 November. They were preceded in August 1834 by a batch of 39 free labourers.[31] Table 5.2 provides a detailed breakdown of the numbers of Indian immigrants who arrived in Mauritius between 1834 and 1910.

Table 5.2 Indian immigrants, arrived at and departed from Mauritius, 1834–1910[32]

Year	*Arrival*			*Departure*		
	Total	*Male*	*Female*	*Total*	*Male*	*Female*
1834	75	75	nil	4	4	nil
1835	1,254	1,182	72	26	25	1
1836	3,823	3,639	184	190	187	3
1837	7,292	6,939	353	134	114	20
1838	11,808	11,567	241	154	148	6
1839	1,035	933	102	173	170	3
1840	116	107	9	422	394	28
1841	542	499	43	1,089	995	94
1842	83	73	10	2,115	2,021	94
1843	34,525	30,218	4,307	2,992	2,884	108
1844	11,549	9,709	1,840	2,461	2,312	149
1845	10,971	8,918	2,053	2,662	2,492	170
1846	7,339	5,718	1,621	2,760	2,556	204
1847	5,830	5,174	656	1,784	1,651	133
1848	5,395	4,739	656	3,015	2,639	376
1849	7,425	6,378	1,047	4,892	4,298	594
1850	10,030	8,436	1,594	3,725	3,283	442
1851	10,020	8,257	1,763	3,269	2,895	374
1852	17,485	13,671	3,814	2,426	2,034	392
1853	12,144	9,877	2,267	2,028	1,767	261
1854	18,484	14,995	3,489	3,675	3,166	509
1855	12,915	9,645	3,270	4,267	3,702	565
1856	12,653	9,130	3,523	4,897	4,220	677
1857	12,725	8,640	4,085	4,603	3,794	809
1858	29,946	20,932	9,014	8,165	6,707	1,458
1859	44,397	31,643	12,754	5,117	4,146	971
1860	13,286	9,070	4,216	2,833	2,290	543
1861	13,985	10,232	3,753	2,257	1,786	471

31 PP 1837–38 (180) (232), p. 77, discussed below. See also Deerpalsingh et al., op. cit., p. 24. Mauritius recognizes the 2nd of November as the arrival of the first indentured labourers with a public holiday. For a statement of the numbers of Indians introduced from Calcutta since 1 August 1834, see Committee on the Export of Coolies to Mauritius and Demerara, *Report of the Committee Appointed to Enquire into Abuses in the Export of Coolies to the Colonies of Mauritius and Demerara* (Calcutta: G.H. Huttmann, Bengal Military Orphan Press, 1840), pp. 286–387.

32 Data compiled from Ferenczi, Imre, and Walter F. Willcox, *International Migrations – Volume 1: Statistics* (New York: National Bureau of Economic Research, 1929), pp. 1041–1042.

Year	*Arrival*			*Departure*		
	Total	*Male*	*Female*	*Total*	*Male*	*Female*
1862	9,893	7,440	2,453	2,212	1,752	460
1863	5,254	3,667	1,587	3,220	2,553	667
1864	7,552	5,626	1,926	3,413	2,692	721
1865	20,283	14,910	5,373	3,521	2,854	667
1866	5,596	3,702	1,894	3,815	2,925	890
1867	350	317	33	3,398	2,571	827
1868	2,608	1,968	640	2,544	1,880	664
1869	1,772	1,182	590	2,320	1,684	636
1870	4,076	2,831	1,245	2,842	2,172	670
1871	3,292	2,318	974	3,074	2,369	705
1872	5,774	4,015	1,759	3,819	2,788	1,031
1873	7,614	5,226	2,388	3,035	2,160	875
1874	7,052	4,818	2,234	4,075	2,874	1,201
1875	2,919	1,996	923	3,423	2,368	1,055
1876	502	330	172	3,271	2,354	917
1877	2,187	1,528	659	2,417	1,794	623
1878	4,826	3,203	1,623	2,352	1,825	527
1879	3,079	2,013	1,066	2,555	1,926	629
1880	742	371	371	2,345	1,731	614
1881	nil	nil	nil	1,551	1,180	317
1882	1,241	805	436	1,863	1,466	397
1883	1,915	1,283	632	2,406	1,766	640
1884	6,389	4,450	1,939	1,853	1,362	491
1885	358	246	112	4,001	2,891	1,110
1886	746	511	235	2,320	1,649	671
1887	264	191	73	2,350	1,707	643
1888	713	482	231	1,731	1,283	448
1889	4,532	3,244	1,298	1,319	990	329
1890	3,025	2,152	873	1,055	827	228
1891	991	713	278	900	716	184
1892	nil	nil	nil	1,478	1,129	349
1893	485	353	132	1,654	1,197	457
1894	1,026	758	268	968	754	214
1895	1,734	1,249	485	1,135	860	275
1896	801	593	208	1,155	858	297
1897	426	314	112	919	671	248
1898	nil	nil	nil	1,106	842	264
1899	nil	nil	nil	746	564	182
1900	2,890	2,094	796	1,151	858	293
1901	4,574	3,265	1,309	631	469	162
1902	2,565	1,875	690	648	462	186
1903	508	374	134	523	383	140
1904	2,057	1,513	544	561	413	148
1905	720	534	186	419	314	105
1906	618	463	155	615	435	180
1907	586	439	147	511	366	145
1908	nil	nil	nil	1,041	775	266
1909	nil	nil	nil	686	512	174
1910	532	397	135	585	403	182

The data in Table 5.2 is included in detail to support the forthcoming analysis. As previously mentioned, 1834 is commonly taken to mark the beginning of Indian indentured labour to Mauritius, whereas 1910 marks its end.[33]

Several general observations can be made from a first glance at these numbers:

- Indian immigration throughout the period rarely followed a steady pattern but shows considerable fluctuations, sometimes drastically from one year to the next.
- Immigration was highest in the years between 1843 and 1865 during which time the annual influx was routinely greater than 10,000. It reached its peak in 1859 and from 1865 onwards tailed off significantly.
- The number of departures were significant but in the early years at least remained low in comparison to the arrivals, generally fluctuating between 1,000 to 4,000 throughout the entire period irrespective of the arrival numbers of any given year. They reached their highest level in 1858 and 1859, with over 8,000 and 5,000 departures respectively. In later years the number of departures was occasionally higher than that of arrivals, but in a broad sense one could imagine that the aggregate population numbers were largely stable.
- Male and female immigration became at no point balanced and remained significantly biased in favour of the former. In most years the male immigration was two to three times that of female immigration.

These prima facie observations will be addressed in this and the next chapter, and the data will be further checked against relevant historical events.

5.4 Making the transition from slavery

Before analyzing the legal framework that governed early indentured labour, and how it related to the apprenticeship system which in Mauritius ran concurrently, it is important to address certain issues which underpinned the introduction of Indian workers to the island.

From Table 5.2, it is evident that what started as an experiment in 1834 was the beginning of an extraordinary project of migration which changed the face of Mauritian society permanently. It also marked the move from slavery to a different labour system. This transition occurring in 19th-century Mauritius is a direct reversal of the American experience of the 17th century. Prior to the introduction of African slavery, labour in the New World consisted primarily of British indentured workers. Russell Menard explains that in some places, such as Barbados, the transition to slavery was effected quickly, while occurring as a

33 After that year, Indians whose contracts had expired continued to depart, but these numbers have not been reproduced here.

more gradual process in areas like Chesapeake, where tobacco was being cultivated.[34] Scholars take different views on the precise causes leading to the move from indentured labour to slavery. Menard divides the arguments into two broad schools of thought. On the one hand, there are those who regard the transition as predominantly an economic process, occurring as a consequence of changes in the supply in labour.[35] On the other hand, the change has been rationalized as having been driven by "planter preference". In this view, the practical differences in keeping "slaves" as opposed to "labourers"[36] is regarded as fundamental, with political and cultural considerations given more relevance. Menard himself supports both approaches and combines them by suggesting that what occurred was a two-stage process. He argues that the transition was lead by an elite, particularly around Chesapeake. Slave ownership became a marker of status and therefore a social aspiration, leading to the expansion of the system and ultimately, a pervasive presence of slavery on the continent.

It is not within the ambit of this thesis to analyze the American experience in detail, but the reversed transition from indentured labour to slavery presents an interesting contrast to the Mauritian example. Specifically, Menard's synthesis of arguments and framework for understanding the change may be borrowed. Applying the categories of either (a) an economically-driven transition or (b) one which occurred through the preference of the planters, it is clear that in the case of Mauritius, in the beginning at least, the change was externally imposed. Slavery was being abolished by imperial law, and thus was no longer available to the planters. The fact that indentured labour immigration began in 1834, the same year in which the Abolition of Slavery Act took effect in the other colonies, suggests that recourse to the new form of labour was a direct result of the end of slavery. It is unlikely that had slavery not been abolished, planters would have sought to replace it with another labour system, at least not at that precise moment in time.

Later developments however reveal that beyond the initial impetus of having to seek alternative labour, planter preference played an important role in the transition, especially with regard to the new workforce's ethnicity. Research has shown that the preference for a specifically Indian workforce manifested itself at different levels, and for different reasons. Taken together, they were responsible for the large influx of Indian workers and thus the subsequent size of the Indian presence in Mauritius.

34 Menard, Russell, 'Making a "Popular Slave Society" in Colonial British America', *Journal of Interdisciplinary History*, XLIII (3) (2013), 377–395.

35 The number of workers dwindled due to certain developments in Europe and indenture to the Americas no longer presented an attractive option. See the comprehensive volume on the subject by Menard, Russell, *Migrants, Servants and Slaves: Unfree Labor in Colonial British America* (Aldershot; Burlington, VT: Routledge, 2001).

36 The designations "servant" and "indentured servitude" appear to be the preferred terminology in the American context. See Chapter 6 for a brief discussion on the choice of appellation.

5.4.1 *Preferences in ethnicity*

In the first instance, it appears that Indian workers were favoured over other ethnicities as a consequence of government policy. A frequently forgotten, yet notable part of the experiment with indentured labour involved the immigration of workers from China. Around 3,000 Chinese labourers, mainly from the regions of Macao, Canton and Penang, were recruited for Mauritius between 1840 to 1843.[37] Marina Carter and James Ng Foon Kwong suggest that Chinese indenture failed largely due to the comparatively higher cost for transportation, as well as Chinese law which hampered the process by requiring special permits for the emigration of workers.[38] Additionally, Chinese workers do not appear to have performed well as plantation labourers in the tropical climate.[39] Ultimately however, Chinese indenture was no longer pursued after the local government decided to decline claims for the bounty due on the introduction of foreign, non-Indian workers as guaranteed under Ordinance No. 8 of 1842.[40] The ordinance was in place during a time when Indian labour immigration to the colony had come to be suspended due to extensive reports of abuse. The brief dalliance with Chinese indenture thus occurred when the access to the Indian labour pool was closed for a brief period, approximately from 1840 to 1842. The aim was therefore to find a possible alternative to Indian indenture, but the Chinese experiment proved disappointing. The choice of Chinese labour was, however, only one alternative to Indian labour.

Several years prior, in 1834 with the abolition of slavery pending, the proposal was made to introduce African indentured labour to Mauritius. Charles Letord, a local inhabitant, made an elaborate appeal to the governor for a scheme which would allow for the introduction of workers from the eastern coast of Africa, extolling the advantages of the project in great detail.[41] The idea was

37 Carter, Marina, and James Ng Foong Kwong, *Forging the Rainbow* (Mauritius: self-published, 1997), p. xii.

38 Ibid., Chapter 2. Carter and Kwong also observe that other workers, in much smaller numbers, were imported from Madagascar, the Comoros and other areas around the Indian Ocean.

39 Ibid., see also Saha, Panchan, *Emigration of Indian Labour (1834–1900)* (Delhi: People's Publishing House, 1970), p. 16.

40 'Extract of the Minute of the Proceedings of the Council of Government on 1st August 1842', regarding the applications of Giquel & Co., and Lecord, in *PP 1844 [530] Emigration. West Indies and Mauritius. Correspondence relative to emigration of labourers to the West Indies and the Mauritius, from the west coast of Africa, the East Indies, and China*, pp. 208–209. The post-1840 bounty system of immigration to Mauritius is discussed in the next chapter.

41 'Projet d'Emancipation présenté à son Exellence le Major Général Sir William Nicolay, Gouverneur et Commondant en Chef de l'Ile Maurice et Dépendances, par M. Charles Letord, Créole de Maurice et Captaine de Marine au Commerce', in *PP 1837–38 (180) (232) British Guiana and Mauritius. Copies of all orders in council, or colonial ordinances for the better regulation and enforcement of the relative duties of masters and employers, and articled servants, tradesmen and labourers, in the colonies of British Guiana and Mauritius, and of correspondence relating thereto*, p. 69.

however emphatically rejected with an "unqualified Refusal", as the governor felt that "however speciously coloured", it amounted to "neither more nor less than a Renewal of the Slave Trade, and therefore entirely inadmissible."[42] Monsieur Letord's proposal may have invited rejection, given his reputation as having been formerly active as a trafficker known by the alias Dorval, a slave dealer of some notoriety during the early years of British occupation.[43] But the fact that his detailed proposal was curtly dismissed and no further attempt was made to introduce African workers at the time[44] demonstrates that in Mauritius, black indenture had been considered as too reminiscent of slavery, and the potential recruitment deemed as resembling too closely the trade in slaves, which in its own time had proven very difficult to suppress, as will be recalled from Chapter 3. This is in contrast to the experience of British Guiana, which following emancipation not only received first a contingent of black workers from Barbados, but also European labourers from Madeira, Portugal, before beginning to import Indians on a significant scale.[45] But in Mauritius, the search for a large pool of inexpensive labour became quickly and firmly fixed towards India, and in the process, the two different forms of labour – slavery and indenture – came to be represented in terms of an ethnic distinction between two categories of worker – those of African and Indian extraction.

If, in the first place the choice of Indian labour was the result of government policy, it then became a self-sustaining policy. Plantation owners had their own reason for encouraging a large influx of workers from the subcontinent, as will become evident when the correlation of the two systems of indentured labour and apprenticeship is considered in the next section.

5.5 Emancipated slaves and indentured labourers working together

5.5.1 Labour control and power

As outlined in Chapter 4, the Abolition Act of 1833 in effect prolonged the condition of slavery by a number of years by keeping the emancipated slaves bound in service. The distinction made between "praedials"[46] and "non-praedials" was designed to keep the former, which were agricultural apprentices, in longer

42 Secretary Dick to Letord, Port Louis (Mauritius), 20 June 1834, in *PP 1837–38 (180) (232)*, above, p. 74.
43 Governor Nicolay to Lord Glenelg, Mauritius, 25 July 1836, in *PP 1837–38 (180) (232)*, above, p. 67.
44 About ten years later, Ordinance No. 59 of 1844 was passed to encourage emigration specifically from Africa, though unsuccessfully so. See also Chapter 6.
45 See Mangru, Basdeo, *Benevolent Neutrality – Indian Government Policy and Labour Migration to British Guiana 1854–1884* (London: Hansib Publications, 1987), pp. 34–37.
46 Further distinguished by either being "attached" to soil or not, see section IV of the 1833 Act.

service, namely until 1 August 1840.[47] Non-praedials were set to be bound until 1 August 1838.[48] In the event, the British West Indies brought the entire system to an end in 1838, and following the example, Mauritius ended apprenticeships in 1839.

In his assessment of the apprenticeship system, Moses Nwulia claims that abolition effectively turned chattel slaves into serfs, which "strengthened rather than weakened the old patterns of master-servant relationships".[49] This, in his opinion, was not conducive to the emerging multi-ethnic society of Mauritius.[50] In his assessment, Nwulia is referring to exclusively to the relationship between French planters and the former slaves, and the development of a community where the latter would be living as free people alongside their previous subjugators. Nwulia's argument is extended here to include the newly arrived Indian labourers of the period, who initially had to operate in the same context as apprentices.

Table 5.2 shows that after a tentative start in 1834, Indian immigration rose rapidly, reaching its first peak of close to 12,000 arrivals in 1838, just before apprenticeships came to an end the following year. The question arises how these two groups of different ethnicities coexisted, and how the planters, of yet another ethnicity, related to them.

The numbers in Table 5.3 derive from the official statistics provided by the Central Statistic Office (CSO) of Mauritius. As can be observed, "Indians" were not counted in 1834 and 1835, even though as previously noted, a considerable Indian presence already existed and indentured immigration from the subcontinent had begun in earnest. It is likely that they were counted under the rubric of "Aliens", which the CSO however defines as "mainly Chinese and Malayans, Malagasies, and some Europeans".[51] The CSO does not provide any numbers

Table 5.3 Population of Mauritius 1834–1840[52]

Year	*White and Free Coloured*	*Apprentices*	*Indians*	*Aliens*	*Total*
1834	26,943	64,331	–	473	91,747
1835	29,612	61,045	–	1,490	92,147
1837	31,672	52,616	11,601	(not available)	95,889
1838	37,865	53,230	23,909	665	115,669

47 Section V of the 1833 Act.
48 Section VI of the 1833 Act.
49 Nwulia, Moses D. E., 'The "Apprenticeship" System in Mauritius: Its Character and Its Impact on Race Relations in the Immediate Post-Emancipation Period, 1839–1879', *African Studies Review*, 21 (1978), 89–101, p. 89.
50 Ibid.
51 Ibid.
52 Adapted from Central Statistical Office, *Natality and Fertility in Mauritius, 1825–1955* (Mauritius: Central Statistical Office, 1956), p. 3.

for 1836. Curiously, as Table 5.3 indicates, in 1837, when 11,601 Indians had been counted, no numbers are available for "Aliens". To ascertain an overview of the population for 1836, the Blue Book of that year has been consulted. It contains a population return of each district of Mauritius, from which it has been calculated that in 1836, the "free population" amounted to 30,411, and the "apprenticed population" 53,791.[53] Further, the return contains the observation that "European Aliens exclusive of children" amounted to 670, and that there were in fact 4,337 "Indian Labourers".[54] This number roughly corresponds to the number of arrivals at that point, minus the departures, with allowances made for mortality and children possibly not counted.

The numbers in Table 5.3 indicate that the increase of indentured labourers was accompanied by a rapid decrease in the numbers of the apprenticed population, which had diminished within four years from 64,331 to 53,230. The question arises as to how the influx of new workers was affecting them.

Marina Carter has pointed out that the recourse to Indian labour was a natural choice in the case of Mauritius, given the geographical proximity as well as the planters' existing familiarity with the subcontinent. But while Indians were initially brought to simply increase the number of workers, the fact that they could be fairly easily and cheaply procured was soon utilized to the disadvantage of the local workforce.[55] Thus, what "came to be seen firstly as an insurance policy pending the freeing of apprentices" later turned into "a means of maintaining a stable wage level."[56]

This early situation of competition and rivalry has been noted by other scholars,[57] but in contemporary records is actually strongly rebuffed, as research shows. In June 1836, the Colonial Office requested circulation of a questionnaire to ascertain the impact of the introduction of Indian labourers to Mauritius. The answers of major firms involved in sugar production such as Blyth, Son & Co. and Hunter, Arbuthnot & Co. were remarkably similar. Both confirmed that apprentices and Indian labourers, male and female, were put to work alongside each other. To the query, "Have the Apprentice Labourers on your Estate shown any Feeling of Ill-Will or Dislike to the Employment of the Indians on your Habitation; and if so to what Cause do you attribute such feeling on their Part?", the existence any ill-feeling whatsoever was emphatically denied.[58]

53 CO 172/62, Blue Book for 1836, 'Return of the Population, and of the marriages, births and deaths', pp. 145–146.

54 Ibid.

55 Carter, Marina, 'The Transition from Apprenticeship to Indentured Labour in Mauritius', in *The Wages of Slavery: From Chattel Slavery to Wage Labour in Africa, the Caribbean and England*, ed. by Michael Twaddle (London: Frank Cass, 1993), pp. 114–130, p. 116.

56 Ibid.

57 See for example the discussion by Khal Torabully in *Coolitude*, op. cit., pp. 162–163, and the enduring legacy for modern societies today in islands like Mauritus, Trinidad and Fiji, where certain sentiments between different ethnicities continue to persist.

58 *PP 1837–38 (180) (232) British Guiana and Mauritius. Copies of all orders in council, or colonial ordinances for the better regulation and enforcement of the relative duties of masters and*

To be sure, both apprentices and Indian labourers were subjected to strict rules, discussed below. Yet how deep the divisions between the two communities actually were is difficult to ascertain. It is clear that any rivalry that may have existed would have been exploited by the planters, as the arrival of indentured labourers in large numbers created competition among the workforce. Sugar production became much less reliant on the availability of apprenticed workers. The decline in the number of apprentices as observable in Table 5.3 is striking, presenting a reduction of 11,101 in their population over a four-year period, with no justifiable cause. The situation only sharpened after the end of the apprenticeship period and indentured immigration was formalized under a state-backed scheme. This development, occurring in the wake of the introduction of indentured labour from India, can be regarded as the beginning of the marginalization of the black community in Mauritius, which during the period of slavery presented the largest ethnic group on the island, only to diminish following their emancipation.

It has been established in the previous chapters that the power balance in Mauritius was largely tied to control over the labouring population, since it was an essential requirement in wealth creation. Both with the abolition of the slave trade and the abolition of slavery, power was being removed from the local oligarchy, with which more often than not, the local British administration had aligned itself. With the arrival of indentured labourers, the power pendulum swung back in their favour, a state of affairs that was anxiously sought to be preserved.

This is particularly illustrated by Ordinance No. 16 of 1835,[59] which the local Council of Government, or Legislative Council, purported to have passed. It will be recalled that the council was composed of local notable inhabitants appointed by the governor, all inevitably linked to the sugar interest. Through Articles 17, 18 and 24, the ordinance made all importation and deportation of workers in and from the colony subject to authorization by the governor. Such power having hitherto been the exclusive prerogative of His Majesty the King, it was not well-received in London.[60] Eventually, the ordinance was disallowed, much to the dismay of Governor Nicolay.[61] A dispatch by Lord Glenelg[62] to Governor Nicolay clearly indicates the power struggle involved:

> You will distinctly understand, that no Law for regulating the Relations between free Labourers and their Employers must be proposed by you, unless with the previous sanction of His Majesty to the Terms of any such Proposal; and that you are not at liberty to assent to any Law of that Nature

---

employers, and articled servants, tradesmen and labourers, in the colonies of British Guiana and Mauritius, and of correspondence relating thereto, pp. 78–81.

59 Actually Ordinance 17, which has been incorrectly cited in most records.

60 Ibid., Hollier Griffiths to Colonial Secretary G.F. Dick, 20 November 1835, pp. 49–50.

61 CO 167/196, Nicolay to Glenelg, 21 January 1837.

62 Charles Grant, Baron Glenelg, Secretary of State for Wars and the Colonies from 18 April 1835 to 20 February 1939, see Panton, Kenneth J., *Historical Dictionary of the British Empire* (London: Rowman & Littlefield, 2015), p. 587.

if proposed by any other Person, unless it contain a Clause suspending its operation until His Majesty's pleasure shall have been signified.[63]

The Colonial Office was thus anxious to maintain its influence, and not inclined to leave the important question of labour regulation to the local officials. It is possible that it feared a repeated version of what occurred in the aftermath of the 1825 equalization of sugar tariffs, discussed in the previous chapter, which led to an entirely unanticipated growth in the sugar industry, and engendered profoundly negative effects for the slave population. In Mauritius, the labour question had been a thorny one ever since Britain sought to abolish the slave trade, with the local government often converging with the local French elite in their interest. Taking these issues into account, it is understandable that the metropolis was not to give up control over regulating the relationship between the planters and the new type of worker.

5.5.2 The legal framework: apprentices

The overarching legal framework for the apprenticeship system in Mauritius derived from an Order in Council dated 17 September 1834, further to the Abolition of Slavery Act.[64] The Order was not easily welcomed in Mauritius. Correspondence between Governor Nicolay and London indicates resistance, and even a level of insubordination, as far as the local administration was concerned. Initially Nicolay sought to pass his own ordinance that would govern emancipated slaves, which was later disallowed.[65] The precise terms of the governor's own regulation do not seem to have been preserved and thus cannot be compared, however his resistance to follow directions from London is quite telling.

When the King's Order arrived in Mauritius, Nicolay provided a set of largely spurious grounds why it could not be put into effect immediately, citing the need to have it "translated into good French, an undertaking of no small magnitude in this Colony, where the work of the most able translator that can be found always requires most careful examination and numerous corrections".[66] He claims that "to promulgate an Order of such extreme importance without having taken all possible precaution to ensure its correctness, might evidently be productive of serious public evil", yet in seeking to justify why his own ordinance would remain in force until after the King's Order "shall have been duly studied and correctly prepared for promulgation", he states that "it is very gratifying to perceive that the Order in Council and the local ordinance are in principle the same, and that the difference between them in matter of detail appear to be but

63 *PP 1837–38 (180) (232)*, above, Glenelg to Nicolay, 20 January 1836, p. 47.
64 *PP 1835 (278-I) (278-II)*, above, pp. 372–389.
65 Ibid., Nicolay to Spring Rice, Mauritius 20 November 1834 and the Earl of Aberdeen to Nicolay, London, 16 March 1835.
66 Ibid., Nicolay to Spring Rice, Mauritius 29 January 1835.

small; the transition from the one to the other will therefore be easy",[67] thereby contradicting his earlier assertion that the Order could only be implemented after great circumspection.

The Colonial Office was evidently not impressed, for in May 1835 it disallowed three out of four locally passed ordinances, the only one passed having been one granting an extension of the period for the return of the lists of slaves.[68] Lord Glenelg took particular issue with an ordinance that sought to regulate marriage between apprentices, whereby the consent of the employer for such a union would be required, but whose refusal, if found inadequate, could be superseded by the consent of a special justice. The desire to control apprentice marriages again appears linked to keeping control over the labouring population. The Act abolishing slavery only turned children above the age of six into apprentices.[69] Children younger than six were free, and therefore, any later offspring would not have been "born into" apprenticeship.

With the end of the apprenticeship period, and therefore full emancipation, in sight, the regulation of marriages would not have been defensible. Glenelg himself felt that the "distinctions" the ordinance contained "tend to impair that great principle of legal equality between all classes of the King's subjects, whatever their origin or colour, which it is so evidently necessary to maintain."[70] This professed desire for parity between the classes notwithstanding, the order governing the apprenticeship system showed little legal equality between emancipated slaves and their employers.

It was specified that apprentices were required to work for 45 hours per week, with heavy penalties for non-performance of duties.[71] For every hour of absence without "reasonable cause", apprentices were required to work two extra hours, and so in proportion of for every hour missed, not exceeding 15 extra hours in any one week.[72]

A classification system was put in place to give apprentices designations signifying their level of contravention. Thus, "for absenting himself without reasonable cause for more than seven and a half hours in any one week", the apprentice was considered a "deserter"; for such absence for two days in a week, a "vagabond"; and for more than six days in one week, he or she was declared a "runaway".[73] The penalties were harsh: "deserters" could be confined to hard labour for any amount of time not exceeding one week, while "vagabonds" could be so confined for up to two weeks and receive "any

67 Ibid.
68 Ibid., Glenelg to Nicolay, London, 31 May 1835.
69 Article I of the Act.
70 Ibid.
71 Order of the King in Council for giving effect in the Colony of the Mauritius to the Statute 3 & 4 Will. IV, c.73, for the Abolition of Slavery throughout the British Dominions, 17 September 1834, Cap. V.
72 Ibid., Article 3.
73 Ibid., Articles 4,5 and 6 respectively.

number of stripes not exceeding 15". Those considered "runaways" could be confined to hard labour for up to one month, and receive "any number of stripes not exceeding 30".[74]

Punishment could also be incurred for work performed "indolently, carelessly or negligently", on the first offence rendering the apprentice liable to extra labour not exceeding 15 hours in any one week, or for non-praedials, to whipping not exceeding 15 stripes. If the second offence occurred within two calendar months, it would draw hard labour confinement for up to one week; for the third offence, within the same time period, the apprentice would incur hard labour for up to a two weeks, "with whipping not exceeding 20 stripes."[75] Other offences incurring punishment included "endangering the property of his employer", "disobeying lawful commands" of the same, states of drunkenness, insolence, insubordination, conspiracy or resistance.[76] Whipping was however restricted to males only; where women would have drawn that punishment, they were punished to confinement in the stocks instead, "for no more than six days on the whole for any one offence".[77]

In comparison, the penalties for non-performance of duties by employers towards apprentices involved a fine, or at most, a term of imprisonment not exceeding one month, in the case of failure to pay the required fine in cases of serious maltreatment of apprentices only.[78]

The fundamental imbalance before the law is thus evident. The fact that non-performance of duties by an apprentice, a nominally free person, could draw significant corporal punishment by his employer, for potentially light or hard-to-prove contraventions (for example, "disobedience" or "insolence"), clearly maintained the power imbalance of slavery.

Similarly, the manner through which the order stipulated apprentices had to be "maintained", namely by direct provisions or via appropriation of ground, rendered the apprentices entirely dependent on their employers for subsistence, and was thus redolent of slavery.

5.5.3 The legal framework: indentured labourers

In contrast to the position of apprentices, the working conditions of indentured labourers from India was primarily governed by the terms of the agreement they had signed. As indicated above with Ordinance No. 16 of 1835, local administration may have sought to impose more restrictive regulations, but it seems the Colonial Office were in this instance more cognizant of the fact that these were indeed "free" workers.

74 Ibid., Article 8.
75 Ibid., Article 9.
76 Ibid., Articles 10 to 15.
77 Ibid., Article 16.
78 Ibid., Cap. VI, Article 13.

The contract of those first 36 labourers arriving in 1834 is indicative of the provisions commonly contained in indenture agreements of the early period.[79] The following terms are noteworthy:

- Indenture was for a period of five years.
- Passage to Mauritius, as well as a return passage, was to be borne by the employer, unless the worker in question sought to return before the expiration of the agreed five years.
- The employing company was held responsible that the workers should not be "a burden to the Colony", for which reason one rupee per month would be retained from pay of each person (representing one-fifth of the worker's salary), until there would be a sufficient amount to return the individual to India. Should that contingency not have had been required, the sum was to be returned at the end of the five years.
- In addition to pay, workers were to receive provisions and clothing.
- Each person received six months pay in advance.

At a first glance, these provisions appear to indicate that the situation of the Indian labourers was preferable to that of the apprentices during the same period. The realities faced by the indentured workforce will therefore be examined next.

5.6 Realities of early indenture

The issues around early indenture immigration in Mauritius are convoluted and at first glance difficult to unravel. There were various concerns and stakeholders involved, and their interplay was not a smooth one. The local British administration had not only to satisfy the metropolitan government in London, but also meet the expectations of the Franco-Mauritian plantocracy, in whose grip the economic prosperity of the island firmly remained. At the same time, following emancipation and the impending end of apprenticeships, former slaves had to be integrated into society, alongside Indian labourers, who took up the role of sugar cane field workers. With the arrival of the latter, the government of India became a further player in the already charged political arena.

Historians have documented to great extent the abuses encountered by indentured labourers,[80] the conceptualization of the system as a "new form of slavery" being based on reports of coercion, misrepresentation, kidnap and violence

79 Reproduced in *PP 1837–38 (180) (232)*, above, p. 77.

80 A selection would include Tinker, op. cit.; Sundararajan, Saroja, *From Bondage to Deliverance: Indentured Labour in Mauritius and British Guiana* (New Delhi: Allied Publishers, 2006); Mangru, Basdeo, *Benevolent Neutrality – Indian Government Policy and Labour Migration to British Guiana 1854–1884* (London: Hansib Publications, 1987); Saha, Panchan, *Emigration of Indian Labour (1834–1900)* (Delhi: People's Publishing House, 1970); Teelock, Vijayalakshmi, Anwar Janoo, Geoffrey Summers, Marc Serge Rivière and Sooryakanti Nirsimloo-Gayan, eds., *Angaje: Explorations into the History, Society and Culture of Indentured*

involved in the recruitment process, with ill-treatment and poor conditions awaiting at the destination. Marina Carter has rationalized these early experiences by stating that slave-keeping is what the planters had been accustomed to, thus the entire system and infrastructure which was in place would naturally have been that of slavery.[81] If this notion is accepted, not as a defence of the practices but simply as an observation of fact, it is fair to assume that the reality of early indenture, particularly on the plantations, may have resembled slavery to a significant extent. For reasons stated previously, an evaluation of the actual experience of indentured labour is not attempted in this thesis, to avoid the pitfall of making value judgements regarding its severity. Such evaluation may lend itself as an apology or justification to any shortcomings in the system. Indeed, a remark frequently encountered in contemporary records and correspondence by British officials is the notion that, whatever harsh conditions the labourers endured, whether during transportation or in the colonies, it would have been still "better" than their situation in India.

In any instance, a clear appraisal of conditions is not easily made, as the recorded evidence of labourers demonstrates. For the large number of people who complained of the experience, listing their various grievances, there were also a considerable number of persons who stated they were fairly satisfied with their sojourn and had returned back to India with their earnings.[82] However, as with all such accounts, the question has to be considered as to how reliable in fact such first-hand testimonies are, given that they were commonly taken by British officials, and it is not unreasonable to assume that a level of intimidation may have been experienced on part of the Indian labourers. Additionally, many labourers had come to associate making complaints not with redress, but punishment, as an 1840 inquiry found.[83] For these reasons, the emphasis in this study is on the official responses and the evolution of the system, though some oral testimony on the transportation experience has been included below.

The year 1837 witnessed the passage of the first relevant piece of Indian legislation in the context of labour immigration to Mauritius.[84] The Act required the emigration of Indian natives to take place under authorization, with permits being required before embarkation, thus introducing a type of licensing system. Echoing the early contract terms, the Act stipulated that service agreements were

---

Immigrants and Their Descendants in Mauritius, 3 vols (Port Louis: Aapravasi Ghat Trust Fund, 2012).

81 See the discussion for example in Carter, Marina, *Lakshmi's Legacy: Testimonies of Indian Women in 19th Century Mauritius* (Mauritius: Editions de l'Ocean Indien, 1994).

82 See the testimonies contained in IOL.1947.b.250 *Evidence of the Committee Appointed by the Supreme Government of India to Enquire into the Abuses Alleged to Exist in Exporting from Bengal, Hill Coolies and Indian Labourers, of Various Classes to Other Countries* (Calcutta: G. H. Huttmann, Bengal Military Orphan Press, 1839).

83 Discussed at 5.6.1 below.

84 Colonial Emigration Act No. V, 1 May 1837. Superseded by Act No. XXXII, 20 November 1837, which was broadly identical.

to be limited to five years.[85] Certain safeguards were also included, such as requiring that a memorandum of the contract was to be written not only in English, but also in the native language of the prospective worker,[86] and that the terms had to be "distinctly explained" to him or her, with the memorandum to be retained by the worker during their years of service.[87] For granting permits authorizing the embarkation of more than twenty Indians, the relevant officers had the power inspect the vessel in question, with the aim to ascertain the adequate provision of accommodation, food and medical attendance,[88] and the clear stipulation that such permits were not to be granted unless the provisions were regarded "sufficient for their [the natives] health".[89] Failure to procure the relevant permit was liable to be punished by a fine not exceeding two hundred rupees per native transported, and in default of such payment, with imprisonment not exceeding 30 days.[90] This legal framework notwithstanding, reports of abuse gained prevalence.

5.6.1 Abuses in the system

The year 1838 proved eventful, in that not only did it witness the end of apprenticeships in the West Indies, it also saw the first spike in Indian arrivals in Mauritius (numbering just over 11,800), while at a public meeting in Calcutta concerns over indenture to the colonies were being voiced, which lead to the formation of an inquiry committee, whose report (the "Bengal Hill Coolie Report") did not however become available before 1840. In the meantime, in 1839 the Indian government sought to suspend labour emigration by rendering it an offence to contract Indian natives for labour overseas, or "aiding or abetting" their emigration "for the purpose of being employed as a labourer."[91] Thus, for a period of roughly two years, from around 1840 to 1842, indentured labour immigration from India was halted. Table 5.2 indeed indicates negligible numbers of arrivals for that period.

Suspension was in line with recommendations contained in a report compiled by T. Hugon in 1839.[92] Hugon's report draws attention to numerous shortcomings, which he felt warranted a temporary prohibition. Incidentally, many of the exploitations he identifies are linked to what otherwise could be regarded as the "advantages" of the early system. However, not all of Hugon's recommendations are intelligible without an understanding of the reports of abuse that were

85 Section III.
86 Section II.
87 Section V.
88 Section VI.
89 Section VII.
90 Section X.
91 Act No. XIV, 27 May 1839, Section II.
92 IOR/F/4/1847/77655, *Report of T. Hugon of Bengal Service upon the Subject of Indian Emigration to Mauritius* (Port Louis, Mauritius, 29 July 1839) (hereafter "Hugon's report").

circulating. Having been most clearly documented in the Bengal Hill Coolie Report,[93] it is therefore considered here first.

The result of an investigation carried out between 22 August 1838 and 14 January 1839, the Bengal Hill Coolie Report presented the views of a committee specifically tasked to inquire into "the abuses alleged to exist in the export of coolies to the colonies".[94] The opinions of the five commissioners were split, with a majority of three believing significant abuses had taken place, with the other two disagreeing.

Commissioners T. Dickens, James Charles and Russomy Dutt made the emphatic observation that

> we conceive it to be distinctly proved beyond dispute that the Coolies and other Natives exported to Mauritius and elsewhere, were (generally speaking) induced to come to Calcutta by gross misrepresentation and deceit practised upon them by native crimps styled Duffadars and Arkotties [note: these terms denote recruiters] employed by European and Anglo-Indian Undertakers and Shippers who were mostly cognizant of these frauds, and who received a very considerable sum per head for each Coolie exported.[95]

The commissioners found that, had the workers "been distinctly made aware that they were to go beyond seas to a great distance and to remain absent for five years, it is probable that not one, or at least very few, would have been induced to take such an engagement."[96]

Testimony suggested that the workers had been persuaded to arrive at the emigration depot in Calcutta by deceptive promises of employment as company peons, road workers, porters, gardeners and the like, and that they were "really incapable of understanding the nature of the contracts they were said to have entered into", despite the opportunity of for clarifications having been offered.[97] Further it was found that "kidnapping prevailed to a very considerable extent", with impotent police authorities unable or unwilling to prevent such occurrences, and perhaps most insidiously, "an impression was successfully created and maintained . . . among the Coolies that they would be liable to penal consequences if they expressed dissatisfaction at being sent on board ship."[98]

Further notable findings were that much of the emigration took place without the required permits and thus in breach of the 1837 legislation.[99] The commissioners hereby highlighted a transnational failure of the police, marked by

93 IOL.1947.b.552 *East India – Report on Hill Coolies, Bengal*, dated 14 October 1840.
94 Ibid., paras. 1 and 5.
95 Ibid., para. 9.
96 Ibid., para.10
97 Ibid., paras. 11–12.
98 Ibid., paras. 13–15
99 Ibid., para.11.

a complacency both in India and in Mauritius whereby the regulations on authorized departures from the former and arrivals at the latter were not being enforced.[100]

Comparing the income of indentured labourers with that of free workers and apprentices, the commissioners demonstrate in their calculations that the wage of the latter group was between four to six-and-half times higher. It should be noted that this point is disputed by one of the dissenting commissioners in his separate opinion. W. T. Dowson in his account sought to demonstrate that the wage of the indentured labourer was the higher one, though it is not entirely clear where he drew his numbers from.[101] Both Dowson and the other dissenting commissioner, J. P. Grant, focused in their separate opinions predominantly on the advantages of free emigration, arguing that even if the opinion of the majority of the commissioners was admitted, the effects of a prohibition would be "to render the Isle of France worthless as a Commercial Colony and to necessitate its being kept up as a political one solely at the expense of England".[102]

The issue of female labourers was not extensively addressed in the report, but some important observations were made. Commissioners Dickens, Charles and Russomy inferred that, in the absence of any restraint on the emigration of women, and the Mauritian government even being desirous of their arrival in larger numbers, it was the planters who did not seek female workers, with effects "most disastrous to the families of those who have emigrated",[103] leaving them in a destitute state back in India. The report also notes that cultural issues[104] are likely to have played a role in the low number of emigrating women, as the conditions of maritime emigration were not conducive to the preservation of certain Asian values.[105]

How could these shortcomings be remedied? Turning now to Hugon's report, it contained several recommendations regarding what an improved system of indenture should entail. As will become evident, it was not only the condition of the workers which was being considered, but also that of the planters. In first instance, Hugon suggested that there was a need for more stringent regulation, and he advocated the formation of a "Committee of Emigration" that would be composed of planters and merchants but should also have at least one "of the most intelligent and best educated natives of India settled in the island",[106] to promote the labourers' interest. While he felt that, thus far the interference

100 Ibid., paras 17–19.
101 Ibid., Minute of W. T. Dowson, p. 22.
102 Ibid., Dowson, p. 17.
103 Ibid., main report, para. 22.
104 Cultural issues relevant to Indian indenture emigration are discussed more fully below at 5.6.3.
105 Main report, para. 28.
106 Hugon's report, para. 2.

of government had been "studiously avoided and even opposed", it should now be introduced "wherever it can prove efficacious in the prevention of abuses".[107]

As a major change, Hugon suggested there be only one emigration agent in each Indian presidency approved by the Indian government. The existence of too many traders was considered a critical issue, as they reputedly employed "extortions" to which planters had to agree or risk not receiving their required number of workers. Competition, it was found, was not beneficial in this type of commerce. Hugon pointed out that any sum charged to planters over and above the expenses actually incurred would be borne by the workers, for their masters "were left to remunerate themselves at the expense of the labourers by taking from them most of the wages given in advance under the pretence of debt."[108] The fact that an acknowledgement had been made in front of a magistrate carried little relevance to an illiterate labourer, who was likely to be easily induced by the descriptions of the advantages of emigrating and, according to Hugon, make "the ignorant dupe consent to the payment of a premium".[109] One of the apparently greatest lures to enter into an indenture contract, advance pay, presented thus one of its major pitfalls. As stated Hugon: "The system of paying in advance is vicious and in India always the cause of great abuse. . . . The fact that only two or at most three months having been received out of the six is an unanswerable argument against the system."[110] The same was also noted by the commissioners of the Bengal Hill Coolie Report, namely that in the system of advance pay, the planter paid the required sum fully, but the worker actually only received a fraction of it.[111]

A further problem arising from the high level of competition in labour trading was the hardship suffered by the workers on the journey to the colonies. The Bengal Hill Coolie Report inquired into the issue, questioning ship captains and relevant officials.[112] It emerged that the stay on the vessel could be considerably longer than just period of the passage. For Mauritius, the actual sea voyage took on average a month, but in the case of the *Cavendish Bentick* for example, sailing in February 1838, Captain Alexander Mackenzie stated that "the passage, including a month's detention in the river, and three days quarantine at Port Louis, lasted from the 19th February to 16th May."[113]

The evidence of Captain Mackenzie as well as others involved in the transportation of workers claimed that the labourers were content, comfortable and

107 Ibid., para 3.
108 Ibid., para 4.
109 Ibid.
110 Ibid.
111 Bengal Hill Coolie Report, para. 16.
112 IOL.1947.b.250 *Evidence of the Committee Appointed by the Supreme Government of India to Enquire into the Abuses Alleged to Exist in Exporting from Bengal, Hill Coolies and Indian Labourers, of Various Classes to Other Countries* (Calcutta: G. H. Huttmann, Bengal Military Orphan Press, 1839).
113 Ibid., p. 33.

reasonably well provided for during the journey, with sufficient food and clean water.[114] However, the account of Indian ship physician Dr Abdoolah Khan, who had been engaged twice on a vessel conveying workers to Mauritius at the time of questioning, paints a very different picture. While he affirmed that they knew where they were going and for what purpose, when asked if the labourers knew whether they would be separated from their families for five years, Dr Khan said they believed they were going be absent only for two months, as stated to them by the "Duffadars".[115]

To the question "Did the Coolies appear to be happy and comfortable?", he replied "What happiness! They were all crying." Dr Khan stated they were crying "for their discomforts, such as want of room for sleeping and for dressing victuals and also for want of utensils for eating from." As to the sufficiency of water, "it was stinking and thick, something like beer foaming up." Finally, to the question "Did the Coolies say they were very sorry for having come?", Dr Khan replied in the affirmative. As to the treatment of labourers by the captain and officers on board, he stated "they used to beat them and drive them from one place to another."[116]

The issue of transportation is frequently neglected in scholarship, invariably because when compared to the slave trade, later conditions appear undoubtedly improved. This illustrates the striking shortcomings when discussing indentured labour with slavery as a benchmark, for despite the ameliorated state, the situation on the vessels was grave. The competition for labour ensured that no real complaint could be laid by planters against the traders, yet the adverse effects of overcrowding could be so severe for the labourers that while "no very great mortality took place on board, they arrived in such a debilitated state as to remain for months unable to perform any work."[117] Such was the seriousness of the issue that Hugon recommended a pecuniary reward for each worker arriving in good health as an incentive for the captain, with penalties where the opposite took place, in addition to a ban on the vessel for further emigration purposes.[118] In the same context he called for greater government regulation regarding health and safety, as well as quarantine procedures at the end of the journey, which could otherwise be very protracted, much to the discomfort of the passengers after a long voyage.

Hugon also felt that labourers should not be bound by an extended contract, but rather be able "to void it at any time by a re-imbursement of the expenses of his introduction reduced at the lowest sum possible by interference of Government", so that "he would in fact be merely indebted for that amount and acquit

114 Ibid., see for example the evidence of sea captain F. W. Birch, and also John Hughes, recruitment agent.

115 Ibid., p. 42. Note: A "Duffadar" was understood to be a man in charge of a group of labourers, also on occasion meant to be a minor officer.

116 Ibid.

117 Hugon's report, para. 5.

118 Ibid.

himself gradually by his labour." Hugon noted however that "this condition I am aware will meet with serious objections on the part of the less enlightened portion of the public of Mauritius but it forms the only guarantee that could possibly be offered to the native against imposition in India and ill-usage here."[119] He favoured a shorter, three-year contract, for while long contracts ensured planters against a rise in the price of labour, such agreements did nothing to secure against the depreciation of it, and the sugar industry was a volatile one, thus not truly requiring long-term contracts.[120] Despite advocating greater government regulation, Hugon was circumspect about the role "Laws and Magistrates" should play, whose intervention he felt was "the surest way of promoting discord" between the parties.[121] Rather he promoted the idea that planters should educate themselves about the customs and habits of their workers, which he felt would guarantee them the long-term fidelity Indian labourers were stereotypically known for.

5.6.2 The nature of coercion and "unfreedom"

How is the first phase of indenture migration to be evaluated from a standpoint of labour relations? These five years, from 1834 to 1839, are easily sidelined in a study on Indian indentured labour, which after the ban on emigration was lifted in 1842, continued for the rest of the 19th century and into the early 20th century. Here, however, it is argued that this early and comparatively short period represents an important foundation on which the later was system built, being the starting point from which it evolved. As already noted, Indian indenture during the 1830s was conducted on an informal basis, sought out by the planters themselves, initially as an insurance against the loss of the apprentices, but later as their preferred pool of labour. The persistent comparisons to slavery invite close scrutiny of the recruitment process, and if the focus is on labour relations as in this study, the question arises as to how that labour relationship was initially formed. With the exception of instances of kidnap and unlawful imprisonment (which according to the contemporary reports and historical opinions discussed above, appears to have existed to a significant, yet uncertain extent), the process could ostensibly be described as a "free" one. As outlined previously, prospective workers were presented with a contract in the presence of a magistrate, upon which they applied their mark. If labourers entered into these contracts voluntarily, is it appropriate to speak of a "coercive" system?

To answer this question, the issue which has to be addressed in first instance is an assessment of the worker in question. Who were those first labourers who arrived in Mauritius? A most vivid description is provided by Leela Gujadhur Sarup. From the Commissioners' Report of 1840 it has already been gleaned that in the early years the workers were known as "Hill Coolies". Sarup states that the

119 Ibid., para 11.
120 Ibid., para 14.
121 Ibid.

first batch hailed from the Chota Nagpur hills,[122] whose inhabitants were reportedly "known to be the most backward tribals of India", who she describes as an "uneducated" and "uncultured" people, who "wore no clothes and roamed the areas" stealing cattle and crops for subsistence, using spears and hatchets.[123] This fairly savage image is not one commonly painted by scholars, who instead tend to merely stress the low economic standing of the Indian recruits. Basdeo Mangru for example simply observes that the hill dwellers were known to habitually leave their homes and families behind in search of work, a reason he gives as to why they were possibly willing to seek labour opportunities outside of India.[124] Sarup's depiction however meshes well with a very telling account contained in an exchange of 1836 between John Gladstone and recruiters in India.

Gladstone,[125] previously a member of the British parliament, owned several plantations in the West Indies. Concerned with the anticipated end of the apprenticeship system in Demerara and Jamaica, he wrote to Gillanders, Arbuthnot & Co., stating "that it is a matter of doubt and uncertainty how far they may be induced to continue their services on the plantations after their apprenticeship expires in 1840", with the planters and merchants thus being "most desirous to obtain and introduce labourers from other quarters, and particularly from climates something similar in their nature." Gladstone's contemplation would appear reasonable enough in seeking to ensure the continued economic viability of his holdings. Another section in his letter however reveals deeper, political considerations. He states: "It is of great importance to us to endeavour to provide a portion of other labourers, who we might use as a set-off, and when the time for it comes, make us, as far as it is possible, independent of our negro population".[126]

Gladstone's ambition, to be "independent" of the black population in the West Indies, echoes the development which eventually occurred in Mauritius, with former apprentices becoming sidelined in favour of Indian labourers, discussed above. The statement suggests that such a course may not have been incidental to the circumstances, but rather consciously pursued from the very outset, in both colonies. Leaving these broader political considerations however aside for the moment, and returning to the new type of worker which was being sought, the

122 Also known as the Chota Nagpur Plateau, situated in the eastern part of the subcontinent and covering several Indian states.

123 Gujadhur Sarup, Leela, *Indentured Labour – Slavery to Salvation* (Kolkata: Aldrich International, 2004), p. 254.

124 Mangru, Basdeo, *Benevolent Neutrality – Indian Government Policy and Labour Migration to British Guiana 1854–1884* (London: Hansib Publications, 1987), p. 54–55.

125 John Gladstone was the father of Prime Minister William Gladstone, see Panton, Kenneth J., *Historical Dictionary of the British Empire* (London: Rowman & Littlefield, 2015).

126 John Gladstone to Messrs Gillanders, Artbuthnot & Co., Liverpool, 4 January 1836, *in PP 1837–38 (180) (232) British Guiana and Mauritius. Copies of all orders in council, or colonial ordinances for the better regulation and enforcement of the relative duties of masters and employers, and articled servants, tradesmen and labourers, in the colonies of British Guiana and Mauritius, and of correspondence relating thereto*, pp. 143–146.

recruiters' provided Gladstone with a favourable reply, outlining how by then, more than 2,000 Indians had been sent to Mauritius. Crucially, they stated that they were "not aware of any greater difficulty [which] would present itself in sending men to the West Indies, the natives being perfectly ignorant of the place they agree to go to, or the length of the voyage they are undertaking." It was noted further that "the tribe that is found to suit best in the Mauritius is from the hills to the north of Calcutta", which had inhabitants of "hardly any ideas beyond those of supplying the wants of nature". Additionally it was stated, "they are also very docile and easily managed, and appear to have no local ties, nor any objection to leave their country." The recruiters noted that "our friends at the Isle of France have always discouraged the men being so accompanied [by their wives]", yet stated "we firmly believe we are breaking no ties of kindred, or in any way acting a cruel part." The answer to Gladstone's enquiry concludes with the summary that

> the Hill tribes . . . are looked down upon by the more cunning natives of the plains, and they are always spoken of as more akin to the monkey than the man. They have no religion, no education, and, in their present state, no wants beyond eating, drinking and sleeping; and to procure which they are willing to labour.[127]

The information provided by the recruiters is highly problematic, for reasons beyond the blatant racism which even by 19th-century standards appears striking. Indentured labour to British Guiana proceeded from John Gladstone's initial efforts,[128] which in the end saw close to a quarter of a million Indians emigrate to the colony situated on the northern coast of South America.[129] Crucially, the recruiters admitted that, despite the geographically much farther distance to the West Indies (as compared to Mauritius), they perceived no significant difficulties in dispatching Indian workers to that part of the world, as, to repeat their own words, "the natives are perfectly ignorant of the place they agree to go to", or even "the length of the voyage they are undertaking". This ignorance and lack of understanding on part of the workers, so obviously known to and exploited by the recruiters, seriously undermines the argument that coercion was absent in this type of contract labour. As Amy Stanley observed, the idea of the contract in labour relations has often been primarily understood as a "metaphor for freedom", in that the obligation to work has been incurred by choice, by volition of the person rather than

127 Messrs Gillanders, Arbuthnot & Co. to John Gladstone, Calcutta, 6 June 1836, *in PP 1837–38 (180) (232),* above.

128 See John Gladstone to Lord Glenelg, Carlton Gardens, 28 February 1838, in *PP 1837–38 (180) (232),* above.

129 See Table 4.2, Chapter 4. The first batch became known as the "Gladstone Coolies", see Look Lai, Walton, *Indentured Labor, Caribbean Sugar* (Baltimore, MD; London: Johns Hopkins University Press, 1993), p. 53.

imposed through force externally.[130] Importantly however, the contract connoted not only freedom, but also exchange. "The mechanism of the exchange established the symmetry of the relation", Stanley notes.[131] Such symmetry was clearly lacking when the labourers in question agreed to depart to destinations they did not know where situated, nor the length of the voyage involved. In the estimation of Guyanese historian Basdeo Mangru, the most operative inducement on the hill coolies had been false statements by the recruiters on the type of journey and work involved, which alongside short, but unlawful imprisonment as a type of coercion were most commonly used to convince Indians to emigrate.[132]

Misrepresentation of this nature was heavily criticized by the Bengal Hill Coolie Report Committee, as noted above. The letter by Gillanders, Arbuthnot & Co. also confirms the committee's suspicion that the emigration of women was being discouraged as a result of planter preference, and while the recruiters did not feel they were "acting a cruel part", the report noted that families left behind often fell into destitution.[133]

It is evident that the labour relationship between the workers and the recruiters was a fundamentally imbalanced one, and that the voluntary aspect, so crucial to the notion of free labour, was being negated through the recruitment practices, even where these did not involve obvious coercion such as the use of force or kidnap. The research presented above indicates that the indentured labourers of the early period did not understand the implications as they applied their mark, commonly a thumbprint, to an agreement of sailing and working abroad. Misrepresentations as to destination, length of voyage and type of work to be undertaken are sufficient to argue that such contracts were effectively void.

The notion of "volition" and "coercion" will be examined further in the next chapter in the context of state-regulated indenture, where certain push factors that drove Indian emigration in the second part of the 19th century are examined.

5.6.3 *Cultural issues relevant to Indian labour migration*

As already noted, scholars debate the extent of fraud and kidnapping that occurred as part of the recruitment of labourers.[134] In this context, aspects of Indian culture are often discussed, for a significant issue implied in the decision to emigrate,

130 Stanley, Amy Dru, *From Bondage to Contract – Wage Labor, Marriage and the Market in the Age of Slave Emancipation* (New York: Cambridge University Press, 1998), p. 2.
131 Ibid.
132 Mangru, op. cit., p. 54.
133 Bengal Hill Coolie Report, para. 21.
134 See for example the different points of view taken by Tinker, op. cit., who emphasizes the element of coercion and fraud, and Emmer and Engerman, who both downplay it. See Emmer, P. C., 'The Meek Hindu: The Recruitment of Indian Labourers for Service Overseas, 1870–1916', in *Colonialism and Migration: Indentured Labour before and after Slavery*, ed. by P. C. Emmer, *Comparative Studies in Overseas History* (Dordrecht; Lancaster: Nijhoff, 1986); and Engerman, Stanley L., 'Contract Labor, Sugar, and Technology in the Nineteenth Century', *The Journal of Economic History*, 43 (1983), 635–659.

whether by inducement or necessity, would have been the inability to maintain certain customs and cultural requirements, notably those relating to caste.

The "loss of caste" involved in crossing the sea as an operative concern on labourers' minds has been both underlined and dismissed.[135] Part of the issue is the symbolism of a sea voyage from a religious point of view (presenting a crossing of the "Kala Pani", meaning "black water"), which is complex and may be difficult to grasp for the uninitiated. However, a more tangible aspect is the way in which the workers were forced to intermingle at the beginning and during the journey, in a manner that in their home societies would have been deemed unacceptable. Leaving a discussion on the prejudices inherent in the caste system aside and focusing merely on the labourers' accustomed way of living, contemporary accounts indicate that a forceful breaking down of social barriers among the workers, ultimately unavoidable in a plantation environment, appears to have been a conscious aim of the recruiters from the outset.

The account of Totaram Sanadhya, a labourer from India who emigrated to Fiji in 1893, is considered a unique narrative, ghost-written by Banarsidas Chaturvedi, which provides insight into the personal experiences of those who participated in indenture migration.[136] Sanadhya recounts the embellished version presented by recruiters to potential draftees of what life in the plantation colonies would be like. He explains that their own clothes were taken away and that they were instructed in how to answer to the magistrate who questioned them prior to registration. The mere lip-service paid to this aspect of safeguarding the independence of recruits is evident in Sanadhya's statement that 165 persons were registered in roughly 20 minutes.[137] Sanadhya himself changed his mind about emigrating after learning that it would involve field labour but was not allowed to leave by the recruiters, and in fact was locked into a room. His subsequent experience is quite telling and illustrative of the issues faced by Indian labourers:

> When I was brought from the cell I saw that Chamar, Koli, Brahman and so forth [note: different groups of caste] were all seated in one place and forced to have their meal together. Just about everyone was forced to have their meal on re-used plates, and was forced to drink water. When anyone said anything, then what, but he was beaten specially. Seeing this situation I said, "I will not eat with these people even if I die of hunger". The officer said, "Die. No one fears that. We'll throw you in the river". In the end I was ordered to eat with the cook.[138]

135 Compare the views presented in the Mauritius Truth and Justice report discounting the relevance of the issue, and the research of Marina Carter indicating the opposite; see Carter, Marina, ed., *Across the Kalapani: The Bihari Presence in Mauritius* (Port Louis: CRIOS, Centre for Research on Indian Ocean Societies, 2000).

136 Sanadhya, Totaram, and Bernarsidas Chaturvedi, *My Twenty-One Years in the Fiji Islands & The Story of the Haunted Line*, ed. by John Dunham Kelly, trans. by Uttra Kumari Singh (Suva: Fiji Museum, 2003).

137 Ibid., p. 36.

138 Ibid., p. 38

John Kelly has described this series of actions experienced by Sanadhya as the process by which "coolies were made, rather than born, and made by pollution and isolation."[139] "Pollution" in this context refers to a forced intermingling of the castes, which the recruits would not otherwise have engaged in. The operative effect of the "isolation" element is the separation from an ordinary societal context. Kelly reiterates that by the time the workers arrived in the colonies, they were under the charge the overseers beyond any cultural sensitivity and knowledge of religious customs, and at that point, "their standardization by law was complete".[140] Indeed, it had to be for their successful integration into the sugar production system.

Cultural homogenization began at the emigration depot and continued on the vessel carrying the workers to their destination. As previously noted, the issue of transportation has not been extensively discussed in scholarship,[141] but contemporary accounts provide a glimpse of the conditions during the long sea voyage which have been recounted above. Cumulatively, the recruitment process and voyage can be regarded as reconstructing the identity of the labourer for the precise needs of his employment. Disturbingly, this took place by elimination of other elements of his identity, such as caste, religious and cultural preferences.

5.5 Conclusion

This chapter demonstrates that the first phase of Indian indenture immigration, taking place in Mauritius from 1834 to 1840, cannot, despite its comparatively short duration, be neglected as a side note in the overall indenture period. It reveals that the choice for specifically Indian labour was a deliberate one, in a move that permanently marked the composition of Mauritian society. While Chinese indenture proved a failure, African indentured labour was not pursued in Mauritius due to its resemblance to the slave trade. Planters, once satisfied with the new type of labourer, used their arrival in greater numbers to depress wages in a move that marks the beginning of the marginalization of former slaves on the island. The transition from slavery to indenture thus, while initially imposed externally by imperial law, was later directed by planter preference.

The concept of post-emancipation apprenticeship betrays itself as extended slavery particularly if attention is paid to the level of corporal punishment apprentices were liable to. An examination of the legal frameworks which governed early indentured labourers and apprentices reveals that while the conditions were

139 Kelly, John D., 'The Other Leviathans: Corporate Investment and the Construction of a Sugar Colony', in *White and Deadly: Sugar and Colonialism*, ed. by Pal Ahluwalia, Bill Ashcroft and Roger Knight (New York: New Science Publishers, 1999), p. 102.

140 Ibid.

141 See Lubbock, op. cit., cited above, who has addressed the question of indentured labour transportation but who focuses predominantly on the fleet involved in emigration.

ostensibly more favourable for the former, in practice this was not automatically the case. A definite consensus on which group was earning more is lacking, though the majority of the commissioners of the Bengal Hill Coolie Report agreed that apprentices obtained higher wages. The concept of advance pay to Indian labourers was an insidious one. Planters made the payment in full to the agents, but only a fraction of it reached the labourers, who then had to work for the first few months after arrival without further wages, under conditions where the planters were seeking to recoup their recruitment expenses. In this context, it emerges that the gender imbalance among labourers was not solely the result of cultural inhibitions, but also a consequence of planter preference and recruitment policies which encouraged the emigration of unaccompanied men, much to the detriment of families left behind.

Deception and exploitation were rife, in an early system that preyed upon the vulnerabilities of certain segments of the Indian population. The issue of consent is thrown into relief when it becomes evident that the labourer in question was not clear what he or she was consenting to, given that both the nature of the work and even the destination was purposefully kept obscure. If place of origin was a key consideration in the decision to seek indentured labour from India, and hence "marked" the system of indenture with ethnic overtones in its distinction from the African apprentices, preparing the Indian worker for the plantation context involved a forceful breaking down of customs and habits which saw the prospective labourer being shaped to the requirements of his future employer. Ethnicity thus appeared to be an important marker through which the two systems of labour would be effectively distinguished, but it was ultimately to be an instrumentalized category – one "imposed" upon the indentured labourer as opposed to being one that reflected the distinctiveness of their own cultures and traditions. The productive encoding of the two labour systems by reference to the putative ethnic identity of the labourers themselves was to lead ultimately to the systematic merging of class and race within a tiered Mauritian society with the white, European, plantation aristocracy at the top, and the black, former slave population at the bottom.

Yet there is one further twist to the story. In Mauritius and elsewhere, it is clear that indentured labour from India had been sought, in part at least, to enable the plantation owners to achieve independence from the labour power of apprentices, whose compulsory term was coming to an end. As in Hegel's famous account of the master and slave dialectic,[142] there was an incipient recognition that the master was not entirely "free" in the sense of being a self-determining and autonomous agent, but was yet dependent upon the labour power of the slave over whom authority was asserted. The formal emancipation of the slaves in Mauritius thus exposed the plantation owners to the very real possibility of a reversal in the

142 Contained in Hegel, G. W. F., *Phenomenology of Spirit*, trans. by A. V. Miller (Oxford: Oxford University Press, 1977).

relationship of power, the danger of which could only be avoided by dint of the identification of an alternative supply of labour. As will be seen in the next chapter, the anxiety of the plantation owners on this score was evidently well-founded insofar as the former slaves showed no inclination to work as "free" people in the same setting as before. The ever-growing number of foreign workers arriving in Mauritius ultimately however proved to be to their significant detriment.

6 State-regulated immigration and the emergence of an Indian peasantry

6.1 Introduction

After a brief suspension of roughly two years, the ban on Indian labour emigration to Mauritius was lifted in 1842. In this second phase, which lasted until the end of Indian indenture to the island around 1910, indentured labour was set on a new footing. The era was marked by significant state involvement, manifesting itself not only in the laws governing immigration, but also in the provisions which regulated labour on the island locally.

This chapter, which examines the final part in the 19th century "assembly process" of Mauritian society, demonstrates the shifts which took place in the labour debate. With the apprenticeship system having ended, emancipated slaves were free from any obligation to work on the sugar plantations and, as will be discussed below, they indeed chose to stay away from the fields. With attempts at importation of workers from other countries having largely failed (as examined in Chapter 5), the focus in Mauritius from the mid-19th century forward was very firmly on Indian immigration. Numerous coercive measures were devised to retain labourers and control their mobility and options in the labour market. Towards the end of the century, this gave way to yet a new way of organization as a local Indian peasantry developed.

6.2 The sugar industry: economics and politics

It has been observed that the analogy between contract labour and slavery derives to a significant extent from the fact that both systems were utilized for the production of sugar.[1] As the sugar industry was the essential reason for the recruitment of workers, it provided the context in which indenture as a system of labour was to develop. For this reason, a brief examination of the sugar industry in the 19th century is included here prior to analyzing the second phase of indentured immigration in Mauritius, expanding on the issues introduced in Chapter 2 which

1 Engerman, Stanley L., 'Contract Labor, Sugar, and Technology in the Nineteenth Century', *The Journal of Economic History*, 43 (1983), 635–659, p. 639.

DOI: 10.4324/9781003313366-8

situated the topic of this study in the broader history of the island. As previously highlighted, by the mid-19th century, Mauritius came to occupy the place of the British Empire's principal sugar producer. The British imperial approach to the recruitment of labour for the island must be understood as reflecting the wider economic and political considerations of the time.

6.2.1 Sugar and the British market

The sugar cane industry itself can be traced back to 700 A.D. in the Mediterranean, and it was not before the 16th century that the region had to give in to competition from the Americas.[2] The world quickly developed an appetite for the commodity, and as observed by Sidney Mintz, "by no later than 1800, sugar had become a necessity – albeit a costly and rare one – in the diet of every English person; by 1900, it was supplying nearly one-fifth of the calories in the English diet." As R. W. Beachey notes, British sugar consumption was on the rise ever since the passage of the 1846 Sugar Duties Act, and continued to rise in parallel to successive reductions in the rate of sugar duties[3] (see Table 6.1).

The 1846 Act had aimed to eliminate preferential rates by 1854, as indeed it did.[4] It should be noted that what is commonly referred to as the "Sugar Duties Act of 1846" was actually a series of Acts which replaced each other,[5] and had further relevant regulations attached to them.[6] The sugar duties legislation was part

Table 6.1 Sugar consumption in the United Kingdom per head, 1840–1880[7]

Year	*Amount of sugar consumed per head in lbs*
1840	15.20
1850	24.79
1860	34.14
1870	47.23
1880	63.68

2 Galloway, J. H., *The Sugar Cane Industry: An Historical Geography from Its Origins to 1914* (Cambridge: Cambridge University Press, 1989), p. 31.
3 Beachey, R. W., *British West Indies Sugar Industry in Late 19th Century* (Oxford: Basil Blackwell, 1957), p. 46.
4 Lobdell, Richard A., 'Patterns of Investment and Sources of Credit in the British West Indian Sugar Industry, 1838–97', *Journal of Caribbean History*, 4 (1972), 31–53, pp. 39–40.
5 'An Act for granting to Her Majesty, until the Fifth day of July One thousand eight hundred and Forty-six, certain Duties of Customs were imposed upon the importation of Sugar and Molasses', 8 & 9 Vict., c. 5; and similarly named Acts, of different dates, during the same session.
6 There were several Orders in Council related to the Act above, which declared the sugars of foreign countries as being admissible in the United Kingdom upon evidence of not being the produce of slave labour, see for instance *PP 1846 (229) Sugar duties. Copies of two Orders in Council.*
7 Numbers reproduced from Beachey, op. cit., p. 47.

of a wider effort of the British government at the time to promote free trade principles and was passed in tandem with the repeal of the "Corn Laws", measures originally designed to regulate the price of grain via tariffs on imports. However, in the period when Britain was expanding its power overseas, the policy of free trade was regarded as adverse to colonial policies.[8] Integral to the Whig policy of the early 1840s was the abandonment of the system of "imperial preference" that had long not only protected sugar but also timber imports and shipping. According to Anthony Howe, "colonial interest groups, like those of industry and agriculture, were to be dethroned in favour of a self-regulating market economy, in which government would respond to the needs of the many (the consumers) by removing the privileges of the few."

The underlying idea had been that with the removal of monopolies, production would increase and prices lower. The lower cost would lead to increased consumption, and in turn greater revenues. In the event, the sugar duties legislation led to "widespread distress" in the West Indies as well as in Mauritius.[9] Duties on foreign sugar and a prohibition of specifically foreign, slave-grown sugar had protected the islands' interest by eliminating competition in the British market.[10] The removal of these protective mechanisms at a time when the sugar colonies were seeking alternatives to slave labour in the aftermath of abolition lead to a crisis, especially in the West Indies, due to its financial encumbrances.

As mentioned in Chapter 2, a Select Committee Report of 1832 indicates that the West Indian economy was at that point already experiencing severe difficulties, which the planters themselves viewed as primarily the result of the abolition of the trade in slaves, but which the report noted had already existed prior to the ban.[11] Having expanded their industry during the war years, it has been observed that falling sugar prices were inevitable during peace time.[12] But to aggravate their situation, with tariff parity achieved by Mauritius in 1825, West Indian planters

8 Fakhri, Michael, *Sugar and the Making of International Trade Law* (Cambridge: Cambridge University Press, 2014), pp. 38–39.

9 Howe, Anthony, *Free Trade and Liberal England, 1846–1946* (Oxford: Oxford University Press, 1998), pp. 50–51.

10 Saha, Panchan, *Emigration of Indian Labour (1834–1900)* (Delhi: People's Publishing House, 1970), p. 4. The issue of protection through tariffs remained complex. Beachey and Lobdell point out that even after 1854, Britain applied a system whereby different qualities of sugar imported would be taxed differently, in a system that favoured the West Indies. Post-1840, their competitors, including Mauritius, were able to produce relatively refined sugar, which was taxed at a higher rate than West Indian muscovado. The spoiling of sugar to deliberately lower its quality was a common charge against planters in British Guiana for example, who through this method sought to continue taking advantage of the lower duties.

11 *PP 1831–32 (381) Report from Select Committee on the Commercial State of the West India Colonies*, p. 21.

12 Lobdell, op. cit., p. 31.

at that time found themselves not only competing for the same market, but also the same sources of investment.[13]

The crisis that followed the 1846 legislation exposed the nature of the West Indian sugar interest. The 19th-century sugar industry there commonly evokes the image of absentee proprietors or impoverished residents.[14] In reality, much investment had been supplied by City of London merchants, not only in the form of capital to support the increasing demand for sugar, but also as standing creditors for the planters' debts which had been secured by the mortgaging of their estates.[15] The merchant agent was the traditional source of credit for the planter and possessed significant influence over consignments.[16] With the crisis, control over the sugar industry came to be concentrated in London, illustrated particularly in the creation of the "West Indian Encumbered Estates Court", set up pursuant to an Act passed in 1854 and entrusted with disentangling the intricate charges with which the colonial estates were burdened.[17]

Mauritius, in contrast, was not encumbered to the same degree as the West Indies. Nevertheless, the investment that the resident French planters had attracted from the metropolis gave them the avenue, via their British associates, to lobby the relevant groups at the Colonial Office in London.[18] This advantage was used in particular following the abolition of slavery, when the Mauritian sugar industry was seeking alternative labour. As Table 2.1 in Chapter 2 indicates, sugar production had been rising dramatically and consistently during the first half of the 19th century.

6.2.2 *Seeking new labour*

In the wake of emancipation, when the world market for sugar opened up, both "new" colonies (which included Mauritius, Natal and Fiji) and "ancient" ones (such as Jamaica, Trinidad and British Guiana) had to find the labour to supply it.[19] Mintz suggests that the political struggle between the metropolis and the colonial planters was partially alleviated by what he describes as "recourse to external but politically accessible labor pools."[20]

13 Ibid., p. 39; see also the evidence by proprietor Matthew Higgins in the 1848 Select Committee Report on Sugar and Coffee Planting, Fourth Report, p. 101, quoted in Chapter 2. This lasted until 1874, when all duties on sugar were abolished, see Lobdell, op. cit., p. 40, and Beachey, op. cit., p. 45.
14 Howe, op. cit., p. 53.
15 Ibid.
16 Green, W. A., *British Slave Emancipation: The Sugar Colonies and the Great Experiment, 1830–1865* (Clarendon Paperbacks; Oxford: Clarendon Press, 1991), pp. 40–41.
17 For a full discussion on the court, see Beachey, op. cit., Chapter 1.
18 North-Coombes, M. D., 'From Slavery to Indenture: Forced Labour in the Political Economy of Mauritius 1834–1867', in *Indentured Labour in the British Empire, 1834–1920*, ed. by Kay Saunders (London: Croom Helm, 1984), pp. 88–89.
19 Mintz, op. cit., p. 70.
20 Ibid.

The case of Mauritius appears to confirm this notion. The British government and the French plantocracy found themselves united over the sugar question, and by introducing Indian labour found a convenient avenue to further their interests. The so-called "labour shortage", which will be addressed separately below, was framed in predominantly racist terms, in which both British and local French stakeholders conveniently converged.[21] Engerman seeks to downplay the racial element, but in doing so actually emphasizes it. He claims: "The explanation for the shifting ethnic composition of the labor force is the attitude of the available labor supply towards plantation work, not some judgment that the Indians worked harder or that it was easier to evaluate and monitor their output potential."[22] However, it is precisely this concern for the "attitude" of the locally available labour, namely former slaves, which was used as a major argument in justifying the introduction of Indian labour, the effect of which operated to the detriment of the resident black population, as discussed below.

6.2.3 The decline of sugar cane

Sugar in the 19th century faced two crises. In the wake of the 1846 sugar duties legislation, there had been a commercial crisis, which had come about as the result of the financial entanglements within the industry. Some colonies weathered the period better than others, as can be seen in the contrasting cases of Mauritius and the West Indies. Towards the end of the 19th century, however, sugar cane itself faced a crisis, with the rising popularity for the production of beet sugar in central Europe. After a brief dalliance with beet during the Napoleonic wars at the turn of the century, interest in its cultivation rose again in the 1830s,[23] and became a definite challenge to cane sugar in 1884–1885.[24] But, as Michael Fakhri observes, "there was though more at stake with the sugar crisis than the price of sugar."[25] Given the economic structure of the West Indies, Britain was aware that, were the sugar industry allowed to collapse, it would have to bear the consequences, both economically and politically.

Sugar cane was originally introduced in Mauritius during Dutch occupation.[26] From the beginning, the European colonist favoured a plantation sys-

21 North-Coombes, M. D., 'From Slavery to Indenture: Forced Labour in the Political Economy of Mauritius 1834–1867', in *Indentured Labour in the British Empire, 1834–1920*, ed. by Kay Saunders (London: Croom Helm, 1984).

22 Engerman, op. cit., pp. 653–654.

23 Perkins, John, and Roger Munting, 'Science versus Nature: The Cane – Beet Sugar Rivalry', Bill Ashcroft, Roger Knight and Pal Ahluwalia, eds., op. cit., p. 159.

24 Fakhri, op. cit., p. 41.

25 Ibid., p. 43

26 In 1650, at the suggestion of the Governor-General Rienertsz of Dutch India, the necessary supplies were sent from Java. Until 1850, only one variety, the *Otaheite*, was cultivated, which then made way for the *Cheribon* and the *Penang* type, both also from Java. The latter half of the 19th century saw the introduction of a multitude of varieties from the Pacific area and the Orient. See Deerr, Noel, *The History of Sugar, Volume I* (London: Chapman and

tem as the preferred method for cultivation, and as explained in Chapter 4, the tariff equalization of 1825 set Mauritius firmly on the path of an imbalanced monoculture. It must be understood that plantations, whether in Mauritius or elsewhere, presented not only an economic but also a social unit.[27] As Tinker emphasizes: "Everybody in a sugar colony from the governor and the wealthiest merchant or landowner down to the meanest field hand was involved in the production of sugar for a distant market."[28] As a consequence, the entire infrastructure was set up with a focus on achieving a desired output. And "unless the economic base was transformed, everything would continue to function to serve that same purpose, whether under a system of slavery or under a system of nominally free labour."[29] In the event, emancipation did not ring the bell for an end of the plantation system. Pal Ahluwalia regards this failure to abandon the plantation system as responsible for the need for new migrants and their subsequent fate,[30] a suggestion which the analysis contained in this chapter supports. It is not until the plantation system was dismantled that also the situation of the Indian immigrants changed. The eventual decline of the industry led to the adoption of a central factory system, in a process that saw cane land being consolidated into large estates. Mauritius and Réunion followed the same approach as that taken in West Indies, in contrast to Hawaii, Natal and Fiji.[31] The plantation system gave way to a different method of sugar cultivation, whereby planters sold off parts of their land. The process, known in Mauritius as the *Grand Morcellement*, is discussed at 6.5 below. The way in which the industry adapted to a lessened demand led to a fall in the need for new immigrant labourers, and to the establishment of a settled, local Indian peasantry, still involved in the sugar production, but as small owners rather than field hands, heralding the eventual end of indentured labour in Mauritius.

6.3 Evolution of the indenture system

The period of formal, organized indenture immigration presented a departure from the previously private attempts to seek an alternative to slavery. Having settled on India as the preferred labour pool, the introduction of overseas workers was no longer experimental but presented a significant investment made by the colony, one from which both planters and the administration were increasingly

Hall, 1949), p. 183, and X. 319/4471 (British Library) *Mauritius and its Sugar Industry*, April 1963.

27 Green, W. A., *British Slave Emancipation: The Sugar Colonies and the Great Experiment, 1830–1865* (Clarendon Paperbacks; Oxford: Clarendon Press, 1991), p. 35.

28 Tinker, op. cit., p. 3.

29 Ibid.

30 See Ahluwalia, Pal, 'Discourses of Discovery: Transculturations and Sugar Plantations in Africa', in Bill Ashcroft et al., op. cit., pp. 51–64.

31 Galloway, op. cit., p. 224.

seeking to maximize their return, as the regulations passed over the following decades demonstrate.

This is in contrast to how early indenture was generally regarded. Correspondence from the period suggests that it was envisaged that the Indian workers would only remain temporarily, since the prime concern in the context of their introduction appears to have been that they should not become "a source of expense to his Majesty's Government on the island" after the expiration of their contract or if their services were no longer required,[32] necessitating assurances that provisions for their return were in place.[33] A similar issue arose in 1835, when the chief commissary of police in Mauritius insisted that recruiters pay the required security for workers imported from abroad.[34] The recruiters did not argue against paying the security as such, but contended that it was not due since the workers were subjects of British India and therefore not foreign.[35] The issue gave *Procureur General* d'Epinay in his legal opinion the opportunity to allude to the possibility of the indentured labourers not being considered "proper" British subjects, however refusing to discuss the point in any detail and without providing a definite answer, he simply insisted the security was required to safeguard the public purse.[36]

This preponderance with ensuring that provisions were in place to guarantee the workers' timely departure changed with the advent of state-regulated indenture. As will be discussed next, several mechanisms were devised over the years to keep the labourers in prolonged contracts, with regulations curtailing both their options to return to India as well as preventing them from seeking an independent livelihood on the island. Thus with the move from informal to formal immigration, the concern moved from regarding the labourers as a potential burden, to how best to compel them to stay in Mauritius for as long as possible, while remaining engaged productively as workers within the sugar industry.

The contemporary account of Reverend Beaton on his missionary service in Mauritius during the mid-19th century gives a telling insight into how important Indian labour had become to the island:

> Coolies from the banks of the Ganges, brought . . . to do the work of Helots . . . and to be so, all but in name. . . . These swarthy Orientals . . . are the muscles and sinews of the Mauritius body politic, the secret source of all the wealth, luxury and splendour with which the island abounds. It is from the labour

32 Secretary H.T. Princep to Chief Magistrate D. McFarlan, 15 September 1834, with respect to the original 36 Hill Coolies, in *PP 1838 Papers respecting the East-India Labourers' Bill*, pp. 88–91.

33 McFarlan to Princep, Calcutta, 19 September 1834, in *PP 1838*, ibid.

34 Finniss to Messrs. P. Froberville, Griffiths, and Co., Port Louis, 25 September 1835, in *PP 1838*, above, p. 52.

35 Froberville, Griffiths, and Co. to Finniss, Port Louis, 4 November 1835, in *PP 1838*, above, p. 54.

36 Translated Opinion of P. d'Epinay, 5 January 1836, in *PP 1838*, above, pp. 55–63.

> of his swarthy body in the cane-fields that gold is extracted more plenteously than from the diggings of Ballarat.[37]

The period of formal indenture immigration to Mauritius until its termination can be divided into three distinct periods: Initially, after immigration resumed following suspension, a "bounty system" was put into place which lasted until 1844, followed by a "contingent system" until 1857, with an overhauled set of new labour laws passed in 1867.[38]

6.3.1 The bounty system

In 1842, the prohibition of Indian emigration was officially lifted, initially exclusively to Mauritius.[39] The procurement of workers was no longer a private matter, but came under official control. This crucial period in Mauritian history saw the tenure of three different administrators in Mauritius, with the most decisive changes occurring during the term of Colonel William Staveley, who was not formally a governor of the island.[40]

The schedule attached to the Order in Council permitting renewed immigration to Mauritius contained numerous regulations which sought to safeguard the interests of the Indian labourers. Notably, it was stipulated that it would be the governor of Mauritius who was to nominate emigration agents in India, at such ports and places designated as embarkation points by the governor general of India.[41] It was also the governor of Mauritius who was authorized to appoint a Protector of Immigrants on the island.[42] Remuneration for the agents was to be by fixed annual salary, and not linked to the number of emigrants sent to Mauritius.[43] The emigration agents' duties included inspecting the fitness of the transporting vessels, ascertaining that sufficient provisions were being carried, as well as verifying the understanding of the intended recruits of their proposed

37 Beaton, Patrick, *Creoles & Coolies – Five Years in Mauritius* (London: James Nisbet and Co., 1859), pp. 10–11.

38 *Report of the Royal Commissioners appointed to inquire into the treatment of Immigrants in Mauritius*, 6 February 1875, (the "1875 Report"), available through the Hathi Trust website <http://babel.hathitrust.org/cgi/pt?id=hvd.hneegi;view=1up;seq=4> [accessed 26 June 2022].

39 Through the Queen's Order in Council dated 15 January 1842, promulgated in Mauritius in May 1842 and passed in India under Act No. XV, 2 December 1842. See also Ordinance No. 11 of 1842, discussed below.

40 Sir Lionel Smith was governor from 6 July 1840 until his death on 2 January 1842. Contemporary legislation refers to Colonel Staveley as the "Officer Administering the Government of Mauritius" in the interim, until the arrival of the next governor, Sir William Gomm, on 21 November 1842; see Macmillan, Allister, *Mauritius Illustrated: Historical and Descriptive, Commercial and Industrial, Facts, Figures and Resources* (New Delhi: Asian Educational Services, 2010).

41 Schedule to Order in Council 15 January 1842, section I.

42 Ibid.

43 Section II.

engagement.[44] Upon arrival, the Protector of Immigrants was "as far possible by personal inspection of the Ship or Vessel", to ascertain that the regulations had been complied with,[45] and no payment from the island's treasury was to be made unless governor of Mauritius was satisfied that this had been the case.[46]

In terms of labour contracts, the schedule importantly provided:

> No Emigrant arriving from India at Mauritius shall be capable of entering into any contract of service to be performed in that Island until he shall have been at least 48 hours on shore there, and every such contract of service made before that time shall be null and void to all intents and purposes.[47]

In the same vein, no liability existed for the emigrants for contracts entered into before their arrival at Mauritius,[48] however they were not able to enter into service contracts except as governed by the local laws for agricultural and manufacturing labourers.[49]

These rules can be understood to have been intended to allow the labourer freedom to choose his engagement carefully, by being able to survey the local situation before committing him- or herself. Unfortunately, the provision did not have the desired effect. As an 1875 report inquiring into the treatment of immigrants in Mauritius states:

> The interval of 48 hours was perfectly illusory as a means of enabling them to obtain information to guide them in their choice of employers, or as to the terms they should accept, while it was one sufficiently long to expose them to the tricks and frauds of crimps and so-called "labour-brokers", whose proceedings proved a fruitful source of scandal and complaint for the next sixteen years.[50]

The rule preventing the worker from entering into a contract within less than 48 hours of arrival may have been intended as a protective measure, but it in practice it proved much too short to help safeguard the labourers' interest. Surveying the local options may also have proven to be impractical, if not outright impossible, for the arriving immigrant. Again, the availability of "choice", like that of the decision to emigrate in the first place, was the merest fiction in the absence of accessible information.

An important issue facing Colonel Staveley and the local council was the issue of costs. Ordinance No. 2 of 1842 established an Immigration Fund from which

44 See sections III to IX.
45 Section XI.
46 Section XXI.
47 Section XVIII.
48 Section XIX.
49 Section XX.
50 1875 report, above, para. 204.

the introduction of immigrant workers was to be financed, allowing the sum of £25,000 annually to be appropriated for that purpose from the revenues of the colony.[51] It was evident however that these funds would be insufficient to meet the expenses involved in labour immigration, in particular, the need to provide a return passage for the workers. To that end, Staveley, with the consent of the Government Council, passed Ordinance No. 7 of 1842, which, for the explicit purpose of financing Indian labour immigration, imposed a consumption tax on liquor, specifically rum or arrack manufactured in Mauritius, and spirits, wines and cordials imported from abroad.[52] The same ordinance stipulated that for each legally introduced labourer, the Immigration Fund would provide £6 for adults (male or female), and £3 for children.[53] The 1875 report states that back in Britain, Lord Stanley[54] felt the notion of "legally introduced" workers was not clear, and in any event regarded the ordinance as unnecessary, and therefore recommended its disallowance.[55] However, it appears the ordinance was eventually approved.[56]

Ordinance No. 11 of 1842 formalized the preceding regulations, specifically declaring the schedule attached to the Queen's Order in Council of 15 January 1842 as carrying the force of law, while also adding further penalties for abuses of the system and specifically granting workers a free return passage. However, since the ordinance never received Her Majesty's approval, for reasons that even contemporary officials could not trace, it lapsed, with the result that its penal provisions remained unenforceable by the Mauritian government.[57]

With a view to increasing the supply of Indian labourers, the indemnity (or "bounty") that was available from the immigration fund was raised from £6 to £7 for male labourers by Ordinance No. 3 of 1843.[58] In a further attempt to increase the number of female recruits, the ordinance also introduced a convoluted provision to the effect that the bounty for male labourers would be increased by a further 5 per cent "whenever the number of females shall be in the proportion of five to every one hundred male labourers brought over in the same ships", provided those females were aged between 12 and 30.[59] However, the indemnity would not be paid for the first ten females, nor for more than 25 females per hundred males, whatever the actual number of females transported.[60]

51 Ordinance No. 2, 28 February 1842, section I.
52 Ordinance No. 7, 23 June 1842.
53 Ibid., section VI.
54 Lord Edward Stanley, Secretary of State for War and the Colonies, 30 August 1841 to 23 December 1845, see Panton, Kenneth J., op. cit., Appendix A.
55 1875 report, above, para. 206.
56 See local government notice of 26 June 1844.
57 1875 report, above, para. 209.
58 Ordinance No. 3 of 1843, 27 February 1843.
59 Ibid., section III.
60 Ibid.

The Indian Act No. XVI of 1843 restricted emigration to Mauritius to the port of Calcutta, with the recruitment of workers taken out of the hands of emigration agents and given to an official appointed by the government of Mauritius, subject to the supervision of a Protector of Immigrations appointed by the government of India, who from January 1844 was to be in sole control of emigration. This shift was hoped to encourage a "superior class of females" to emigrate, as well as more families, thus encouraging permanent settlement on the island instead of temporary migration.[61] Incidentally, the number of female arrivals did not rise; in fact, for the years 1847 and 1848, it fell drastically to a mere 656, from 4,307 females in 1843, as can be gathered from the data contained in Table 5.2.[62]

The period of the "bounty" system can be wrapped up by noting that recruitment from other countries, such as China and certain parts of Africa, was not deemed successful or desirable.[63] As discussed in the previous chapter, the prospect of importing workers from the African continent in particular was considered too reminiscent of slavery, and there were suspicions that it would have been nearly impossible to ascertain whether the workers obtained from that area were actually "free.[64] In the light of these concerns, the recruitment of labour from India was preferred insofar as the officials could satisfy themselves, simply from the place of origin, that it was "free".

6.3.2 The contingent system

In 1845, ten years after slavery had ended and the steady introduction of indentured labourers had begun, the demand for workers in Mauritius continued unabated. This persistent need for labour sparked the establishment of a committee set up by Governor William Gomm,[65] with the specific purpose of inquiring into "the causes of the continued demand for labour, notwithstanding the already extensive introduction of immigrants into the colony."[66] The report of the Rawson Committee addressed two main questions: first, whether or not there existed sufficient labour in Mauritius in order to meet the needs of the island; and second, whether the regulation that limited engagements to one year should be

61 1875 report, above, para. 220. See also Carter, Marina, and James Ng Foong Kwong, *Forging the Rainbow* (Mauritius: Self-published, 1997).

62 Table 5.2 shows the immigration numbers and is contained in Chapter 5.

63 See the disallowances of Ordinance No. 8 of 1842, which aimed to provide for the immigration of free labourers from other countries than British India, and of Ordinance No. 59 of 1844, which was designed to encourage emigration specifically from Africa.

64 1875 report, above, para. 228.

65 Sir William Gomm was governor of Mauritius from 21 November 1842 until 5 May 1849.

66 Governor William Gomm to Lord Stanley, Mauritius, 20 March 1845, in *PP 1845 (641) Mauritius, copies or extracts of the despatch from the Governor of Mauritius.*

Table 6.2 Abstract of the population of Mauritius on 1 August 1846[67]

		Male	*Female*	*Total*
General Population		30,225	25,246	55,471
Ex-apprentices	*Adults*	23,879	15,610	39,489
	Children born since 1 February 1835	5,325	5,600	10,905
Indians		48,726	7,309	56,035

rescinded.[68] Following calculations that considered mortality, illness, persistent absenteeism as well as departures, the report concluded that

> the total number of labourers now engaged on estates, including the ex-apprentices, is 40,000; that of these 9,450 are, from various causes withdrawn from such labour; and that the value of the labour of the remainder is only equal to that yielded by 23,000 slaves, making no allowance for the diminished amount of labour rendered at the present time by the ex-apprentices.[69]

As the Rawson report notes, while this number roughly corresponded to the number of slaves available just a few years prior to emancipation, the capacity of Mauritius for sugar production had drastically increased since then, and would no longer satisfy the demands of the island's economy.[70] The committee made a number of findings, notably that the number of Indian arrivals was an erroneous basis on which to estimate the available labour, especially since workers were not only required for the sugar industry, but also other kinds of employment, especially public works (such as the maintenance of roads, etc.). It was thought that "the urgent demand for labourers has led to many of the evils under which the planters labour", amongst which predominantly the issue was "the enhancement of wages", and that "many of the evils complained of by the planters would be remedied by the further introduction of labourers 'to such an extent as to create competition for employment' ". However it was recognized that under the present system that level of immigration was impossible to reach.[71] The committee suggested that if engagements were to last longer than a year, planters would feel a greater incentive to invest in immigration.

Based on the recommendations of the report, and with the aim of making labour immigration more cost-effective for planters, Ordinance No. 1 of 1846 was passed. However, its provisions were found to be so "unjust and oppressive"

67 CO 172/12, compiled from data printed in a *Mauritius Times* newspaper supplement of 12 August 1848.

68 Enclosure of Gomm to Lord Stanley, 20 March 1845, in *PP 1845* above, p. 4.

69 Ibid., p. 7.

70 Ibid.

71 Ibid., Resolutions 3 and 7, p. 16.

to the Indian labourers that it was disallowed by the Colonial Office.[72] Earl Grey[73] objected, in particular to Article 4 of that ordinance[74] which sought to make every oral engagement binding for a month, and would further continue every month unless either the master or servant gave a 14-day notice before the expiration of the month. In Earl Grey's view this would likely place an Indian immigrant in a position of perpetual engagement, given his likely ignorance of the language and requirements of the law.

However, Article 4 was by no means the only objectionable provision. Article 7 aimed to severely punish desertion from work. A labourer absent for one calendar month was liable to imprisonment with hard labour for between one and two months, or a fine of 5 *l.*, or both. Where absence had been for three months, a labourer was liable upon conviction to "confinement in any legal house of correction", as well as hard labour on the public streets and highways, for a period between two to four months, or a penalty of 10 *l.* or both.[75]

Further, Article 8 subjected workers to the formality of obtaining a Certificate of Discharge at the end of their contract. Specifically within 48 hours of discharge, they were required to apply for it from a stipendiary magistrate, in default of which their engagement "shall be deemed unfinished", and additionally rendering liable to certain penalties.[76] Article 9 further stipulated that without such a certificate, a labourer was prohibited to enter a new contract of service, except if he was re-engaging with the same master. The effect of that would have been, as noted by Earl Grey, a compulsion to re-engage with the same employer.[77]

Earl Grey made the insightful observation that

> the original error to which all the objectionable provisions of the Ordinance are to be traced, is that it proceeds upon the principle of endeavouring by law to enforce upon the immigrants the due performance of the obligations to labour which they have contracted by accepting a free passage to the colony.[78]

He regarded this as a "great mistake", for "all experience tends to prove that no legal regulations, however severe, if they stop short of the extreme compulsion

72 Earl Grey to Governor William Gomm, Downing Street, 29 September 1846, in *PP 1847–48 (419) West India colonies and Mauritius. Copies of any Acts for the suppression of vagrancy, for the prevention of Squattting, or for the Encouragement and Enforcement of Labour Contracts, Passed by any of the Colonial Legislatures or Council since the Year 1834, but Disallowed by the Secretary of State for the Colonies,* p. 144.

73 Henry Grey, the Earl Grey, Secretary of State for War and the Colonies, from 6 July 1846 to 21 February 1852, see Appendix A in Panton, Kenneth J., *Historical Dictionary of the British Empire* (London: Rowman & Littlefield, 2015).

74 Ordinance No. 1 of 1846, 16 February 1846, enclosure to dispatch of Grey to Gomm, above.

75 Ibid.

76 Ibid.

77 Grey to Gomm, above, p. 144.

78 Ibid., p. 145.

which is the characteristic of slavery, can succeed in enforcing really efficient labour".[79] Instead he suggested that policies be pursued that would encourage the industry of the labourers by working in their interest.

The provisions of the disallowed ordinance demonstrate the pervading paradigm of labour relations persisting a decade into indentured labour immigration, which rendered the fulfilment of the contract a public, or criminal, law matter instead of a private law relationship between employer and employee. Further, Articles 8 and 9 clearly sought to take advantage of the labouring population by introducing a level of bureaucracy that they were unlikely to have been able to navigate. This strategy however was strongly applied in subsequent years, under the new labour regulations discussed below.

Ordinance No. 24 of 1847 was designed to re-enact the provisions of Ordinance No. 1 of 1846, taking into account some of Earl Grey's objections. Nevertheless, the content of Article 4 on oral contracts was basically left intact, and whilst Article 7 on desertions was withdrawn, the new articles merely replaced the penalty of imprisonment for system of fines.[80] In substance thus, the labour contract remained subject to a punitive system of enforcement in which the administration clearly stood behind the interests of the planters.

Meanwhile, the Indian government was apprehensive about the slowly changing system of immigrant labour in Mauritius. Since emigration had been allowed by the Indian legislature for the purpose of increasing available labour on the island, it was felt that the freedom of the labourer to choose his engagement and obtain the highest pay possible should not be curtailed in any way.[81] In the context of Ordinances No. 22 and No. 24 of 1847, the board of directors of the East India Company regarded with concern the endeavour to increase immigration for the purpose of creating competition among labourers and depress wages; for if Mauritius proved to be unable to compete with other sugar producers in the following years, the island would fall into crisis, and would lack sufficient means to return the workers to India.[82]

The arrangement of the "contingent system" that dominated this period is best illustrated through certain provisions in the ordinances passed during the 1850s. Under Article I of Ordinance No. 15 of 1854,[83] it fell to the governor to determine, on a yearly basis, the number of immigrants to be introduced to the island, which thus provided a basic contingent of workers. Workers were distributed according to a quota which, in the case of sugar manufactures, was

79 Ibid.
80 1875 report, p. 70.
81 Ibid., p. 71.
82 Ibid.
83 SD 48/70 (Mauritius Archives), Ordinance No. 15, 8 April 1854, reproduced in Deerpalsingh, Saloni, and Marina Carter, *Select Documents on Indian Immigration, Mauritius, 1834–1926 – The Despatch and Allocation of Indentured Labour* (Volume II) (Moka: Mahatma Gandhi Institute, 1996).

calculated on the basis of the estate's output from the previous year.[84] Any employer seeking to engage more workers than they had been assigned was able to do so by paying £3 for each extra immigrant allocated.[85] The latter provisions were repealed by Ordinance No. 22 of 1857, so that employers had to bear the full cost of the introduction of the extra immigrants they wished to engage beyond their allocated quota.[86] This system induced a high level of competition between the planters, who as Mauritius was producing more and more sugar, vied for labourers to join their estates, and in the long term it did not prove tenable.

6.3.3 Regulating labour

During those decades, regulations regarding immigration presented merely one aspect by which the labour market was being controlled. Another strategy was, of course, to introduce legislation to regulate conditions of the workers after arrival.

As mentioned previously, the fact that contracts were limited to one year was regarded as a great inconvenience, whether under the bounty system or the contingent system. It was found that "this period was quite insufficient to reimburse the colony or the planter, for the expenses of the introduction", since, with the labourer being under no obligation to re-engage, the only right he lost if he chose to return to India at that point was his free passage.[87]

In response, Ordinance No. 3 of 1849 extended contracts, which then still had to be entered into in Mauritius and no earlier than after 48 hours after the immigrant had arrived, to a period of three years.[88] This frame was further extended by Ordinance No. 16 of 1862 to five years,[89] thus equalizing the engagement with the period for required residence (contemporarily referred to as "industrial residence", clarified further below.) Importantly, in 1858, Ordinance No. 15 legalized contracts made in India, provided these did not exceed three years.[90]

84 Ibid., Section II.
85 Ibid., Sections VI and VII.
86 SA 59/53 (Mauritius Archives), Ordinance No. 22, 14 July 1857, reproduced in Deerpalsingh and Carter, Volume II above. See also Ordinance No. 12 of 1855, which was an earlier provision that allowed the introduction of immigrants outside the government's contingent.
87 1875 report, p. 98.
88 SD 35/13 (Mauritius Archives), Enclosure of Governor Anderson to Earl Grey, Mauritius, 10 July 1849: Ordinance No. 3, 2 July 1849, Article 1, reproduced in Deerpalsingh, Saloni, and Marina Carter, *Select Documents on Indian Immigration: Mauritius, 1834–1926 – Living and Working Conditions under Indenture* (Volume III) (Moka: Mahatma Gandhi Institute, 1996).
89 SA 76/794 (Mauritius Archives), Enclosure of Newcastle to Stevenson, Mauritius, 11 October 1862: Ordinance No. 16, 2 April 1862, reproduced in Deerpalsingh and Carter, Volume III above.
90 SA 64/27 (Mauritius Archives), Enclosure of Newcastle to Stevenson, Mauritius, 21 August 1859, Ordinance No. 30 of 1858, reproduced in Deerpalsingh and Carter, Volume II above.

An enduring distinction was introduced in 1847 by Ordinance No. 22 which, for the first time, differentiated between "Old" and "New" immigrants.[91] Article 1 defined "New Immigrants" as Indian labourers who immigrated into Mauritius after the promulgation of the Order in Council of 15 January 1842, and for whose introduction the government had paid. The term "Old Immigrant" was applied to those Indian labours who had immigrated prior to that time, "or for whose introduction no public money was paid."[92]

The distinction was an important one, for those deemed "Old Immigrants" would have completed their initial engagement and were essentially bond-free. They could return to India or seek alternative means of subsisting on the island, whether in different branches of employment or by acquiring a small plot of land for self-cultivation. They were no longer obliged to work on the sugar estates, the original reason for which they had been introduced to the colony. For "New Immigrants", by contrast, opportunities were decisively curtailed, directing them exclusively to the sugar industry by stipulating that "no male immigrant of 14 years of age or above, arriving in this Colony after the passing of this Ordinance, shall engage himself otherwise than with a sugar planter."[93]

Through formalizing the distinction between old and new immigrants, Ordinance No. 22 introduced a level of bureaucracy which the labourers had to navigate henceforth, and which with time became more convoluted, as discussed below. To start with, in order to prove their status, the workers were issued with tickets bearing their name, immigration number and other identifying details, such as age, "stature" and "marks".[94] The ordinance made clear that until five years of industrial residence had been completed, no labourer would be entitled to a free passage back to India.[95] The period of industrial residence began on the first day after which the immigrants were allowed to leave the arrival depot,[96] and consisted of residence in the colony either in the employment "under a stamped engagement with a sugar planter", or by the payment of a monthly tax "in lieu thereof . . . during any part of the above period of five years in which the immigrant is not so employed."[97]

However, in an evident bid to further control the available labour on the island, Ordinance No. 16 of 1852 abolished the right to a free return passage,[98] with only those who had arrived since 1 May 1847 entitled to one if they had

91 SA 41/181 (Mauritius Archives), Enclosure of Grey to Gomm, 2 January 1848: Ordinance No. 22 of 1847, 3 May 1847, reproduced in Deerpalsingh and Carter, Volume III above.

92 Ibid., Article 1.

93 Article 7.

94 The ticket for Old Immigrants was called "Form A" and for New Immigrants "Form B". The latter also detailed the labourer's caste.

95 Article 4.

96 Article 6.

97 Article 5.

98 SD 43/301 (Mauritius Archives), Enclosure of Higginson to Parkington, 17 May 1852: Ordinance No. 16, 14 April 1852, to take effect 1 May 1852, in Deerpalsingh and Carter, above, Volume III.

completed their five-year industrial residence,[99] but for other new immigrants the entitlement ceased.[100]

These regulations, along with the immigration restrictions lifted as already discussed, lead to a significant increase in available labour. As a result, the production of sugar in the following years was "of an amount . . . without parallel", peaking in 1862–1863 with the hitherto largest crop ever achieved.[101]

The following years however, rather unexpectedly, proved difficult. Natural calamities in India such as hurricanes and floods caused an increase in emigration to Mauritius, which the planters only too readily sought to absorb. However, the increase of emigrants was also accompanied by a decrease of grain and crops exportation from presidencies like Bengal, on which Mauritius had come to rely on to feed its population. With an unfavourable season marked by droughts on the island, as well as greater competition on the sugar market from the cultivation of European beet, the situation in Mauritius became one of "general distress", for both food and work was suddenly hard to come by for the many labourers.[102] It is in this climate of a large and depressed population that the new labour laws of 1867 were introduced.

6.4 The new labour laws

6.4.1 The pass system

The most significant piece of legislation consolidating previous enactments was Ordinance No. 31 of 1867,[103] as supplemented by Government Notice 166 of 11 November 1868. The ticket requirement introduced 20 years earlier was still in place[104], with Article 39 of the 1867 ordinance further making it compulsory for Old Immigrants to have a portrait affixed to it. No fee was chargeable for the ticket itself, but the cost of the photo was to be borne by the immigrant.[105] Article 41 sought to take greater control of the movements of Old Immigrants by requiring that any of them not under a written contract of service had to appear at the central police station of his district and declare "his place of abode, and occupation, employment, or other means of subsistence." The same declaration was required of every immigrant on completion of his industrial residence

99 Article 4.
100 Article 7.
101 1875 report, p. 99.
102 Ibid., p. 101.
103 Came into force 2 May 1868. For the text of the regulations, see Greene, W., and L. E. Schmidt, eds., *Labor Laws of Mauritius – A Collection of the Laws Specifcally Relating to Masters and Servants at Mauritius* (Mauritius: L. Channell's Printing Establishment, 1869).
104 Ordinance No. 22 of 1847, and repeated in Ordinance No. 25 of 1848 and Ordinance No. 16 of 1852.
105 By virtue of Government Notice No. 166 of 11 November 1868, Article 82, the Protector of Immigrants had the power to exempt infirm or destitute immigrants from payment the fee for the portrait.

acquiring Old Immigrant status, as well as of every Old Immigrant on the expiry of this written service contract.

Old Immigrants orally engaged would be unable to acquire their pass unless the job contractor personally appeared in front of the police,[106] and those occupied as day labourers or similar had first to procure a license to authorize them exercising their chosen trade.[107] Further, it was stipulated that "every Immigrant licensed to work by the day, or to perform job-work, shall be bound to wear conspicuously on his right arm a badge bearing upon it the word 'Job-man' and the number of his license."[108] The regulations provided that a new pass had to be applied for in a number of circumstances, such as change of residence[109] or occupation,[110] the failure of which was punishable by a fine.[111] Additionally, the immigrant was under the obligation to inform the police of his mere intention to change abode, following which such intention would be noted on his pass. The provision was quite strict, for it provided that "no new pass shall be issued to any Immigrant who has removed from one District to another unless such notice has been previously given by him."[112]

The pass system created many difficulties for the largely illiterate workforce. The procurement of photos was expensive,[113] and the need to apply for these passes required them to travel to the main police station of their district, which could involve a considerable distance and would in most cases inevitably require an absence from work. It has been observed that it was not unusual for labourers to be arrested for vagrancy (discussed next) on the way to have these passes made,[114] thus making a mockery of the entire process.

6.4.2 Vagrancy

Regulations related to vagrancy can be traced back to the Order in Council of 7 September 1838, and were largely repeated by Ordinance No. 42 of 1844.[115] While the order and the ordinance were primarily geared towards establishing vagrancy as an offence, with varying custodial sentences including hard labour for the categories of "idle and disorderly persons",[116] "vagabonds"[117] and "incor-

106 Government Notice 166, Article 49.
107 Ibid., Article 54.
108 Ibid., Article 56.
109 Ordinance No. 31 of 1867, Article 44.
110 Government Notice 166, Article 43.
111 Ibid.
112 Ibid., Article 44.
113 Fixed at four shillings in 1868.
114 Mishra, Amit Kumar, 'Indian Indentured Labourers in Mauritius: Reassessing the "New System of Slavery" vs. Free Labour Debate', *Studies in History*, 25 (2009), 229–251, p. 239.
115 Passed 10 June 1844.
116 Section I, sentence not to exceed one calendar month.
117 Section II, sentence not to exceed 60 days.

rigible rogues",[118] in the 1867 new labour legislation the issue of vagrancy was approached from the context of compelling the population to labour. Unlawful absence led to loss of wages and allowances for the time of such absence, in addition to forfeiture of a certain amount of the worker's monthly wages for each day of absence.[119] This mechanism is frequently described by scholars as the notorious "double-cut", by which the worker was effectively punished twice. Upon his employer's complaint, instead of forfeiture, the labourer was liable to be sentenced to imprisonment,[120] "or (at the option of the employer) to a prolongation of the Contract equivalent to the time of absence".[121] The reported case of *Itoo* demonstrates that where there was repeated refusal to work on prolongation, the labourer was liable for imprisonment on each refusal.[122]

Where absence from work without justifiable cause was accompanied with absconding from his dwelling for more than three consecutive days, the labourer in question was deemed a "deserter", and liable to imprisonment no exceeding three months,[123] and could be lawfully apprehended by his employer or anyone acting with his employer's authority.[124]

Particularly harshly, an Old Immigrant, who was unable to produce his passes on demand, was liable to be detained and kept at the Immigration Depot until enquiries were made about his means to subsistence. Unless these were found satisfactory, either through bona fide employment or service, he was deemed a "vagrant".[125] Thus where a labourer was on his way to have a pass made, he could be detained and be not only punished for "vagrancy", but also lose his wages accordingly.

Article 48 of the 1867 order excessively curtailed immigrants movements, for it provided that "any Immigrant found in a District where he has no residence, or in any house or premises, and being unable to give a satisfactory reason for his being in such a District, house, or premises, as the case may be, may be arrested by any Officer or Constable of Police, without warrant". What was considered "satisfactory" was not defined, and thus left the labourer liable to punishment in almost

118 Section III and VII, sentenced not to exceed 6 months.
119 Enacted by Article 18 of Ordinance No. 16 of 1862, to which Article 49 of Ordinance No. 31 of 1867 referred.
120 Ibid., not exceeding 14 days.
121 Article 18 of Ordinance No. 16 of 1862.
122 On release of their first custodial sentence for refusing to work on prolongation, the labourers refused again and were imprisoned for a second term. The Supreme Court dismissed their appeal brought on the ground of having been sentenced twice for the same offence, see *Itoo and others v. Barron, Moon and others* [Piston's Reports, 1862], also cited in IALS GM2.H.3, Greene, W., *Digest of the Reported Criminal Jurisprudence of the Supreme Court of Mauritius from 1842 to 1883* (Port Louis, Mauritius, 1884), p. 102.
123 Ordinance No. 31 of 1867, Article 50.
124 Ibid., Article 51.
125 Ibid., Article 46.

any instance where he was not found at this place of work. These, among other instances, rendered the position of Indian labourers in Mauritius very precarious.

6.4.3 Wages

Payment of wages differed considerably among the colonies, as Governor Gordon[126] observed in an 1871 despatch to the Earl of Kimberley.[127] In Jamaica and Demerara, labourers were paid weekly, in Trinidad fortnightly, and in St. Lucia payments were to be made twice a month under penalty, imprisonment or, under the governor's discretion, cancellation of the contract. In Mauritius however, payment was due only once a month, though crucially, as Governor Gordon pointed out, a local enactment in form of Ordinance No. 15 of 1852 prevented a worker from suing for cancellation of contract on the ground of nonpayment of wages until at least three months had expired from the day the payment was due. This was confirmed 15 years later by Ordinance No. 31 of 1867, with the governor observing that "it has been lately ruled by the Supreme Court that cancellation of contract cannot be claimed under this clause unless a period of four months has elapsed since the last payment of wages."[128]

The reported case of *Belloguet v. Pyndugadoo* in 1870 corroborates the account of Governor Gordon, stressing the interval of three months since the payment was due before the right to cancellation of contract would arise, though noting that the contract could be cancelled at any time at the discretion of the magistrate for non-execution.[129] It seems unlikely though that the magistrates would have exercised their power in favour of the labourer however, for Governor Gordon also observed that once

> a labourer obtains a Judgment against his master for wages due, the Magistrate is authorized to grant the master a delay, and, as in the schedule, the blank to be filled up by the Magistrate is followed by the world "months", it is clear that a long delay is contemplated. This delay is capable of further extension with the consent of the coolie.[130]

126 Sir Arthur Hamilton Gordon, governor of Mauritius from 1871 to 1874, see Macmillan, Allister, *Mauritius Illustrated: Historical and Descriptive, Commercial and Industrial, Facts, Figures and Resources* (New Delhi: Asian Educational Services, 2010).

127 John Wodehouse, Earl of Kimberley, Secretary of State for the Colonies, July 1870 to February 1874 and April 1880 to December 1882, see Appendix A in Panton, Kenneth J., *Historical Dictionary of the British Empire* (London: Rowman & Littlefield, 2015).

128 CO 882/2 Governor Gordon to the Earl of Kimberley, Mauritius, 18 August 1871.

129 Greene, W., *Digest of the Reported Criminal Jurisprudence of the Supreme Court of Mauritius from 1842 to 1883* (Port Louis: Mercantile Record Company's Printing Establishment, 1884), p. 106.

130 CO 882/2 Governor Gordon to the Earl of Kimberley, Mauritius, 18 August 1871.

It is difficult to fathom under this regime how long labourers may have had been obliged to work without payment of wages. Coupled with the rules that allowed wages to be cut in a variety of circumstances as well as the instances that granted the employer a prolongation of contract in his favour, it is clear that the situation the labourers found themselves in did not, by any account, amount to an equitable service agreement. The case of *Thamun v. D'Emmerz* of 1861 in this context reveals an interesting aspect as to how the relationship between labourers and their employers was being conceived. It was held that upon an employer's death, and the estate passing by inheritance, "the right to the services of the labourers engaged under written contract is transmitted to the heirs."[131] This, of course, is reminiscent of the situation of slaves, who under the *Code Noir* were inheritable as chattels.

Overall, it is evident that whatever Indian labourers may have expected from agreeing to work in Mauritius, the conditions they were faced with were harsh and difficult to bear. This is most unfortunately reflected in the high rates of suicides among the workers during the period in question.

6.4.4 Incidents of suicide

In 1871, newly appointed Governor Gordon expressed his concern at what he regarded an "extraordinary frequency of suicide among the Indian immigrants in this Colony", noting that "the vast majority occur among the indentured labourers on estates."[132] The governor observed with dismay the inconsistencies between the returns of the Civil Status Office and the police records on the numbers of deaths. Yet irrespective of which set of numbers could have been considered more reliable, the governor believed "we must consider the heavier return to be the truer one".[133] He included the return shown in Table 6.3 with his correspondence:

Table 6.3 Probable motives – return of suicides amongst Indian nationals 1 January 1861–31 December 1870[134]

Jealousy	*Revenge*	*Poverty*	*Sickness*	*Temporary Insanity*	*Discontent and Ill-Treatment*	*Unknown*
83	26	28	189	82	17	217

131 Greene, W., *Digest of the Reported Criminal Jurisprudence of the Supreme Court of Mauritius from 1842 to 1883* (Port Louis, Mauritius, 1884), p. 99.

132 CO 882/2 Governor Gordon to the Earl of Kimberley, Mauritius 28 July 1871, in Correspondence relating to Indian Immigrants in Mauritius and Its Dependencies, February 13, 1872, p. 90.

133 Ibid.

134 CO 882/2 Enclosure 1 in No. 6, Return of Suicides committed in the Island of Mauritius from January 1, 1861, to December 31, 1870.

Governor Gordon stated that he did not place reliance on the classification provided, and in particular did not believe that "jealousy" was a decisive cause to any large degree. Taking into account proportional variations in the number of male and female immigrants among the Indian population over the decade, he noted that suicides were committed predominantly among men. From the current set of data, the governor observed that "the suicides are almost all those of males, only 17 suicides of women having occurred out of a total of 642".[135] In closing Governor Gordon made the observation that "I myself believe that a very large portion of these suicides are due to nostalgia, or an intense desire to return to India, which they have no means of gratifying."[136] In his reply, the Earl of Kimberley instructed the governor to establish a "system of proper inquiry into sudden deaths either by a coroner or by a magistrate" which did not exist at the time on the island, and expressed regret at the discrepancies between the returns of the police and the Civil Status Office respectively, which he felt "must be due to want of care either in the Department in question or on the part of those whose duty it is to report the occurrence of deaths on estates."[137]

Analyzing the numbers contained in Table 6.3, it appears striking that the smallest number of suicides is attributed to "discontent and ill-treatment", enumerated at only 17 out of 642, whereas the largest number, at 217, is considered to have occurred due to "unknown" causes, raising the suspicion that the circumstances leading to the suicide may have well been known, but neither overseers nor officials were prepared to record them precisely. Instead, there seems to have been resort to less intelligible rubrics, such as "jealousy" and "temporary insanity", each ostensibly responsible for a large number of deaths. But whatever the precise reasons, the high level of incidents does not reflect positively on the indentured labour experience, including the apparent carelessness with which the deaths were recorded.

6.4.5 "Unfree" labour

The above analysis demonstrates that the exploitative nature of a labour system was not solely dependent upon the legal status of the worker. An important question relates to the consequences for non-performance of contract (whether actual or fabricated), which in the case of indentured labourers in Mauritius entailed criminal penalization as punishment.

As elucidated by Ralph Shlomowitz, employers of long-term indenture workers were generally concerned with two matters: retention of the worker until the end of the contract and extraction of a satisfactory amount of labour

135 CO 882/2, Gordon above.
136 Ibid.
137 CO 882/2 The Earl of Kimberly to Governor Gordon, Downing Street, 11 September 1871.

for the duration of the same.[138] According to him, it was precisely the availability of a criminal remedy for what would be actually a civil offence that was the most distinctive feature of indenture. Providing employers with such a level of control over their workforce is thus what differentiated this system from free labour.[139]

It is submitted that criminal penalization is but one aspect which rendered indentured labour in Mauritius coercive. Rejecting the notion that free labour always implies non-coercion and protection of the worker, Amrit Mishra stipulates two indicators in particular, in addition to moral domination, which he deems as the determinants of freedom: mobility and wage payments.[140] As noted above, vagrancy laws were employed to drastically restrict the movement of indentured labourers. Thus, any activity that was not directly work-related (such as visiting friends and relatives on other estates, going to register grievances with the protector or magistrate or seeking alternative work after the end of a contract) was deemed criminal. These oppressive measures were extended when it became compulsory for the labourers, through the ticketing system introduced in 1867, to carry passes at all times. Any default resulted in imprisonment, which inevitably amounted to a "double-punishment" as a result of the attending wage cut (itself quite drastic, as it involved two days wages lost for each day missed), as per Ordinance No. 22 of 1847.

On the basis of these oppressive regulations, Mishra argues that indentured labour was not free, as it denied economic independence as well as mobility of occupation and place.[141] However, given that the idea of "free labour" may encompass a number of exploitative and coercive instances it may be better understood as an "ideological construct".[142] Stanley Engerman seeks to resolve the inherent tensions and contradictions by drawing a distinction between "liberty of the person" and "liberty of contract".[143] Yet in the absence of available alternatives to the worker (as has been observed in the case of the labourers once they became employed on the plantations), Engerman states that "the value of legal freedom is weakened."[144] In Mauritius a greater semblance of freedom was achieved when resources were made available to the imported workers, most notably land.

138 Shlomowitz, Ralph, 'On Punishments and Rewards in Coercive Labour Systems: Comparative Perspectives', *Slavery & Abolition*, 12 (1991), 97–102.

139 Ibid., p. 100.

140 Mishra, Amit Kumar, 'Indian Indentured Labourers in Mauritius: Reassessing the "New System of Slavery" vs. Free Labour Debate', *Studies in History*, 25 (2009), 229–251.

141 Ibid., p. 250

142 See Craven, Paul, and Douglas Hay, 'The Criminalization of "Free" Labour: Master and Servant in Comparative Perspective', *Slavery & Abolition*, 15 (1994), 71–101, p. 72.

143 Engerman, Stanley L., 'Introduction', in *Terms of Labor: Slavery, Serfdom and Free Labor*, ed. by Stanley L. Engerman (Stanford: Stanford University Press, 1999), pp. 11–12.

144 Ibid.

6.5 Emergence of an Indian peasantry

The establishment of a settled population made of imported workers was initially not an aim actively pursued by the local authorities. As mentioned at the beginning of this chapter, the main concern in the 1830s, when the first indentured labourers began arriving in larger numbers, had been to ensure that their return was provided for. Research suggests that the possibility of a self-reliant population which could subsist independently was perceived as a threat to the sugar economy. Early evidence of this can be found in an Order in Council in 1838, which prohibited squatting on pieces of land, a measure largely ignored by the ex-apprentices against whom the regulations were directed.[145] Former slaves however strongly resisted a return to the sugar cane fields, and retreated to the mountain regions, trying to establish independent livelihoods as artisans, day workers and the like. The data contained in Table 6.2 shows that in 1846, the total population of ex-apprentices (excluding children born since emancipation) amounted to 39,489. This is in contrast to the 64,331 apprentices counted in 1834.[146] As noted in the previous chapter, the number of apprentices began to reduce quite rapidly with the introduction of indentured labourers, during the period of apprenticeship itself. Post-apprenticeship, Moses Nwulia describes the situation as one where "the eyes of the planter and of the ex-slave were averted from each other."[147] Neither were planters seeking out ex-apprentices as workers, nor were the latter willing to engage in the labour they equated with slavery. Nwulia links the drop in numbers to cholera and small pox outbreaks among the former slave population,[148] indicating the difficult living conditions they found themselves in. Ordinance No. 10 of 1841 is a further example of the regulations which sought to keep the workers within the sugar economy system.[149] Applying equally to former apprentices and indentured labourers, it defined vagrancy in broad terms, thus potentially applicable to anyone not engaged on a sugar estate.[150]

As noted in the discussion above, attempts to influence the labour market were not limited to local regulation, but were also to be found in the immigration rules. This becomes particularly evident with respect to the right of a free return passage. Initially part of the original agreement, the concept underwent considerable changes. Ordinance No. 2 of 1845 introduced a number of formalities which had to be met before an immigrant was allowed to return, such as certified fitness of

145 Order in Council of 8 October 1838, see Nwulia, Moses D. E., 'The "Apprenticeship" System in Mauritius: Its Character and Its Impact on Race Relations in the Immediate Post-Emancipation Period, 1839–1879', *African Studies Review*, 21 (1978), 89–101, p. 100.

146 See Table 5.3, Chapter 5.

147 Nwulia, op. cit., p. 100.

148 Ibid.

149 "For the more effectual repression of Vagrancy", subsequently disallowed.

150 See also Reddi, S. J., 'The Establishment of the Indian Indenture System 1834–1842', in *Indians Overseas – The Mauritian Experience*, ed. by U. Bissoondoyal (Moka: Mahatma Gandhi Institute, 1984).

health before embarkation,[151] due notice given to the Protector of Immigrants[152] and penalties for ship masters conveying immigrants from Mauritius in breach of the conditions set out in the ordinance.[153]

Ordinance No. 2 was passed in February 1845 and gives no indication that the right to a free return passage would be curtailed. In May of the same year however, Governor Gomm made the suggestion to Lord Stanley that

> the claim to the free return passage . . . should be considered as cancelled with regard to individuals not continuing in the service of cultivation, and that the local government should be empowered to notify to each individual departing from the service for which he was specially introduced at so heavy an expense, that in so doing he forfeits his claim to the prospective advantage. Such notices might, in various instances, have the effect of retaining the fickle labourer in agricultural employ.

Despite such concerns, the governor reports to be "highly satisfied" with the general progress of the labourers, and in closing makes the brief observation that the workers were increasingly placing their earnings in a local savings bank, a development which he deemed "evidence of increased confidence".[154] As will be discussed in the next section, the slow accumulation of savings by Indian workers would prove crucial several decades later.

Governor Gomm's suggestion at providing an incentive to agricultural work by restricting the entitlement to a free return passage was not immediately given effect. Instead, subsequent to the introduction of the ticketing requirements which created the distinction between "Old" and "New" immigrants, Ordinance No. 16 of 1852 extended the formalities governing travel further, notably requiring every immigrant to obtain a passport before leaving the colony.[155] As noted earlier, Ordsssinance No. 16 for the first time restricted the right to a free return passage by stipulating that "no New Immigrant who may have arrived since the 1st May 1847 shall be entitled to a free passage back to India unless he has completed an industrial residence of five years".[156] The entitlement to a free return passage was eventually discontinued altogether in 1853.[157]

151 Article I.
152 Ibid.
153 Article V.
154 Governor Gomm to Lord Stanley, 16 May 1845, in *PP 1845 (641) Mauritius. Copies or Extracts of the Despatch from the Governor of Mauritius*, p. 52.
155 Article III.
156 Article IV.
157 By virtue of a dispatch from the Secretary of State, see Rouillard, John, ed., *A Collection of the Laws of Mauritius and Its Dependencies, Volume VI* (Mauritius: Published by the Authority of the Government, 1866), p. 123 <http://catalog.hathitrust.org/Record/011570339> [accessed 26 June 2022].

The completed withdrawal of the right to a free return passage in 1853 can be viewed as a clear attempt to encourage the labourers to settle on the island, particularly if viewed with another legal advance occurring the same year.[158] Ordinance No. 22 of 1853 made simplified provisions for the solemnization of marriages of immigrants, no longer requiring them to comply with the requirements of the local French Civil Code, but simply having to produce certificates from the Protector of Immigrants confirming that to the best knowledge of the protector, the persons in question were not married, obtainable at one shilling per certificate.[159] Further, in 1856, provisions were finally made to recognize marriages entered into in India. Pursuant to Ordinance No. 3 of that year, any Indian immigrant "having been legally married in India according to the Forms and Ceremonies of his Religion" accompanied by his wife became able to make a declaration, under formalities as prescribed that they were lawfully married,[160] and such a declaration "shall be deemed for all purposes sufficient prima facie evidence of the Marriage of the Parties and of the Legitimacy of the Issue of the Children (if any) named therein."[161] Thus, in the 1850s, with a free return passage no longer offered, but stability to family life through legislation being introduced, indentured labourers from India were encouraged to remain and settle in Mauritius. By 1861, the island had developed into a very cosmopolitan colony, as a return on the countries of birth of the resident population shows (see Table 6.4).

Table 6.4 Countries of birth of resident population in Mauritius, 1861[162]

Country	*Population*		
	Male	*Female*	*Total*
EUROPE			
England	642	210	852
Scotland	154	35	189
Ireland	204	86	290
British Possessions and Dependencies	20	8	28
TOTAL	*1,020*	*339*	*1,359*
France	873	303	1,176
Spain	21	2	23
Portugal	58	2	60
Italy	40	4	44
Germany	45	8	53

158 See also the discussion by Gunputh, Veena Devi, 'Sex Disproportion among Indian Immigrants', in *Indians Overseas – The Mauritian Experience*, ed. by U. Bissoondoyal (Moka: Mahatma Gandhi Institute, 1984), pp. 213–222.

159 Article VIII, subsection 3.

160 Article I.

161 Article V.

162 Data taken from Appendix No. 5, Statement Showing the Countries of Birth of Resident Population of Mauritius on the 8th April 1861, contained in C.S.D.364/2 Report of the Commissioners appointed to take a Census of the Island of Mauritius and its Dependencies, April 1861.

Country	*Population*		
	Male	*Female*	*Total*
Holland	10	2	12
Belgium	19	6	25
Other parts of Europe	77	21	98
TOTAL	*1,143*	*348*	*1,491*
AFRICA			
Mauritius	58,699	58,190	116,889
Seychelles and other Dependencies	295	284	579
Réunion	412	331	743
Madagascar	2,270	1,115	3,385
Mozambique	1,909	458	2,367
Cape Colony	23	19	42
Other parts of Africa	295	50	345
TOTAL	*63,903*	*60,447*	*124,350*
ASIA			
Bengal	75,902	24,126	100,028
Madras	41,019	15,456	56,475
Bombay	11,516	4,406	15,922
Singapore, Penang and Malacca	91	11	102
China	1,900	4	1,904
Other parts of Asia	5,241	1,242	6,483
TOTAL	*135,669*	*45,245*	*180,914*
AMERICA			
United States	81	5	86
British Colonies	30	7	37
Other parts of America	13	4	17
TOTAL	*124*	*16*	*140*
AUSTRALIA	7	9	16
Not Stated	1,095	685	1,780
TOTAL	**202,961**	**107,089**	**310,050**

As the numbers show, out of a resident population of 310,050, only 116,889 were actually born in Mauritius. By far the greatest number of residents were born in India, with 172,425 from Bengal, Madras and Bombay combined, and just over 3,000 had arrived from various parts of Europe, America and Australia.

Despite its diverse outlook and evident attraction, as noted above, the 1860s proved a challenging period for the island, creating a crisis in the local sugar economy through a mixture of natural catastrophes affecting the agricultural sector, and a reduced demand for cane sugar with the ascent of beet in Europe. This hit the Indian population particularly hard. As an employment return for 1861 shows, 90,621 residents were occupied in agriculture on the sugar estates alone,[163] and 84,548 of these belonged to the Indian population (84,380 male

163 See Appendix No. 9, Statement Showing the Employments of the Population of Mauritius on the 8th April 1861, contained in C.S.D.364/2 Report of the Commissioners

and 168 female).[164] In other words, just over 93 per cent of workers in the sugar industry were of Indian extraction. A further 89,851 Indians (89,492 male and 359 female) were employed in general agriculture (as gardeners, woodcutters, cowherds and the like),[165] with another 12,229 (11,808 male and 421 female) working as general labourers (such as workmen, stonecutters, etc.).[166]

The way in which the planters sought to address the crisis in Mauritius has been described as "a process of economic retrenchment".[167] Planters began to subdivide their sugar estates, a period commonly referred to as the *Grand Morcellement*, which involved selling off parts of their land. While this development is often stated to have begun in earnest in the 1880s, Richard Allen dates the beginning of the process as early as 1862 on the basis of his research into contemporary notarial acts.[168]

William Storey, in his assessment of the period, states that by the 1860s, "the sugar industry was chronically starved of finance capital", which he accounts to decline in the price of cane sugar and the "remoteness" of metropolitan investors.[169] Whether the "remoteness" refers to the geographical distance between the island and London, or is more indicative of a disinterest in an industry that began to show definite signs of decline is not evident from Storey's observation, though an argument can be made for the latter. Either way, to ease the distress, planters turned to Indian labourers who had been able to save their earnings. By selling off parcels of their land, they were able to both raise capital and cut costs.

To fully appreciate the development, a general understanding of the sugar production process may be helpful. In Mauritius, sugar estates traditionally carried out both the agricultural cultivation of cane as well as the mechanical production of sugar. At the turn of the decade in 1850, it had been assessed that the agricultural phase involved two-thirds of the total cost of sugar production, since the rocky, volcanic soil of the island precluded extensive use of machinery and remained heavily reliant on manual labour. The manufacturing process itself only represented one-fifth of the total cost of production.[170]

The *morcellement* was an experience not limited to Mauritius, but also occurred on its neighbouring island Réunion. On both islands, the process gave rise to

---

appointed to take a Census of the Island of Mauritius and its Dependencies, April 1861.

164 See Appendix No. 17, Statement Showing the Employment of Indian Population of Mauritius on the 8th April 1861, contained in C.S.D.364/2 Report of the Commissioners appointed to take a Census of the Island of Mauritius and its Dependencies, April 1861.

165 Ibid.

166 Ibid.

167 Allen, Richard B., 'Indian Immigrants and the Beginning of the Grand Morcellement 1860–1885', in *Indians Overseas – The Mauritian Experience*, ed. by U. Bissoondoyal (Moka: Mahatma Gandhi Institute, 1984), p. 340–347.

168 Ibid.

169 Storey, William Kelleher, *Science and Power in Colonial Mauritius* (Rochester, NY: University of Rochester Press, 1998), p. 41.

170 Ly-Tio-Fane Pineo, Huguette, *Lured Away: The Life History of Indian Cane Workers in Mauritius* (Moka: Mahatma Gandhi Institute, 1984), pp. 43–44.

a growing class of cane farmers.[171] Another, similar development was that of *métayage*, which after the end of indentured labour was particularly pervasive in Réunion. *Métayage* involved agreements whereby a tenant consented to cultivate cane on agreed portions of land held by the owner. Described by J. Galloway as "usually verbal, informal" contracts, the arrangement benefitted landowners by guaranteeing the supply of cane for their sugar mill while allowing the tenant to receive the advantage of owning part of the crop and thus profiting from his personal labour.[172]

The *morcellement* process in Mauritius was complex and could involve further on-selling of increasingly smaller plots. While there is the argument that only low-yielding plots were sold by the planters, Storey states that the land acquired by the emerging class of smallholders was not always necessarily inferior.[173]

Irrespective of the quality of the land acquired, Indians had made an enormous leap by becoming owners of the same. This contributed to the growth of settlements, which while in the vicinity of sugar estates, were nevertheless outside of them, marking "a form of liberation" for the former labourers.[174] Yet, while it signified an important transition for the labourers, they continued to rely on the estate owners for the processing of their cane. With the mills remaining a crucial part of the sugar production process, the economic power of the white planter class remained unchallenged. As Tijo Salverda observes, while the Franco-Mauritian elite had had to lessen their grip on the very resource that had guaranteed their superior position, namely land, their standing was barely challenged as a consequence of retaining ownership of the mills.[175]

Economic power was thus embedded in the manufacture of sugar, not in the cultivation of it. By divesting themselves of the agricultural part, the plantation owners were able to consolidate their operations to their advantage. In spite of this fundamental retention of control by the Franco-Mauritian oligarchy, landownership was an important milestone for the Indian segment of Mauritian society. Richard Allen calculates that by the end of the 19th century, nearly one-half of independent proprietors were of Indian origin. That group would come to cultivate about a third of all cane land within the first decade of the 20th century, reaching 45 per cent by the 1920s.[176]

171 Galloway, J. H., *The Sugar Cane Industry: An Historical Geography from Its Origins to 1914* (Cambridge: Cambridge University Press, 1989), pp. 224–225.

172 Ibid.

173 Storey, op. cit., p. 41. See also the discussion in Allen, Richard B., *Slaves, Freedmen and Indentured Laborers in Colonial Mauritius* (Cambridge: Cambridge University Press, 2006).

174 Salverda, Tijo, *Franco-Mauritian Elite: Power and Anxiety in the Face of Change* (New York: Berghahn Books, 2015), p. 47.

175 Ibid., p. 48.

176 Allen, Richard B., *Slaves, Freedmen and Indentured Laborers in Colonial Mauritius* (Cambridge: Cambridge University Press, 2006), p. 74.

6.6 Conclusion

This chapter has revealed the restrictive aspects of the regime of state-regulated indentured labour as it was experienced in Mauritius. The succession of various schemes shows that indentured labour as a system was not static, but evolved as the needs of the sugar industry required. In the aftermath of the abuses encountered during the first phase of indenture, calls were made for greater state involvement, regarded as the best protection for the emigrating labourers. Yet far from remedying the shortcomings of the informal system, the official scheme proved more coercive with legislative measures employed to retain workers or prolong their stay on the island. As has become clear, the question inquiring into the "freedom" of the worker is not satisfied simply by reference to legal status. Absence of freedom is not only denoted by overt coercion or use of force, but also in the level of exploitation experienced. The most striking aspect which marks indentured labour as an "unfree" system was the availability of criminal sanctions for breach of contract on part of the workers. Thus not only did workers continue to enter into contracts without clear understanding, the service agreements were also being prolonged under any available pretext. Additionally, the enforcement of these contracts was moved out of the private, civic sphere and became a matter of public law, with lenient provisions for non-execution by employers and harsh punishment for breach of contract by the labourers. Vagrancy laws were used to regulate the options and mobility of workers, severely curtailing the ability to choose their occupation. To this end, a complex level of bureaucracy was employed throughout the period, as evidenced by the ticket, certificate and pass requirements, which were difficult to navigate for a largely uneducated workforce. With the introduction of a legal distinction between "Old" and "New" immigrants, the system sought to control even those who had already completed their contracts in a bid to further bind them to the sugar industry. The high rates of suicides on sugar estates reflects negatively on the experience of indentured labour as a whole.

This chapter also shows how the large influx of Indian workers operated to the detriment of ex-apprentices, who found themselves increasingly marginalized from society in a dynamic which not only saw this group, but also the plantation owners, turn away from the plantations. Crucially, in terms of post-emancipation development, an Indian peasantry had been encouraged as the indentured labour period was drawing to a close, which contrasts with the experience of apprentices in the post-abolition period. Yet even with the end of indentured labour, the Franco-Mauritian oligarchy found a way to maintain their superior economic status by holding on to sugar manufacturing while divesting themselves of their land holdings. Even as the Indian population advanced in their economic standing on the island, their progress continued to be tightly bound to sugar cane cultivation.

7 Conclusion

> "*Such is the picture presented to the eye by the mixed and motley population of Mauritius – a picture unique in itself, such as no other country in the world can supply.*"
>
> –Reverend Patrick Beaton, 1859[1]

7.1 Recapitulation of research

7.1.1 Aims and objectives revisited

The research at hand has sought to demonstrate the profound influence law has upon the development of society. Specifically, the argument which has been pursued is that the impact of law may not only prove formative, but also constitutive. The history of the island of Mauritius provides an ideal illustration. Presenting the uncommon scenario of a society which has been created ex nihilo as a direct consequence of colonialism and home today to a unique demographic, in the absence of an indigenous population the modern nation has emerged from the coming together of different groups arriving on its shores during the period of colonization. The need for labour to support the colonial project acted as the driving force behind the importation of first slaves and later indentured labourers, and the successive waves of immigration served to shape and segment Mauritian society.

This work has sought to illuminate the processes which have led to the "assembly" of Mauritian society via an examination of the 19th-century colonial laws which governed the workforce. Underpinning the research is the suggestion that labour management acted as the principal legal technology through which the composition and development of Mauritian society was influenced, impacting both the island's economy as well as social identities in a lasting fashion. Crucial hereby has been the concept of jurisdictional tensions, identified here as a series

1 Beaton, Patrick, *Creoles & Coolies – Five Years in Mauritius* (London: James Nisbet and Co., 1859), p. 15.

DOI: 10.4324/9781003313366-9

of contestations themselves born from the contradictory aims of the British colonial endeavour, which shaped that development. What emerges is that the two labour systems in question – slavery and indenture – far from being self-contained paradigms, fundamentally interconnected and created in Mauritius a society with very specific attributes.

The argument is not that Mauritian society of today is the direct result of 19th-century events. This would be to utterly disregard the developments of the 20th century, which witnessed the rise of communal politics, an increased relevance of religion, as well as the decolonization process. The last few decades in particular have seen the development of new industries which have accelerated the island's transition to a modern and largely stable multi-ethnic nation. The circumstances of the 19th century, however, while presenting only one part in this long-term evolution, did lay the decisive groundwork by drawing the fundamental lines upon which Mauritian society would develop and continues to be impacted by.

7.1.2 Research summary

Following colonization attempts by both the Portuguese and the Dutch, the first permanent settlers were the French in 1715, who from the beginning used predominantly African slave labour to support their colonial endeavour. This marked the beginning of Mauritian society, initially established for the purpose of extending French imperial power, given the island's strategic position in the southern Indian Ocean. Under French governance, Mauritius was transformed from wild territory to a settled colony with infrastructure, enterprise and commerce. Some sources describe Mauritius in the late 18th and early 19th century as a flourishing French community, while others emphasize poverty and squalor. In any instance, it is clear that at British takeover in 1810, French life was well-established with a strong local administration and judiciary.

British occupation had been originally pursued primarily to obtain a military advantage in the region, and while the neighbouring island of Bourbon (modern Réunion) was returned to France, Mauritius was retained. The situation faced by the first British administrator, Governor Farquhar, was complex. He was charged with implementing British policy in a French-dominated colony while rendering this foreign rule palatable to its inhabitants. The defining issue of his governorship and indeed of the early years of British administration was the abolition of the slave trade. Representing the first legal change which would significantly affect the labour supply on the island, as discussed in Chapter 3, the prohibition had been passed in Britain in 1807 by imperial statute. However, the 1810 Mauritian Terms of Capitulation preserved local French laws, which at the time still recognized the trade. This gave rise to the question whether the ban was of legal effect on the island. Farquhar sought to argue that it did not, and in fact delayed proclamation of the Act to 1813. Did the slave trade remain legal for the first few years of British colonization, as the governor argued throughout his life despite numerous controversies? Historians and commentators, even in a legal context,[2] commonly state that in Mauritius the ban took effect in 1813 subsequent to the belated proclamation of the Act abolishing the trade. In Chapter 3, it has been argued with reference to case law and custom, that the abolition was legally effective immediately upon British conquest, and was neither affected by the Terms of Capitulation, nor dependent upon local proclamation, subverting historical canon. The slave trade's immediate illegality, and known as such to the governor, is important, for it marks the first of many divergences between metropolitan policy and local government, highlighting the precedence given to the needs of the French oligarchy, a theme followed by successive British administrators.

However, the ban proved largely ineffective in practice, with slave traffic continuing clandestinely in and around Mauritius. As outlined in Chapter 3, the persistence of the slave trade was the result of the combination of a number of factors. Firstly, there existed an undeniable need for workers, to enable and maintain colonization of the island. Secondly, the geographic location of Mauritius, southeast of Madagascar, allowed the African slave trade to continue with relative ease due to close proximity to the markets. Additionally, the southern part of the Indian Ocean (unlike the northern part) was dominated by the French, and with the slave trade remaining legal for several more years on the neighbouring French-occupied island of Réunion, perhaps inevitably, the French inhabitants of Mauritius, who had remained the ruling class, were unwilling to adapt to the ban imposed by the British. The prohibition of the trade, once proclaimed on the island, had the effect of merely rendering the traffic surreptitious instead of preventing it. As a consequence, the number of slaves in Mauritius increased without official oversight, and the clandestine nature of their import can only be viewed as rendering the situation of the trafficked persons as more precarious. It could be argued that this situation is one that Farquhar was seeking to avoid by claiming the continued legality of the slave trade. Regulation may only be introduced where the conduct in question is legal; abolition removed the possibility of a controlled trade. Farquhar's general failure to ameliorate slave conditions, however, does not suggest that managed slave traffic, at least in the sense that it could have served to protect slaves, was a genuine concern to the governor.

On the wider issue of slave welfare and the ostensible purpose of the Act banning the trade as an ameliorative measure, Chapter 3 in first instance questions the humanitarian objective behind the prohibition. Not only did the abolition in practice serve to expand the investigative powers of the British navy, the enforcement of the slave-trade ban introduced the new concept of "Prize slaves". After being "liberated" from an illegal ship-trading vessel, slaves were not set free, but became subject to a labour system akin to slavery, and were thus essentially

2 See Mathur, Hansraj, *Parliament in Mauritius* (Rose-Hill, Mauritius: Editions de l'Ocean Indien, 1991), who unequivocally states the law became applicable in Mauritius in 1813, note 6, p. 24.

"recaptured", though instead of belonging to an individual owner, they were considered as property of the Crown.

The abolition of the trade in slaves was thus a complex issue, itself not adopted by the metropolis for purely compassionate reasons. In this research, the Act banning the slave trade is conceived primarily as an instrument which was designed to increase imperial power, an interpretation supported by the work of scholars such as Lauren Benton. However, it is further argued here, that in the case of Mauritius, the Act had the effect of weakening local British authority vis-à-vis the French ruling class, for not only did the trade continue unabatedly, in a failure to seize the opportunity to assert British supremacy locally, judicial enforcement of the ban was frequently transferred to London by the colonial government.

As recounted in Chapter 4, the eventual announcement of the abolition of slavery itself was received badly in Mauritius. In the preceding decade, amelioration policies as directed from Britain had not resulted in noticeable improvements in the conditions of slavery. With the planters' focus firmly on the cultivation of sugar cane, much of the island's wealth and investment had become dependent on the availability of coercible, inexpensive labour, and the local British administration loathed to interfere. This development caused much the concern of the Colonial Office, with Viscount Goderich coming to express regret at the 1825 equalization of sugar tariffs, which he felt had operated to the profound disadvantage of the slave population.

Thus, ironically, the most decisive measure which influenced labour migration in Mauritius was not any major imperial statute, nor a regulation directly related to labour issues as such. Instead, it was the decision to allow Mauritius to export sugar to the British market at the same rate as the West Indies. The tariff parity provided further impetus to ignore the prohibition on the slave trade. Planters on the island achieved the utterly unexpected by drastically increasing the capacity of Mauritius to cultivate sugar. Another unintended consequence of metropolitan policy, equalization had the effect of rendering sugar cane the main crop and steered Mauritius towards a monoculture. In pursuance of profits, other crops were ignored, as were any measures designed to improve the conditions of slavery. The events in Mauritius subvert the traditional markers for the existence of slavery in societies as articulated by Nieboer, for despite limited resources and the sole motivating factor being an external one (tariff parity), the importance of slave-keeping and retention increased, more than a decade after the proclaimed abolition of the slave trade.

The Abolition of Slavery Act 1833 came into force in Mauritius in 1835, and the apprenticeship system, which delayed the actual emancipation of slaves by several years, gave the planters the possibility of experimenting with the introduction of indentured labour from India, discussed in Chapter 5. Quoting the Nigerian historian J. F. Ade Ajayi, who raises the issue of "initiative" in the colonial relationship,[3] Jürgen Osterhammel stresses that the colonial situation was

3 Ajayi, Jacob Festus Ade, 'Colonialism: An Episode in African History', in *Colonialism in Africa 1870–1960*, ed. by Lewis H. Gann and Peter Duigan (Cambridge: Cambridge University Press, 1969), p. 505, as quoted in Osterhammel, op. cit., p. 27.

not a simple dichotomy of oppressor and oppressed, where the powerful western powers acted and the natives merely reacted, but rather should be understood in terms of a continuous striving of all involved for "opportunities to act".[4] For Mauritian slaves, the chance to act (or rather, to act through omission) arrived when abolition was effected and they refused to be employed on the same plantations where they had previously toiled. Full emancipation witnessed a near complete withdrawal of former slaves from plantation labour.

Mauritian historian Vijaya Teelock argues that the experience of plantation slavery left a strong desire for independence and freedom with the former slaves.[5] Her suggestion is supported by an analysis of the aftermath of abolition in the Indian Ocean by Martin Klein.[6] Klein concludes that while the slave trade initially persisted in Mauritius and its neighbouring islands due to the needs of the sugar economy, the disappearance of slavery was more complete because "the forms of slavery found there were more onerous".[7] This is in contrast to other geographical areas where certain types of slavery could frequently afford protection and security. According to Klein: "Wherever plantation slavery existed, former slaves resisted not only disguised forms of slavery, but the plantation system itself."[8] This work agrees with this assessment, but expands this view by observing that the retreat of former slaves cannot be understood as merely a unilateral decision on their part. The planters were only too willing to exchange their black workforce for an Asian one. Instead of offering better conditions and acceptable wages, they increased the number of Indian labourers and attempted to control labour costs by maximizing supply. Rendering planters independent of their former slaves, the process, if not solely responsible, must be regarded as significantly contributory to the marginalization of the black population.

Chapter 5 argues that the first phase of indenture, which in Mauritius occurred at the same time as the apprenticeship period, can therefore also be seen as the time when racial rivalries were first introduced and exploited. Consequentially, the most profound effect of the abolition of slavery in Mauritius was not the emancipation of slaves as such, but the impetus it gave to alter the composition of the island's inhabitants by the introduction of a new type of worker.

As Mauritius was ascending in its role as an important sugar producer at a time when other colonies went into decline, economic interests converged with political considerations and found expression in laws which over the years proved increasingly coercive on the nominally free labourers from India. While indentured labourers were not "chattels" in the sense of being slaves, the research

4 Osterhammel, ibid.

5 Teelock, Vijaya, 'The Influence of Slavery in the Formation of Creole Identity', *Comparative Studies of South Asia, Africa and the Middle East*, 19 (1999), 3–8.

6 Klein, Martin A., 'The Emancipation of Slaves in the Indian Ocean', in *Abolition and its aftermath in Indian Ocean Africa and Asia*, ed. by Gwyn Campbell (Milton Park: Routledge, 2005), pp. 198–218.

7 Ibid., p. 213

8 Ibid.

presented in Chapter 5 demonstrates that they were by no means "free" workers. The evident deceit and coercion present in the recruitment process amounted to exploitation of the most vulnerable segments of Indian society, sought out primarily for their physical constitution and attitude. Whilst the end of slavery was externally motivated, through the passage of imperial law, the transition from slavery to indentured labour was effected predominantly through planter preference. The local planters had some familiarity with Indian workers, and sought them out in greater numbers after the Act abolishing slavery was passed. Notably, African indenture was not pursued in Mauritius, due to its resemblance to the practice of slavery, and after experiments with Chinese indentured labour (during a suspension period) proved unsatisfactory, India became established as the preferred labour pool.

In preparing Indian workers for plantation conditions, social and cultural norms were purposefully broken, and qualities sought in the prospective labourer, such as adaptability and docility, were created by eliminating other aspects of his or her identity, for instance caste or family status. Reports of severe shortcomings in the recruitment process in the form of kidnap, unlawful imprisonment, deception and misrepresentation lead to the suspension of Indian labour migration. Greater state involvement was being called for, as a way to prevent future abuses.

Chapter 6, which examines the period of government-sponsored indenture, shows however state involvement did not prevent abuses, but rather allowed for new types to emerge. An analysis of the relevant legislation shows that immigration and labour regulation worked together to limit both mobility and employment options of the workers in Mauritius, creating conditions that tied them to sugar plantation work and operated to extend their contracts or disincentivize their return to India. With the introduction of a legal distinction between "Old Immigrants" and "New Immigrants", vagrancy laws were applied to compel even those who had already completed their contracts back into work on the sugar estates. The penal framework in particular was noteworthy for creating a public law relationship between employer and employees instead of a private law relationship based on the labour contract. Enforcement of contracts was skewed in favour of employers, as non-execution on their part (such as nonpayment of wages) was treated leniently, whereas breach of contract on part of the labourers resulted in criminal penalization. A high level of bureaucracy was employed to not only control the labour options available to the workers, but also their mobility generally, with heavy penalties (such as a double loss of wages in case of imprisonment) as well as prolongation of their contract in instances of contravention. As the number of indentured labourers increased to become the largest ethnic group on the island, the situation was severe, reflected in the high suicide rates among the Indian population at the time.

When worldwide demand for tropical sugar waned towards the end of the 19th century, so did the demand for workers to occupy the plantations of the colonies. Management of the sugar industry transformed, giving birth to a new Indian peasantry where land ownership and marriage laws encouraged labourers to settle, which is in marked contrast to the policy at the very beginning of indenture, when the main consideration was to ensure the workers' return after contract completion. Towards the end of the 19th century, Mauritius found itself with a large Indian population on an upward trajectory, an ever-more-marginalized group of slave descendants, and a white minority struggling, yet firmly keeping hold of its influential position as the ruling class.

Two general conclusions may be drawn from this account. In the first place, and as it has been suggested in this work, the composition of early Mauritian society was fundamentally influenced, and effectively constituted, by reference to economic concerns, validating Karl Polanyi's argument which regards society as indivisible from its economic system. Recalling Duncan Kennedy's conceptualization of the distributive effect of the law, it has been demonstrated that the law influenced the distribution not only of rights and privileges, but also incentives and inducements, often with unforeseen effect. During the first few decades of the 19th century, the slave trade was regarded as essential to the very existence of colonial society in Mauritius, and thus was perpetuated by the French ruling class even after British conquest and the prohibition of the traffic this entailed. When Mauritian sugar was admitted at preferential rates to the British market 1825, the economic stimulus not only provided further reason to ignore the ban, but the creation of a monoculture that followed acted to the fundamental disadvantage of the slave population, with imperial ameliorative policies remaining largely without effect. The legal abolition of slavery a decade later merely closed one pool of labour, for in the continued endeavour of pursuing a profit-extracting strategy, the sugar interest in Mauritius simply sought out another pool. The size of the Indian population and the marginalization of former slaves and their descendants has its roots in the labour policy pursued during the mid-19th century.

In the second place, it may be observed that the autonomous, yet constitutive quality of law is to be understood not merely by reference to how effective legal interventions of one kind or another were, but also by reference to their unanticipated consequences. The abolition of the slave trade, which as has been argued was not an entirely humanitarian measure in itself, led in Mauritius to an exceedingly detrimental position by simply rendering the trade secret, resulting in very high numbers of unregistered slaves, the number of which scholars are able to only estimate. The abolition of slavery itself did effect the legal emancipation of slaves, but also gave impetus to the introduction of another type of worker which contributed significantly to the ostracism of former slaves and their descendants, thus effectively proving detrimental to social emancipation. The structures designed for the introduction of free contract workers led to an extraordinarily coercive system, which with greater government involvement became not less so, but even more restricting for workers. As regards the classification of labour, or rather "labour power" as per Marx, as a commodity, the research at hand has demonstrated that commodification is not dependent on legal status of the worker. In Mauritius, the indentured labourer was as much a commodity as the slave as a result of the seemingly inexhaustible pool of potential workers in close proximity to the island by virtue of its geographical position. The attitude towards the labouring population, whether as evidenced through the failed amelioration policies during slavery or lack of care in investigating suicides on estates during indenture, demonstrates that workers, during either epoch, were considered expendable. This was despite the ban on slave trading during the former era, and irrespective of the recruitment costs of Indian labourers during the second.

7.2 Contemporary relevance of Mauritian colonial research

It has been observed that laws, particularly those relating to labour, have enormous influence both economically and socially. During the period of slavery, the question of labour was subsumed in the context of property, specifically ownership in the slave and his labour, whereas the epoch of indenture saw the enactment of a system of abstract labour, whereby the work produced by the immigrant was commoditized. The effect of these systems has been enduring. Two sets of observations regarding colonial legacies arise from this research, one related to Mauritius specifically and the other to the modern relevance of such inquiry more generally. The latter has been published and discussed elsewhere,[9] with the focus here on the Mauritian context.

7.2.1 Legacies of slavery and indentured labour in Mauritius

Colonial legacies remain visible in Mauritius, as discussed in Chapter 1. Discrimination and persistent disadvantage suffered by certain parts of society are observable, if not always quantifiably so. The year 2009 saw the establishment of a Truth and Justice Commission ("TJC") in Mauritius. Notably, under the relevant Act, the commission had as its mandate "to make an assessment of the consequences of slavery and indentured labour during the colonial period up to the present" by conducting the necessary inquiries, and further, to "determine appropriate reparative measures to be extended to descendants of slaves and indentured labourers".[10] The resulting report was submitted by the TJC in November 2011.

The historical research undertaken and collated renders the report a valuable contribution and resource for the study of the history of Mauritius. It examines the context of the slave trade and traces in detail the origins of the labourers from India. In particular, the report is to be commended for highlighting certain less-well-known aspects of Mauritian history. For example, the arrival of a small number of French contract workers and orphaned children to support French

9 Boodia-Canoo, Nandini S, 'Researching Colonialism and Colonial Legacies from a Legal Perspective', *The Law Teacher*, 54 (2020), 517–546.

10 *Report of the Truth and Justice Commission* (Mauritius, November 2011), Volume I (main submissions), p. 1 <www.usip.org/sites/default/files/ROL/TJC_Vol1.pdf> [accessed 3 June 2015].

colonization in the early 18th century is a noteworthy finding, demonstrating that labour migration to the island was more varied than is commonly assumed.[11] In the same vein, the report pays necessary attention to the historical role of the *gens de couleur*, the free people of colour, who, while not directly part of either imported labour system, present a relevant part of Mauritian society which, highly diverse within itself, has suffered its own share of discrimination as a group.[12]

The work of the TJC has the potential to dismantle the pervasive conceptions as outlined in the introductory chapter of this work, by showing that the island's history is more complex and the origin and composition of each social stratum more intricate than most Mauritians believe. Unfortunately, this important aspect of their findings is obscured by the conclusions reached on the contemporary situation involving the descendants of slaves and indentured labourers.

In its chapter on the continuities and consequences of slavery and indenture,[13] the TJC draws a highly contentious link between the slavery period and the later family setting of slave descendants. Claiming that "slavery has affected the family institution the most", the report outlines the slave-holder practice of "selective breeding", which it states "deprived [some slaves] of the right to develop monogamous family relationships." Arguing that "psychologically, selective breeding influenced slaves to believe that family relationships were of little value", the TJC contends that "the destruction of the role of the father during slavery would have a major impact decades and centuries later". A primary consequence is identified in the existence of "single-parent households" as well as "the isolation of the males".[14] There are several issues in this claim made by the TJC. First, it raises the issue of selective breeding as a slave-holder practice without reference or documentation. Therefore the very existence of this practice, much less its prevalence, cannot be independently ascertained. It may be argued that by their nature, certain slave-holding practices are not verifiably documented, yet in that instance to make a broad claim as the TJC has done on the basis of unascertainable evidence renders their conclusion tenuous indeed. Second, and perhaps more seriously, the report effectively pathologizes the Afro-Malagasy Mauritian community. Whilst it does not clearly pronounce that the socioeconomic disadvantage suffered by descendants of slaves is directly the result of a lack of family cohesion inherited from the slavery period, it gets very close to suggesting as much.

Addressing the situation of the descendants of indentured labourers in the same chapter, the TJC makes the important observation that not all of these "succeeded" in the conventional sense: not all acquired land, not all became urbanized, not all became educated. In this part, the report denounces the stereotypical depiction of the progress made by labourers, claiming that it is one

11 TJC Report, Volume I, p. 147.
12 Ibid., pp. 243–250.
13 Chapter Four, Volume I, of the TJC Report.
14 TJC Report, Volume I, p. 227.

"regularly reproduced by those of non-indentured ancestry."[15] Yet this depiction is one which the TJC in another part of its report actually endorsed, as noted in Chapter 1 of this study.[16] The remainder of the section in the report depicts the living conditions of workers in the sugar industry subsequent to the end of indenture, to support the underlying argument that the Indian labour transition was not an easy one.

In summary, the TJC's findings can be regarded as largely stating what had been generally "known" to anyone familiar with the societal composition of the island. Certainly, as a result of the numerous interviews undertaken, these observations are now substantiated with a volume of oral testimonies on record, and no longer rely on the reiteration of anecdotes, but otherwise they do not reveal a very great deal. Indeed, one is tempted to say that the TJC found what it was looking for and no more. In the process, however, the TJC missed an important opportunity to fully evaluate the connections between the 19th and the 21st century, and in the process of doing so, resorted to the articulation of simplified links which were responsible for the creation of harmful stereotypes in the first place.

Writing in an newspaper article in 2015, a former commissioner of the TJC expressed his disappointment at the lack of governmental action in the aftermath of the publication of the report with its approximately 300 recommendations, describing the setup of various ineffective committees as "an eyewash", meaning a process of mere lip service with no substance.[17] Co-chairperson of TJC and local historian Vijaya Teelock provided her own assessment in a conference paper published in 2014.[18] In it, she outlines the many practical difficulties and hurdles the establishment of a truth commission engenders, ranging from funding, to staff recruitment, to internal disagreements. Importantly, Teelock notes that "in the process of [the commission's] creation, there was little real discussion of *how* one was to investigate a system that existed 200 years ago, with no surviving victims or perpetrators."[19] As observed above, the absence of a defined epistemology is certainly noticeable in the TJC's report. Nevertheless, as Teelock states: "It was clear that the focus was not to be those who endured slavery at first hand, but rather on their living descendants and those consequences of the slave trade that are believed to have an enduring impact on life in Mauritius today."[20] The problem with that approach apparently became evident at an internal workshop

15 Ibid., p. 229.
16 See the TJC Report's Executive Summary, discussed at 1.3.3.
17 Veerapen, Parmaseeven Pillay, 'Labour and the Truth and Justice Commission', *Le Mauricien*, 2 May 2015 <www.lemauricien.com/article/labour-and-truth-and-justice-commission> [accessed 26 June 2022].
18 Teelock, Vijayalakshmi, 'The Mauritius Truth and Justice Commission: "Eyewash", "Storm in a Teacup" or Promise of a New Future for Mauritius?', in *Emancipation and the Remaking of the British Imperial World* (Manchester: Manchester University Press, 2014), pp. 207–222.
19 Ibid., p. 209. (Emphasis in original)
20 Ibid.

held to answer the question "Who is a descendant?", with Teelock noting the somewhat acrimonious exchanges which ensued.[21] As discussed previously, the question is a complex one in the Mauritian context, and in the absence of clear statistical data (which is difficult to obtain given that former slaves were counted as "General Population" alongside white inhabitants from the mid-19th century onwards, as explained in Chapter 2), the issue invariably engenders a discussion of discrimination and stereotypes. Teelock observes that the issue of racism is highly fraught, and in Mauritius commonly boils down to two aspects: phenotype and name.[22]

This, it is submitted, is quite possibly the main difficulty which arises in the context of Mauritian history and which has filtered into popular Mauritian consciousness: the idea that there are separate descendants of any group. As described in Chapter 1, the TJC itself notes the widespread *métissage* which took place in the 19th century, rendering ideas of racial purity within Mauritian society obsolete. Yet if that is the case, should not all Mauritians be considered descendants of a single colonial past? An unfortunate heritage from the colonial period, and quite possibly a significant block the establishment of a unified Mauritian consciousness, appears to exist in form of a sense of distrust and competition among the different segments of society. However this state cannot be alleviated by tackling Mauritian history in the way it has been dealt with hitherto.

Vijaya Teelock commends the TJC for being the first commission to cover not only the legacies of slavery, but also those of indenture.[23] Nevertheless, she notes that "the inclusion of indenture in the original mandate reflects the official tendency to 'balance' different ethno-cultural forces in Mauritius and avoid the criticism of favouritism towards any particular group", stating that whether locally or internationally, the desire for "truth" or reparation in the context of indenture is much lower than with slavery.[24] Herein, it is submitted, lies a major fallacy. If regard is paid to the indenture experience merely as an exercise to provide a "balanced" view of history by giving equal attention to each epoch and to appease calls of favouritism, the idea of separate histories becomes actually entrenched. This approach may appear inclusive, but actually obscures the fact that the colonial experience was a common, shared one.

In researching the 19th-century history of Mauritius, it became evident to the author of this study that the experience of indentured labour could not be truly appreciated without reference to slavery. Similarly, the aftermath of slavery could not be properly evaluated without reference to indentured labour. As has been demonstrated throughout the chapters, in the Mauritian context, these two labour systems influenced each other in important ways. A failure to fully

21 Ibid., p. 213.
22 Ibid., p. 218.
23 Ibid., p. 209.
24 Ibid.

appreciate their interconnectedness is a significant shortcoming in the TJC's report, even more lamentable since its mandate covered an investigation of both.

It is submitted that any examination Mauritian history needs to follow an approach which examines how the existence of one part of society is affecting another at any given time, instead of seeking to find causes within one system singularly. The research at hand has shown that the arrival of Indian indentured labour in large numbers worked to the detriment of the ex-apprentices. Laws at the end of the 19th century, when the indentured labour period was drawing to a close, clearly favoured the establishment of a free and settled population, a boon which was not granted to slaves in 1835 post-emancipation, nor from 1839 onwards when apprenticeships had ended. This is because slavery had ended, yet bondage had not. Bondage continued to exist, because a colonial system based on exploitation continued to exist. Therefore complete emancipation in the sense of free and full participation in society by ex-apprentices was discouraged. As long as indentured labourers were subject to a coercive regime, former slaves could never achieve full freedom.

By the time the situation of Indian labourers had improved, the situation of slave descendants had deteriorated. Their numbers had dwindled and their participation in the mainstream economy was small. The report notes that land-possession existed among the group, but was subsequently lost, in a process that the TJC was unable to clearly identify and ascribes to illiteracy and the "greed of neighbouring estates", as well as expansion of the sugar industry.[25] A clearer image emerges upon perusal of Volume II of the report, which addresses the issue of land dispossession.

It is clear from the report as well as Teelock's paper that the "blame" for dispossession suffered is put squarely at the door of the law,[26] in a theme which emerges to be highly critical of the legal system overall. In first instance, the concept of "prescription", derived from the French Civil Code as a way to obtain rights over land, has been criticized.[27] Teelock simplifies the issue thus: "Prescription is a method of acquiring rights over property by occupying a portion of land for a fixed period of time. The rationale is to 'punish' those who abandon their land."[28] The latter statement is not an entirely accurate observation. In fact, the French legal concept of prescription as described appears much in line with the English legal concept of adverse possession (and not to be confused with the English version of prescription, which is a method to obtain easements, meaning rights over land, but not to land itself). The rationale for the concept of adverse possession is not "punishment", but rather, an incentive not to leave land (representing a valuable resource) unused. Certainly, nothing prevented the land being acquired by the wealthy on the pretext that it was not being used. The lack of safeguards against abuse however does not

25 TJC Report, Volume I, pp. 221–222.
26 TJC Report, Volume II, Chapter 1 <www.researchgate.net/publication/278512677_Truth_and_Justice_Commission_Report_Vol_2_Land_Issues> [accessed 26 June 2022].
27 Teelock, op. cit., p. 215.
28 Ibid.

mean the law was designed to be punitive against a particular section of society at a specific point in time; indeed, as indicated, the concept, for all its shortcomings, has existed for a long time across legal traditions and locations.

The assault on the law extends further, as Teelock claims: "the legal system and those who work within it are still perceived as an elite group that turns a blind eye to the injustices perpetrated in the name of the law." It is evidently a perception she shares, for she concludes: "To put it simply, the law recognised slavery and the law thus contributed to the harm done to slaves."[29] Teelock is thus venting her frustration against "the bad lawyers with their bad laws". Yet is the solution "better lawyers and better laws"? Abolition, whether of the trade in slaves or slavery itself, could be deemed "good law". But as has been seen, both bans simply incentivized a behaviour of avoidance: the trade continued and later, slavery was replaced with indenture. Most strikingly, the sugar tariff equalization of 1825, a measure which could be considered benevolent or at the very least neutral, had harsh consequences for the slave population, as discussed in Chapter 4. What this work has sought to highlight is the way in which law is imbricated in political and economic calculation – and in the way in which it incentivizes and disincentivizes and produces differentially articulated outcomes such that even an ostensibly "good law" might have profoundly negative effects on a certain segment of the population.

The role of the law, its utility and potential, may capture the attention of non-lawyers, but is easily misinterpreted. Teelock's observations were made with reference to a TJC contribution written by Joyce Fortune, who attempted to make an evaluation of the role of law during slavery from a historian's perspective.[30] Fortune raises the possibility of establishing slavery as a social tort in the Mauritian context,[31] an idea which Teelock believes merits further investigation.[32] Fortune's claim draws on Keith Hylton's work regarding slavery reparations in the United States, though it appears her understanding of his argument is somewhat confused: "Keith Hylton proposes . . . that the litigants in the reparations suits should instead concentrate on the Social Torts, that slavery involves a category of Social Torts which are according to him more harmful and to which the tort law appears to be an inadequate means of seeking damages."[33] In a footnote she observes:

> Note that using Tort Law alone as a means of redressing the injuries incurred during slavery in the reparations suits is insufficient for converting the abuses suffered into claims for damages. Tort doctrine involves "*concrete*" injuries

29 Ibid., p. 217.

30 Fortuné-Pope, Joyce, *Reparations – An Multidisciplinary Approach*, TJC Report Volume III, <www.researchgate.net/publication/278516321_Truth_and_Justice_Commission_report_Volume_3_Contemporary_History_Culture_and_Society_-_research_Reports_Technical_studies_and_Surveys> [accessed 26 June 2022]

31 Ibid., pp. 269–270, p. 281

32 Teelock, op. cit., p. 217.

33 Fortuné-Pope, op. cit., p. 281.

> verifiable by means of forensics, psychiatric and or medical examination, which are to be carried out during the time before the expiration of the statute of limitation to file a claim for compensatory damages. . . . However, in the case of slavery the perpetrators as well as the victims are long deceased and with them are buried all traces of malfeasance and under Federal Tort Law, there can be no crime because the defendants and the plaintiffs are no longer with us.[34]

Fortune thus expressly acknowledges both the inadequacy and the inapplicability of tort law in the context of Mauritian slavery. Why the idea is therefore presented as a viable avenue for redress in her main submissions and promoted as such by Teelock is not clear.

Taking up Hylton's proposal for claims against continually existing beneficiaries of slavery, such as corporations, Fortune notes that such entities may be difficult to identify in the United States, "but in Mauritius, the case is very different." She identifies the Mauritius Commercial Bank, and states that it "was founded in 1838 from compensatory funds obtained from the British Government as reparations for the loss of slaves after the abolition of slavery."[35] Unfortunately, this assertion is made without clear source attribution. As discovered in the course of research for this work, and noted in a footnote on the compensation process in Chapter 4, the Mauritius Commercial Bank was cofounded by Englishman James Blyth, who made significant profits from negotiating debentures (in which slavery compensation had been paid) in London on behalf of Mauritian slave-holders. The bank was created in direct competition to the French planter-controlled *Banque de Maurice*. Whether Blyth, as a handler of the debentures, may be considered a slavery beneficiary is a possible, though not inevitable, argument. In any instance, it is submitted that the Mauritius Commercial Bank does not have as straightforward a claim against it as Fortune maintains, not morally and much less legally.

With reference to the abolition of the slave trade, Fortune's paper fails to appreciate the wider context in which it took place. Thus she states: "Farquhar did not enforce the Slave Trade Abolition Act, which took effect in all British colonies in 1810 and nor was the Slave Trade Felony Act of 1813 ever enforced in Mauritius."[36] As discussed in detail in Chapter 3 of this work, while proclamation of the 1807 Act abolishing the trade was delayed until 1813 following the 1810 conquest, and local enforcement remained weak in subsequent years, it cannot be said that it was not "ever enforced". It will be recalled that the issue of enforcement of the ban was tightly interlinked with the establishment of British authority on the island, in a process which had to ensure not only a peaceful transfer of power from the former colonists, but

34 Ibid., Footnote 1, p. 289.
35 Ibid., p. 282.
36 Ibid.

also the viability of the colony, all while attending to the implementation of imperial policy.

An in-depth legal analysis of the issues around Mauritian slavery has evidently been hitherto missing. It should be noted that Teelock in her paper repeatedly laments the complete absence of legal historians in Mauritius. The criticism of the function of the law as presented by both Teelock and Fortune reveals an unfortunate lack of legal scholarship which would provide the local discourse with a clearer understanding of legal mechanisms and jurisprudence. This work endeavours to make a contribution in this respect, by bringing a nuanced account of the operations of law which reveals aspects of the history of slavery and its abolition that are not evident to those who think about law only in terms of being "good" or "bad", enforced or unenforced. It is hoped that the current research proves helpful to further multidisciplinary research on the history of Mauritius.

Bibliography

Books and Journal Articles

Abbott, Elizabeth, *Sugar: A Bittersweet History* (London; New York: Gerald Duckworth & Co Ltd, 2009)

Addison, J., and K. Hazareesingh, *A New History of Mauritius*, Revised Edition (Rose-Hill, Mauritius: Editions de l'Ocean Indien, 1989)

Adolphe, Harold, *Les Archives Démographique de L'ile Maurice: Registres Paroissiaux et D'état Civil (1721–1810)* (Mauritius: Mauritius Archives Publications, 1966)

Ahluwalia, Pal, 'Discourses of Discovery: Transculturations and Sugar Plantations in Africa', in *White and Deadly: Sugar and Colonialism*, ed. by Bill Ashcroft, Roger Knight, and Pal Ahluwalia (New York: Nova Science Publishers, 1999), pp. 51–64

Ahmad, Aijaz, *In Theory: Nations, Classes, Literatures* (London; New York: Verso, 2008)

Ajayi, Jacob Festus Ade, 'Colonialism: An Episode in African History', in *Colonialism in Africa 1870–1960*, ed. by Lewis H. Gann and Peter Duigan (Cambridge: Cambridge University Press, 1969)

Alcoff, Linda, 'The Problem of Speaking for Others', *Cultural Critique* (1991), 5–32

Allain, Jean, ed., *The Legal Understanding of Slavery: From the Historical to the Contemporary* (Oxford: Oxford University Press, 2012)

Allain, Jean, ed., 'The Nineteenth Century Law of the Sea and the British Abolition of the Slave Trade', *British Yearbook of International Law*, 78 (2008), 342–88

Allen, Richard B., *Creoles, Indian Immigrants and the Restructuring of Society and Economy in Mauritius, 1767–1885 (PhD Thesis)* (Chicago: University of Illinois, 1983)

Allen, Richard B., 'Indian Immigrants and the Beginning of the Grand Morcellement 1860–1885', in *Indians Overseas – The Mauritian Experience*, ed. by U. Bissoondoyal (Moka, Mauritius: Mahatma Gandhi Institute, 1984), p. 340

Allen, Richard B., 'Licentious and Unbridled Proceedings: The Illegal Slave Trade to Mauritius and the Seychelles during the Early Nineteenth Century', *Journal of African History*, 42 (2001), 91–116

Allen, Richard B., *Slaves, Freedmen and Indentured Laborers in Colonial Mauritius* (Cambridge: Cambridge University Press, 2006)

Allen, Richard B., 'The Mascarene Slave-Trade and Labour Migration in the Indian Ocean during the Eighteenth and Nineteenth Centuries', in *The Structure of Slavery in Indian Ocean Africa and Asia*, ed. by Gwyn Campbell, Studies in Slave and Post-Slave Societies and Cultures (London: Frank Cass, 2004)

Allott, Philip, *Eunomia: New Order for a New World* (Oxford: Oxford University Press, 1990)

Alpers, Edward A., Gwyn Campbell, and Michael Salman, eds., *Resisting Bondage in Indian Ocean Africa and Asia* (London: Routledge, 2007)

Anderson, Clare, 'Convicts and Coolies: Rethinking Indentured Labour in the Nineteenth Century', *Slavery & Abolition*, 30 (2009), 93–109

Anderson, Clare, *Convicts in the Indian Ocean: Transportation from South Asia to Mauritius, 1815–53* (Basingstoke: Macmillan, 1999)

Anderson, Clare, *Legible Bodies: Race, Criminality and Colonialism in South Asia* (Oxford: Berg, 2004)

Anderson, Clare, 'The Bel Ombre Rebellion: Indian Convicts in Mauritius, 1815–535', in *Abolition and Its Aftermath in Indian Ocean Africa and Asia*, ed. by Gwyn Campbell (Milton Park: Routledge, 2005), pp. 50–65

Anderson, Clare, *Subaltern Lives: Biographies of Colonialism in the Indian Ocean World, 1790–1920* (Cambridge University Press, 2012)

Angelo, A. H., 'Mauritius: The Basis of the Legal System', *The Comparative and International Law Journal of Southern Africa*, 3 (1970), 228–241

Angelo, Tony, 'Mauritius: Capitulation, Consolidation, Creation', in *A Study of Mixed Legal Systems: Endangered, Entrenched or Blended*, ed. by Sue Farran, Esin Örücü, and Seán Patrick Donlan (Farnham, Surrey; Burlington, VT: Ashgate, 2014), pp. 117–138

Anghie, Antony, Bhupinder Chimni, Karin Mickelson, and Obiora Okafor, eds., *The Third World and International Order: Law, Politics, and Globalization* (Developments in International Law, v. 45; Leiden: Kluwer Law International, 2003)

Anghie, Antony, 'Francisco De Vitoria and the Colonial Origins of International Law', *Social & Legal Studies*, 5 (1996), 321–336

Anghie, Antony, *Imperialism, Sovereignty, and the Making of International Law* (Cambridge Studies in International and Comparative Law, 37; Cambridge: Cambridge University Press, 2005)

Ashcroft, Bill, Gareth Griffiths, and Helen Tiffin, *Post-Colonial Studies: The Key Concepts* (Routledge Key Guides; London: Routledge, 2000)

Ashcroft, Bill, Roger Knight, and Pal Ahluwalia, eds., *White and Deadly: Sugar and Colonialism* (New York: Nova Science Publishers, 1999)

Ashiagbor, Diamond, Prabha Kotiswaran, and Amanda Perry-Kessaris, 'Introduction: Moving Towards an Economic Sociology of Law', *Journal of Law and Society*, 40 (2013), 1–6

Austen, H. C. M., *Sea Fights and Corsairs of the Indian Ocean: The Naval History of Mauritius from 1715 to 1810* (Port Louis; Mauritius: R. W. Brooks Government Printer, 1934)

Avins, Alfred, 'Involuntary Servitude in British Commonwealth Law', *International & Comparative Law Quarterly*, 16 (1967), 29–55

Bahadur, Gaiutra, *Coolie Woman: The Odyssey of Indenture* (Chicago: University of Chicago Press, 2014)

Baker, John, 'Reflections on "Doing" Legal History', in *Making Legal History Approaches and Methodologies*, ed. by Anthony Musson and Chantal Stebbings (Cambridge: Cambridge University Press, 2012)

Baker, Sherston Sir, *Halleck's International Law – Rules Regulating the Intercourse of States in Peace and War, Volume I*, 3rd Edition (London: Kegan Paul, Trench, Trübner & Co. Ltd, 1893)

Baker, Sherston Sir, *Halleck's International Law – Rules Regulating the Intercourse of States in Peace and War, Volume II*, 3rd Edition (London: Kegan Paul, Trench, Trübner & Co. Ltd, 1893)

Banner, Stuart, 'Legal History and Legal Scholarship', *Washington University Law Review*, 76 (1998), 37–44

Banton, Mandy, *Colonial Office Supervision of the Introduction and Revision of Labour Legislation in British Africa: With Special Reference to the Use of Penal Sanctions in Master and Servant Ordinances (PhD Thesis)* (London: SOAS University of London, 1993)

Banton, Mandy, 'The "Taint of Slavery"', in *Slavery, Diplomacy and Empire: Britain and the Suppression of the Slave Trade, 1807–1975*, ed. by Keith Hamilton and Patrick Salmon, Reprint Edition (Brighton: Sussex Academic Press, 2009), pp. 143–164

Barker, A. J., *Slavery and Antislavery in Mauritius, 1810–33: The Conflict between Economic Expansion and Humanitarian Reform under British Rule* (Basingstoke: Macmillan, 1996)

Bauman, Whitney, *Theology, Creation, and Environmental Ethics: From Creatio Ex Nihilo to Terra Nullius*, 1st Edition (New York: Routledge, 2009)

Baumgart, Winfried, *Imperialism: The Idea and Reality of British and French Colonial Expansion, 1880–1914*, Revised Edition (Oxford: Oxford University Press, 1982)

Beachey, R. W., *British West Indies Sugar Industry in Late 19th Century* (Oxford: Basil Blackwell, 1957)

Beaton, Patrick, *Creoles & Coolies – Five Years in Mauritius* (London: James Nisbet and Co., 1859)

Benton, Lauren, 'Abolition and Imperial Law, 1790–1820', *The Journal of Imperial and Commonwealth History*, 39 (2011), 355–374

Benton, Lauren, 'Colonial Law and Cultural Difference: Jurisdictional Politics and the Formation of the Colonial State', *Comparative Studies in Society and History*, 41 (1999), 563–588

Benton, Lauren, 'Historical Perspectives on Legal Pluralism', in *Legal Pluralism and Development: Scholars and Practitioners in Dialogue*, ed. by Brian Z. Tamanaha, Caroline Sage, and Michael Woolcock (Cambridge: Cambridge University Press, 2013)

Benton, Lauren, *Law and Colonial Cultures: Legal Regimes in World History, 1400–1900* (Cambridge; New York, NY: Cambridge University Press, 2001)

Benton, Lauren, and Richard J. Ross, 'Empires and Legal Pluralism: Jurisdiction, Sovereignty and Political Imagination in the Early Modern World', in *Legal Pluralism and Empires, 1500–1850*, ed. by Lauren Benton and Richard J. Ross (New York, NY; London: New York University Press, 2013)

Benton, Lauren, and Richard J. Ross., eds., *Legal Pluralism and Empires, 1500–1850* (New York, NY; London: New York University Press, 2013)

Bethencourt, Francisco, and Diogo Ramada Curto, eds., *Portuguese Oceanic Expansion, 1400–1800*, 1st Publ. (Cambridge; New York: Cambridge University Press, 2007)

Birla, Ritu, 'Maine (and Weber) against the Grain: Towards a Postcolonial Genealogy of the Corporate Person', *Journal of Law and Society*, 40 (2013), 92–114

Bissoondoyal, U., ed., *Indians Overseas – The Mauritian Experience* (Moka; Mauritius: Mahatma Gandhi Institute, 1984)

Bix, Brian, *Jurisprudence: Theory and Context*, 6th Edition (London: Sweet & Maxwell, 2012)

Black, Professor Jeremy, ed., *The Atlantic Slave Trade*, I–IV vols (Aldershot: Ashgate Publishing, 2006)

Blackburn, Robin, *The Overthrow of Colonial Slavery, 1776–1848* (London: Verso, 1988)

Blaut, James M., *The Colonizer's Model of the World: Geographical Diffusionism and Eurocentric History* (New York; London: Guilford Press, 1993)

Bogdan, Michael, *The Law of Mauritius and Seychelles: A Study of Two Small Mixed Legal Systems* (Skrifter Utgivna Av Juridiska Föreningen I Lund = Acta Societatis Juridicae Lundensis, nr. 106; Lund: Juristiförlaget, 1989)

Bolker, Joan, *Writing Your Dissertation in Fifteen Minutes a Day: A Guide to Starting, Revising, and Finishing Your Doctoral Thesis* (New York: H. Holt, 1998)

Boodia-Canoo, Nandini S, 'Researching Colonialism and Colonial Legacies from a Legal Perspective', *The Law Teacher*, 54 (2020), 517–546

Boomgaard, Peter, 'Human Capital, Slavery and Low Rates of Economic and Population Growth in Indonesia, 1600–1910', in *The Structure of Slavery in Indian Ocean Africa and Asia*, ed. by Gwyn Campbell (Studies in Slave and Post-Slave Societies and Cultures; London: Frank Cass, 2004), pp. 83–96

Bourdieu, Pierre, *Distinction: A Social Critique of the Judgement of Taste* (New York, NY: Routledge, 2010)

Boxer, C. R., *The Dutch Seaborne Empire, 1600–1800* (History of Human Society Series; London: Hutchinson, 1965)

Boxer, C. R., *The Portuguese Seaborne Empire, 1415–1825* (The History of Human Society; London: Hutchinson, 1969)

Boyce, David George, *Decolonisation and the British Empire, 1775–1997* (Basingstoke: Macmillan, 1999)

Brass, Tom, and Marcel van der Linden, eds., *Free and Unfree Labour: The Debate Continues*, International and Comparative Social History (Bern; New York: Peter Lang, 1997), p. 5

Bull, Hedley, 'Foreword', in *The Standard of 'Civilization' in International Society*, ed. by Gerrit W. Gong (Oxford: Clarendon, 1984)

Burnard, Trevor, 'The Planter Class', in *The Routledge History of Slavery*, ed. by Gad Heuman and Trevor Burnard (London: Routledge, 2012), pp. 187–203

Burroughs, Peter, 'The Mauritius Rebellion of 1832 and the Abolition of British Colonial Slavery', *The Journal of Imperial and Commonwealth History*, 4 (1976), 243–265

Burton, Antoinette M., *Empire in Question: Reading, Writing, and Teaching British Imperialism* (Durham, NC: Duke University Press, 2011)

Campbell, Gwyn, ed., *Abolition and Its Aftermath in Indian Ocean Africa and Asia* (Milton Park: Routledge, 2005)

Campbell, Gwyn, ed., 'Introduction: Abolition and its Aftermath in the Indian Ocean World', in *Abolition and Its Aftermath in Indian Ocean Africa and Asia*, ed. by Gwyn Campbell (Milton Park: Routledge, 2005), pp. 1–28

Campbell, Gwyn, ed., 'Introduction: Slavery and Other Forms of Unfree Labour in the Indian Ocean World', in *The Structure of Slavery in Indian Ocean Africa and Asia*, ed. by Gwyn Campbell, Studies in Slave and Post-Slave Societies and Cultures (London: Frank Cass, 2004)

Campbell, Gwyn, ed., 'Servitude and the Changing Face of the Demand for Labor in the Indian Ocean World, c. 1800–1900', in *Indian Ocean Slavery in the Age of Abolition*, ed. by Robert W. Harms, Bernard K. Freamon, and David W. Blight (New Haven, CT: Yale University Press, 2013)

Campbell, Gwyn, ed., *The Structure of Slavery in Indian Ocean Africa and Asia*, Studies in Slave and Post-Slave Societies and Cultures (London: Frank Cass, 2004)
Campbell, Gwyn, and Alessandro Stanziani, eds., *Bonded Labour and Debt in the Indian Ocean World*, Financial History (London: Pickering & Chatto, 2013)
Carter, M., V. Govinden, and S. Peerthum, *The Last Slaves: Liberated Africans in 19th Century Mauritius* (Mauritius: CRIOS, Centre for Research on Indian Ocean Societies, 2003)
Carter, Marina, ed., *Across the Kalapani: The Bihari Presence in Mauritius* (Port Louis: CRIOS, Centre for Research on Indian Ocean Societies, 2000)
Carter, Marina, ed., *Lakshmi's Legacy: Testimonies of Indian Women in 19th Century Mauritius* (Stanley; Rose-Hill; Mauritius: Editions de l'Ocean Indien, 1994)
Carter, Marina, ed., *Servants, Sirdars and Settlers : Indians in Mauritius, 1834–1874* (Oxford: Oxford University Press, 1995)
Carter, Marina, ed., 'The Transition from Apprenticeship to Indentured Labour in Mauritius', in *The Wages of Slavery: From Chattel Slavery to Wage Labour in Africa, the Caribbean and England*, ed. by Michael Twaddle (London: Frank Cass, 1993), pp. 114–30
Carter, Marina, ed., *Voices from Indenture: Experiences of Indian Migrants in the British Empire* (London: Leicester University Press, 1996)
Carter, Marina, and James Ng Foong Kwong, *Forging the Rainbow* (Mauritius: Self-published, 1997)
Carter, Marina, and Khal Torabully, *Coolitude: An Anthology of the Indian Labour Diaspora* (London: Anthem Press, 2002)
Carter, Marina, and Raymond D'Unienville, *Unshackling Slaves: Liberation and Adaptation of Ex-Apprentices* (London: Pink Pigeon Books, 2001)
Carter, Marina, M. S. Hall, V. Govinden, R. Ramasawmy, and E. Richon, *Kaleidoscopic Conquest, Mauritius – 1810* (London: CRIOS, Centre for Research on Indian Ocean Societies, 2010)
Cell, John W., *British Colonial Administration in the Mid-Nineteenth Century: The Policy-Making Process* (New Haven, CT; London: Yale University Press, 1970)
Césaire, Aimé, *Discourse on Colonialism*, trans. by Joan Pinkham (New York: Monthly Review Press, 1972)
Chakrabarty, Dipesh, *Provincializing Europe: Postcolonial Thought and Historical Difference*, Princeton Studies in Culture/Power/History (Princeton, NJ; Oxford: Princeton University Press, 2000)
Chakravorty Spivak, Gayatri, 'Can the Subaltern Speak?', in *Colonial Discourse and Post-Colonial Theory: A Reader*, ed. by Patrick Williams and Laura Chrisman, 1st Edition (New York: Columbia University Press, 1994), pp. 66–111
Chan Low, Jocelyn, 'The Making of the Chagos Affair: Myths and Reality', in *Eviction from the Chagos Islands: Displacement and Struggle for Identity against Two World Powers*, ed. by Sandra Evers and Marry Kooy, African History, vol. 1 (Leiden ; Boston: Brill, 2011), pp. 61–79
Chatterjee, Partha, *The Partha Chatterjee Omnibus: Comprising Nationalist Thought and the Colonial World; The Nation and Its Fragments; A Possible India* (New Delhi; Oxford: Oxford University Press, 1999)
Chelin, Antoine, *Supplement to Une Ile et Son Passe: Ile Marice (1507–1947)* (Quatre-Bornes, Mauritius: Michel Robert & Cie, 1982)
Chelin, Antoine, *Une Ile et Son Passé* (Port Louis, Mauritius: Claude Marrier d'Unienville – The Mauritius Printing CY. Ltd, 1973)

Chenny, Shirley, Pascal St-Amour, and Désiré Vencatachellum, 'Slave Prices from Succession and Bankruptcy Sales in Mauritius, 1825–1827', *Explorations in Economic History*, 40 (2003), 419–442
Chimni, B. S., 'Third World Approaches to International Law: A Manifesto', in *The Third World and International Order: Law, Politics, and Globalization*, ed. by Antony Anghie and Others Developments in International Law, vol. 45 (Leiden: Kluwer Law International, 2003), pp. 47–73
Chitson, Dorish, 'Labour Laws in Mauritius during French Colonial Time', *Journal of Mauritian Studies*, 4 (2009), 70–88
Clarence-Smith, William Gervase, *The Economics of the Indian Ocean Slave Trade in the Nineteenth Century* (London: Frank Cass, 1989)
Cohen, Robin, ed., *African Islands and Enclaves*, Sage Series on African Modernization and Development, vol. 7 (Beverly Hills; London: Sage Publications, 1983)
Collingwood, R. G., *The Idea of History*, Revised Edition, with lectures 1926–1928 (Oxford; New York : Clarendon Press, 1994)
Cook, S. B., *Colonial Encounters in the Age of High Imperialism*, Longman World History Series (New York; Harlow: Longman, 1996)
Cooper, Frederick, *Beyond Slavery: Explorations of Race, Labor, and Citizenship in Postemancipation Societies* (Chapel Hill, NC: University of North Carolina Press, 2000)
Costello, Cathryn, 'Migrants and Forced Labour: A Labour Law Response', in *Autonomy of Labour Law*, ed. by Alan L. Bogg and others (Oxford: Portland, OR: Hart Publishing, 2015)
Cotterrell, Roger, 'Law in Social Theory and Social Theory in the Study of Law', in *Blackwell Companion to Law and Society*, ed. by Austin Sarat (Malden, MA: Blackwell Publishing, 2004)
Cotterrell, Roger, 'Rethinking "Embeddedness": Law, Economy, Community', *Journal of Law and Society*, 40 (2013), 49–67
Cotterrell, Roger, 'Why Must Legal Ideas Be Interpreted Sociologically?', *Journal of Law and Society*, 25 (1998), 171–192
Craven, Matthew, 'Between Law and History: The Berlin Conference of 1884–85 and the Logic of Free Trade', *London Review of International Law*, 3 (1) (2015), 31–59
Craven, Matthew C. R., M. Fitzmaurice, and Maria Vogiatzi, eds., *Time, History and International Law*, Developments in International Law, vol. 58 (Leiden ; Boston, MA: M. Nijhoff, 2007)
Craven, Paul, and Douglas Hay, 'The Criminalization of "Free" Labour: Master and Servant in Comparative Perspective', *Slavery & Abolition*, 15 (1994), 71–101
Crouzet, Guillemette, 'Chapter 16: "A Slave Trade Jurisdiction" – Attempts against the Slave Trade and the Making of a Space of Law (Arabo-Persian Gulf, Indian Ocean, Red Sea, circa 1820–1900)', in *Legal Histories of the British Empire: Laws, Engagements and Legacies*, ed. by Shaunnagh Dorsett and John McLaren (Abingdon; New York, NY: Routledge, 2014)
Cryer, Pat, *The Research Student's Guide to Success*, 2nd Edition (Buckingham: Open University Press, 2000)
Cryer, Robert, Tamara Hervey, Bal Sokhi-Bulley, and Alexandra Bohm, eds., *Research Methodologies in EU and International Law* (London: Hart Publishing, 2011)
Curtin, Philip, *The Atlantic Slave Trade – A Census* (Madison, WI: The University of Wisconsin Press, 1969)

Darwin, John, *Britain and Decolonisation: The Retreat from Empire in the Post-War World* (The Making of the 20th Century; Basingstoke: Macmillan Education, 1988)

Darwin, John, 'Decolonization and End of Empire', in *The Oxford History of the British Empire: Historiography*, ed. by Robin W. Winks and Alaine M. Low (Oxford, New York: Oxford University Press, 2001)

Darwin, John, *Unfinished Empire: The Global Expansion of Britain* (London: Penguin, 2013)

Daudet, Yves, 'L'enseignement Du Droit À Maurice', *Mauritius Law Review*, 1 (1988), 131–154

Davidov, Guy, and Brian Langille, eds., *The Idea of Labour Law* (Oxford; New York: Oxford University Presss, 2011)

Davies, A. C. L., *Perspectives on Labour Law*, 2nd Edition (Cambridge: Cambridge University Press, 2009)

Davies, Margaret, *Asking the Law Question* (North Ryde: London: Law Book Company; Sweet & Maxwell, 1994)

Davies, Margaret, *Asking the Law Question*, 3rd Edition (Pyrmont: Lawbook Co, 2008)

Day, Clive, *The Dutch in Java* (Oxford in Asia, Historical Reprints; New York: Oxford University Press, 1966)

de Jong, H. G., 'Coercion in the Conclusion of Treaties: A Consideration of Articles 51 and 52 of the Convention on the the Law of Treaties', *Netherlands Yearbook of International Law*, 15 (1984), 209–47

Dedijer, Vladimir, 'Legal Character of the Capitulation of Norwegian Armed Forces on June 10, 1940', *Nordic Journal of International Law*, 30 (1960), 39–51

Deerpalsingh, Saloni, and Marina Carter, *Select Documents on Indian Immigration: Mauritius, 1834–1926 – Living and Working Conditions under Indenture* (Moka, Mauritius: Mahatma Gandhi Institute, 1996), p. III

Deerpalsingh, Saloni, and Marina Carter, *Select Documents on Indian Immigration: Mauritius, 1834–1926 – The Despatch and Allocation of Indentured Labour* (Moka, Mauritius: Mahatma Gandhi Institute, 1996), p. II

Deerpalsingh, Saloni, J. Ng Foong Kwong, V. Govinden, and V. Teelock, *Labour Immigrants in Mauritius – A Pictoral Recollection* (Mauritius: Mahatma Gandhi Institute, 2001)

Deerr, Noel, *The History of Sugar*, 2 vols. (London: Chapman and Hall, 1949)

Delgado, Richard, 'Two Ways to Think about Race: Reflections on the Id, the Ego, and Other Reformist Theories of Equal Protection', *Georgetown Law Journal*, 89 (2001), 2279

Diffie, Bailey W., and George D. Winnius, *Foundations of the Portuguese Empire, 1415–1580*, Europe and the World in the Age of Expansion (Minneapolis, MN: University of Minnesota Press, 1977)

Dinan, Monique, *Mauritius in the Making across the Censuses 1846–2000* (Mauritius: Nelson Mandela Centre for African Culture, Ministry of Arts & Culture, 2002)

Domar, Evsey D., 'The Causes of Slavery or Serfdom: A Hypothesis', *The Journal of Economic History*, 30 (1970), 18–32

Domingue, P. R., 'The Historical Development of the Mixed Legal System of Mauritius during the French and British Colonial Periods', *Law, Management and Social Sciences*, 4 (2002), 61–93

Domingue, P. R., 'The Historical Development of the Mixed Legal System of Mauritius since Independence', *Law, Management and Social Sciences*, 4 (2002), 95–117

Dorsett, Shaunnagh, and John McLaren, 'Chapter 1: Laws, Engagements and Legacies', in *Legal Histories of the British Empire: Laws, Engagements and Legacies*, ed. by Shaunnagh Dorsett and John McLaren (Abingdon; New York, NY: Routledge, 2014)

Dorsett, Shaunnagh, and John McLaren., eds., *Legal Histories of the British Empire: Laws, Engagements and Legacies* (Abingdon; New York, NY: Routledge, 2014)

Draper, Nicholas, *The Price of Emancipation: Slave-Ownership, Compensation and British Society at the End of Slavery* (Cambridge: Cambridge University Press, 2009)

Dukes, Ruth, 'Hugo Sinzheimer and the Constitutional Function of Labour Law', in *The Idea of Labour Law*, ed. by Guy Davidov and Brian Langille (Oxford; New York: Oxford University Press, 2011), pp. 57–68

D'Unienville, Raymond, *L'Evolution Du Droit Civil a l'Ile Maurice (1721–1968)* (Mauritius: Temple Law Books, LexisNexis, 1994)

Earally, Abdoollah, 'L'UCL diffuse les noms des propriétaires d'esclaves compensés par Londres à Maurice', *L'express* (Mauritius, 28 February 2013) www.lexpress.mu/story/47537-l-ucl-diffuse-les-noms-des-proprietaires-d-esclaves-compenses-par-londres-a-maurice.html#2%27

Elias, T. O., *British Colonial Law: A Comparative Study of the Interaction between English and Local Laws in British Dependencies* (Hoboken, NJ: Stevens, 1962)

Eltis, David, and Stanley L. Engerman, 'Dependence, Servility, and Coerced Labor in Time and Space', in *The Cambridge World History of Slavery: Volume 3, AD 1420–AD 1804*, ed. by David Eltis and Stanley L. Engerman (New York: Cambridge University Press, 2011)

Emmer, P. C., ed., *Colonialism and Migration: Indentured Labour Before and After Slavery* (Comparative Studies in Overseas History, vol. 7; Dordrecht; Lancaster: Nijhoff, 1986)

Emmer, P. C., ed., 'The Meek Hindu: The Recruitment of Indian Labourers for Service Overseas, 1870–1916', in *Colonialism and Migration: Indentured Labour before and after Slavery*, ed. by P. C. Emmer, Comparative Studies in Overseas History (Dordrecht; Lancaster: Nijhoff, 1986)

Emrith, Moomtaz, *History of the Muslims in Mauritius* (Vacoas, Mauritius: Editions Le Printemps, 1994)

Engerman, Stanley L., 'Contract Labor, Sugar, and Technology in the Nineteenth Century', *The Journal of Economic History*, 43 (1983), 635–659

Engerman, Stanley L., 'Introduction', in *Terms of Labor: Slavery, Serfdom and Free Labor*, ed. by Stanley L. Engerman (Stanford: Stanford University Press, 1999)

Engerman, Stanley L., 'The Rise, Persistence, and Slow Decline of Legal Slavery', in *The Legal Understanding of Slavery: From the Historical to the Contemporary*, ed. by Jean Allain (Oxford: Oxford University Press, 2012)

Esmeir, Samera, *Juridical Humanity: A Colonial History* (Stanford: Stanford University Press, 2014)

Etemad, Bouda, *Possessing the World: Taking the Measurements of Colonisation from the Eighteenth to the Twentieth Century*, European Expansion and Global Interaction, vol. 6 (New York; Oxford: Berghahn Books, 2007)

Evers, Sandra, and Marry Kooy, eds., *Eviction from the Chagos Islands: Displacement and Struggle for Identity against Two World Powers*, African History, vol. 1 (Leiden; Boston: Brill, 2011)

Fakhri, Michael, *Sugar and the Making of International Trade Law* (Cambridge: Cambridge University Press, 2014)

Fanon, Frantz, *Black Skin, White Masks* (London: Pluto Press, 1986)
Fantasia, Rick, 'From Class Consciousness to Culture, Action, and Social Organization', *Annual Review of Sociology*, 21 (1995), 269–287
Farran, Sue, Esin Örücü, and Seán Patrick Donlan, *A Study of Mixed Legal Systems: Endangered, Entrenched or Blended*, New Edition (Farnham; Burlington, VT: Ashgate, 2014)
Fassbender, Bardo, Anne Peters, Simone Peter, and Daniel Högger, eds., *The Oxford Handbook of the History of International Law* (Oxford: Oxford University Press, 2014)
Ferenczi, Imre, and Walter F. Willcox, *International Migrations: Volume I – Statistics* (New York: National Bureau of Economic Research, 1929)
Finkelman, Paul, 'Slavery in the United States', in *The Legal Understanding of Slavery: From the Historical to the Contemporary*, ed. by Jean Allain (Oxford: Oxford University Press, 2012)
Fisk, Catherine L., and Robert W. Gordon, '"Law As . . .": Theory and Method in Legal History', *UC Irvine Law Review*, 1 (2011), 519–541
Fitzmaurice, Andrew, 'Liberalism and Empire in Nineteenth-Century International Law', *The American Historical Review*, 117 (2012), 122–140
Fitzmaurice, Andrew, 'The Genealogy of Terra Nullius', *Australian Historical Studies*, 38 (2007), 1–15
Fitzpatrick, Peter, 'Terminal Legality: Imperialism and the (De)composition of Law', in *Law, History, Colonialism: The Reach of Empire*, ed. by Diane Elizabeth Kirkby and Catharine Coleborne, Studies in Imperialism (Manchester: Manchester University Press, 2001), pp. 9–25
Fogel, Robert, and Stanley L. Engerman, *Time on the Cross – The Economics of American Negro Slavery* (New York: Norton, 1995)
Fortuné-Pope, Joyce, *Reparations – An Multidisciplinary Approach*, TJC Report Volume III, www.researchgate.net/publication/278516321_Truth_and_Justice_Commission_report_Volume_3_Contemporary_History_Culture_and_Society_-_research_Reports_Technical_studies_and_Surveys [accessed 26 June 2022]
Foucault, Michel, 'Governmentality', in *The Foucault Effect: Studies in Governmentality*, ed. by Graham Burchell, Colin Gordon, and Peter Miller (Chicago: The University of Chicago Press, 1991), pp. 87–104
Foucault, Michel, *The Birth of Biopolitics: Lectures at the Collège de France, 1978–1979*, ed. by Michel Senellart (Basingstoke: Palgrave Macmillan, 2010)
Foucault, Michel, *The Essential Foucault: Selections from the Essential Works of Foucault, 1954–1984* (New York; London: New Press, 2003)
Freedland, Mark, and Nicola Kountouris, 'The Legal Characterization of Personal Work Relations and the Idea of Labour Law', in *The Idea of Labour Law*, ed. by Guy Davidov and Brian Langille (Oxford; New York: Oxford University Press, 2011), pp. 190–208
Frerichs, Sabine, 'From Credit to Crisis: Max Weber, Karl Polanyi, and the Other Side of the Coin', *Journal of Law and Society*, 40 (2013), 7–26
Frerichs, Sabine, *Studying Law, Economy, and Society: A Short History of Socio-Legal Thinking* (Rochester, NY: Social Science Research Network, 2012)
Fryer, Peter, *Black People in the British Empire* (London: Pluto Classic, 1988)
Galloway, J. H., *The Sugar Cane Industry: An Historical Geography from Its Origins to 1914* (Cambridge: Cambridge University Press, 1989)

Ginzburg, Carlo, 'Our Words, and Theirs – A Reflection on the Historian's Craft, Today', in *Historical Knowledge: In Quest of Theory, Method and Evidence*, ed. by Susanna Fellman and Marjatta Rahikainen (Newcastle upon Tyne: Cambridge Scholars Publishing, 2012)

Goldin, Ian, Geoffrey Cameron, and Meera Balarajan, *Exceptional People – How Migration Shaped Our World and Will Define Our Future* (Princeton, NJ; Oxford: Princeton University Press, 2011)

Gong, Gerrit W., *The Standard of 'Civilization' in International Society* (Oxford: Clarendon, 1984)

Green, W. A., *British Slave Emancipation: The Sugar Colonies and the Great Experiment, 1830–1865* (Oxford: Clarendon Press, 1991)

Greene, W., *Digest of the Reported Criminal Jurisprudence of the Supreme Court of Mauritius from 1842 to 1883* (Port Louis: Mercantile Record Company's Printing Establishment, 1884)

Greene, W., and L. E. Schmidt, eds., *Labor Laws of Mauritius – A Collection of the Laws Specifically Relating to Masters and Servants at Mauritius* (Mauritius: L. Channell's Printing Establishment, 1869)

Gujadhur Sarup, Leela, *Indentured Labour – Slavery to Salvation* (Kolkata: Aldrich International, 2004)

Gunaratnam, Yasmin, *Researching 'Race' and Ethnicity: Methods, Knowledge and Power* (London: Sage Publications, 2003)

Gunputh, Veena Devi, 'Sex Disproportion among Indian Immigrants', in *Indians Overseas – The Mauritian Experience*, ed. by U. Bissoondoyal (Moka; Mauritius: Mahatma Gandhi Institute, 1984), pp. 213–222

Hall, Catherine, Nicholas Draper, Keith McClelland, Katie Donington, and Rachel Lang, *Legacies of British Slave-Ownership* (Cambridge: Cambridge University Press, 2014)

Hall, Stuart, 'The Multi-Cultural Question', in *Un/settled Multiculturalisms: Diasporas, Entanglements, Transruptions*, ed. by Barnor Hesse (London; New York: Zed Books Ltd, 2000)

Hamilton, Keith, and Patrick Salmon, eds., *Slavery, Diplomacy and Empire: Britain and the Suppression of the Slave Trade, 1807–1975*, Reprint Edition (Brighton: Gazelle, 2012)

Hamilton, Paul, *Historicism*, The New Critical Idiom, 2nd Edition (London: Routledge, 2003)

Harford, Tim, 'The Sweatshop Dilemma', *FT Magazine*, 22 October 2016

Harms, Robert W., 'Introduction: Indian Ocean Slavery in the Age of Abolition', in *Indian Ocean Slavery in the Age of Abolition*, ed. by Robert W. Harms, Bernard K. Freamon, and David W. Blight (New Haven, CT: Yale University Press, 2013)

Harms, Robert W., Bernard K. Freamon, and David W. Blight, eds., *Indian Ocean Slavery in the Age of Abolition* (New Haven, CT: Yale University Press, 2013)

Haudrere, Philippe, '*La Compagnie Française Des Indes Au XVIIIe Siècle (1719–1795) – Tome 1' (unpublished Thèse pour le Doctorat d'Etat ès lettres)* (Paris: Université de Paris – Sorbonne, 1987).

Haugaard, Mark, ed., *Power: A Reader* (Manchester; New York: Manchester University Press, 2002)

Hazareesingh, K., ed., *Selected Speeches of Sir Seewoosagur Ramgoolam* (London and Basingstoke: Macmillan, 1979)

Hearn, Jonathan, *Theorizing Power* (Houndmills; Basingstoke; New York: Palgrave Macmillan, 2012)
Hegel, G. W. F., *Phenomenology of Spirit*, trans. by A. V. Miller (Oxford: Oxford University Press, 1977)
Hepple, Bob, 'Factors Influencing the Making and Transformation of Labour Law in Europe', in *The Idea of Labour Law*, ed. by Guy Davidov and Brian Langille (Oxford; New York: Oxford University Press Oxford, 2011), pp. 30–42
Heuman, Gad, and Trevor Burnard, eds., *The Routledge History of Slavery* (London: Routledge, 2012)
Hindess, Barry, *Discourses of Power: From Hobbes to Foucault* (Oxford: Blackwell Publishers, 1996)
Hobsbawm, E. J., and T. O. Ranger, eds., *The Invention of Tradition* (Cambridge: Cambridge University Press, 1992)
Hochschild, Adam, *Bury the Chains: The British Struggle to Abolish Slavery* (Basingstoke: Macmillan, 2005)
Hohfeld, Wesley, 'Fundamental Legal Conceptions as Applied in Judicial Reasoning', *Yale Law Journal*, 710 (1917) http://digitalcommons.law.yale.edu/fss_papers/4378
Hollingworth, Derek, *They Came to Mauritius* (London: Oxford University Press, 1965)
Honoré, Antony, 'The Nature of Slavery', in *The Legal Understanding of Slavery: From the Historical to the Contemporary*, ed. by Jean Allain (Oxford: Oxford University Press, 2012)
Houbert, Jean, 'Mauritius: Independence and Dependence', *The Journal of Modern African Studies*, 19 (1981), 75–105
Hourani, George Fadlo, *Arab Seafaring in the Indian Ocean in Ancient and Early Medieval Times*, revised and expanded (Princeton, NJ: Princeton University Press, 1995)
Howe, Anthony, *Free Trade and Liberal England, 1846–1946* (Oxford: Oxford University Press, 1998)
Howe, Stephen, *Empire: A Very Short Introduction* (Oxford: Oxford University Press, 2002)
Ibbetson, David, 'What Is Legal History a History Of?', in *Law and History*, ed. by Andrew Lewis and Michael Lobban, Current Legal Issues, vol. 6 (Oxford; New York: Oxford University Press, 2004), pp. 33–40
Jahangeer-Chojoo, Amenah, and Diana Bablee, 'Outer Islands of Mauritius, Historical Overview', *Journal of Mauritian Studies*, 3 (2007), 2–43
Jawatkar, K. S., *Diego Garcia in International Diplomacy* (London: Sangam, 1982)
Jeffery, Laura, '"A Lost People"? Chagossian Onward Migration and Echoes of Marginalisation in Crawley', in *Eviction from the Chagos Islands: Displacement and Struggle for Identity against Two World Powers*, ed. by Sandra Evers and Marry Kooy, African History, vol. 1 (Leiden; Boston, MA: Brill, 2011), pp. 219–238
Jeffery, Laura, *Chagos Islanders in Mauritius and the UK: Forced Displacement and Onward Migration*, New Ethnographies (Manchester: Manchester University Press, 2011)
Jeffery, Laura, and David Vine, 'Sorrow, Sadness, and Impoverishment: The Lives of Chagossians in Mauritius', in *Eviction from the Chagos Islands: Displacement and

Struggle for Identity against Two World Powers, ed. by Sandra Evers and Marry Kooy, African History, vol. 1 (Leiden; Boston: Brill, 2011), pp. 83–102

Jenkins, Keith, *Re-Thinking History* (London; New York: Routledge, 2003)

Jeremie, Sir John, and John Reddie, *Recent Events at Mauritius* (London: Hatchard and Son; J. & A. Arch, S. Bagster, 1835)

Jung, Moon-Ho, and Ebrary Sub, *Coolies and Cane Race, Labor, and Sugar in the Age of Emancipation* (Baltimore, MD: Johns Hopkins University Press, 2006) http://site.ebrary.com/lib/soas/Doc?id=10188507 [accessed 16 September 2013]

Jureidini, Ray, *Ways Forward in Recruitment of Low-Skilled Migrant Workers in the Asia-Arab States Corridor* (Beirut: International Labour Organization, 2016)

Kazmin, Amy, and Simeon Kerr, 'India Sends Aid to Stranded Workers in S Arabia', *Financial Times*, 2 August 2016, p. 6

Kelly, John D., 'The Other Leviathans: Corporate Investment and the Construction of a Sugar Colony', in *White and Deadly: Sugar and Colonialism*, ed. by Pal Ahluwalia, Bill Ashcroft, and Roger Knight (New York: New Science Publishers, 1999)

Kennedy, Duncan, 'The Stakes of Law, or Hale and Foucault!', *Legal Studies Forum*, XV (1991), 327

Kirk, Jerome, *Reliability and Validity in Qualitative Research* Qualitative Research Methods, vol. 1 (Newbury Park, CA; London: Sage Publications, 1986)

Kirkby, Diane Elizabeth, and Catharine Coleborne, eds., *Law, History, Colonialism: The Reach of Empire*, Studies in Imperialism (Manchester: Manchester University Press, 2001)

Klein, Martin A., 'The Emancipation of Slaves in the Indian Ocean', in *Abolition and Its Aftermath in Indian Ocean Africa and Asia*, ed. by Gwyn Campbell (Milton Park: Routledge, 2005), pp. 198–218

Knight, G. Roger, 'The Language of Colonial Power: The Sugar Industry's "Coolies" in Colonial Java', in *White and Deadly: Sugar and Colonialism*, ed. by Bill Ashcroft, Roger Knight, and Pal Ahluwalia (New York: Nova Science Publishers, 1999), pp. 65–82

Koskenniemi, Martti, *The Gentle Civilizer of Nations: The Rise and Fall of International Law, 1870–1960*, Hersch Lauterpacht Memorial Lectures (Cambridge: Cambridge University Press, 2002)

Kuczynski, Robert R., *Demographic Survey of the British Colonial Empire. Volume II: South Africa High Commission Territories, East Africa, Mauritius and Seychelles* (Oxford: Oxford University Press, 1949), p. II

Laidlaw, Zoë, '"Justice to India – Prosperity to England – Freedom to the Slave!" Humanitarian and Moral Reform Campaigns on India, Aborigines and American Slavery', *Journal of the Royal Asiatic Society*, 22 (2012), 299–324

Lamusse, Roland, 'Labour Policy in the Plantation Islands', *World Development*, 8 (1980), 1035–1050

Lebedeva, Nina, 'American Military Base on Diego Garcia: What's Next?', *New Eastern Outlook* http://journal-neo.org/2016/12/01/american-military-base-on-diego-garcia-what-is-next/ [accessed 15 December 2016]

Leiter, Brian, *Naturalizing Jurisprudence* (Oxford: Oxford University Press, 2007)

Lobban, Michael, 'The Tools and Tasks of the Legal Historian', in *Law and History*, ed. by Andrew Lewis and Michael Lobban, Current Legal Issues, vol. 6 (Oxford; New York: Oxford University Press, 2004)

Lobdell, Richard A., 'Patterns of Investment and Sources of Credit in the British West Indian Sugar Industry, 1838–97', *Journal of Caribbean History*, 4 (1972), 31–53

Look Lai, Walton, *Indentured Labor, Caribbean Sugar* (Baltimore, MD; London: Johns Hopkins University Press, 1993)
Lowenthal, David, *The Past Is a Foreign Country* (Cambridge; New York: Cambridge University Press, 1985)
Lubbock, Basil, *Coolie Ships and Oil Sailers*, Reprint (Glasgow: Brown, Son and Ferguson Ltd, 1981)
Lucassen, Jan, and Leo Lucassen, 'Measuring and Quantifying Cross-Cultural Migrations: An Introduction', in *Globalising Migration History – The Eurasian Experience (16th – 21st Centuries)*, ed. by Jan Lucassen and Leo Lucassen (Leiden: Brill, 2014), pp. 3–54
Luhmann, Niklas, *Law as a Social System*, ed. by Fatima Kastner and others, trans. by Klaus Ziegert (Oxford; New York: Oxford University Press, 2004)
Ly-Tio-Fane Pineo, Huguette, *Lured Away: The Life History of Indian Cane Workers in Mauritius* (Moka, Mauritius: Mahatma Gandhi Institute, 1984)
Macmillan, Allister, *Mauritius Illustrated: Historical and Descriptive, Commercial and Industrial, Facts, Figures and Resources* (New Delhi: Asian Educational Services, 2010)
Madeley, John, *Diego Garcia: A Contrast to the Falklands*, Report, Minority Rights Group, no. 54, New Revised Edition (London: Minority Rights Group, 1985)
Mamdani, Mahmood, *When Does a Settler Become a Native? Reflections of the Colonial Roots of Citizenship in Equatorial and South Africa*, presented at the inaugural lecture (Cape Town: University of Cape Town, 1998) http://citizenshiprightsinafrica.org/docs/mamdani%201998%20inaugural%20lecture.pdf
Mangru, Basdeo, *Benevolent Neutrality – Indian Government Policy and Labour Migration to British Guiana 1854–1884* (London: Hansib Publications, 1987)
Marius, Richard, *A Short Guide to Writing about History*, 6th Edition (New York: Pearson/Longman, 2007)
Martin, Gaston, *Histoire de L'esclavage Dans Les Colonies Françaises*, Colonies et Empires: Collection Internationale de Documentation Coloniale. 1. Sér.: Études Coloniales, 4 (Paris: Presses universitaires de France, 1948)
Marx, Karl, 'Wage Labour and Capital', in *Wage Labour and Capital & Wages, Price and Profit* (London: Bookmarks, 1996)
Mathur, Hansraj, *Parliament in Mauritius* (Rose-Hill, Mauritius: Editions de l'Ocean Indien, 1991)
Maturana, Humbert R., and Francisco J. Varela, *Autopoiesis and Cognition: The Realization of the Living* (Dordrecht; Boston, MA: D. Reidel Publishing Company, 1980)
McHugh, Paul, 'The Politics of Historiography and the Taxonomies of the Colonial Past: Law, History and the Tribes', in *Making Legal History Approaches and Methodologies*, ed. by Anthony Musson and Chantal Stebbings (Cambridge: Cambridge University Press, 2012)
McKeown, Niall, 'Greek and Roman Slavery', in *The Routledge History of Slavery*, ed. by Gad Heuman and Trevor Burnard (London: Routledge, 2012)
Menard, Russell, 'Making a "Popular Slave Society" in Colonial British America', *Journal of Interdisciplinary History*, XLIII (2013), 377–395
Menard, Russell, *Migrants, Servants and Slaves: Unfree Labor in Colonial British America* (Aldershot; Burlington, VT: Routledge, 2001)
Miers, Suzanne, 'Slavery: A Question of Definition', in *The Structure of Slavery in Indian Ocean Africa and Asia*, ed. by Gwyn Campbell, Studies in Slave and Post-Slave Societies and Cultures (London: Frank Cass, 2004), pp. 1–16

Miller, Robert J., 'The Doctrine of Discovery', in *Discovering Indigenous Lands: The Doctrine of Discovery in the English Colonies*, by Robert J. Miller and others, Reprint Edition (Oxford: Oxford University Press, 2012)

Miller, Robert J., Jacinta Ruru, Larissa Behrendt, and Tracey Lindberg, *Discovering Indigenous Lands: The Doctrine of Discovery in the English Colonies*, Reprint Edition (Oxford: Oxford University Press, 2012)

Minogue, M. M., and S. K. Joypaul, *Notes on the Constitution of Mauritius – Occasional Paper No. 3* (Mauritius: School of Administration, University of Mauritius, 1973)

Mintz, Sidney W., *Sweetness and Power: The Place of Sugar in Modern History* (New York: Penguin Books, 1986)

Mishra, Amit Kumar, 'Indian Indentured Labourers in Mauritius: Reassessing the "New System of Slavery" vs. Free Labour Debate', *Studies in History*, 25 (2009), 229–251

Morgan, Kenneth, *Slavery and the British Empire: From Africa to America* (Oxford: Oxford University Press, 2007)

Muir, Augustus, *Blyth, Greene, Jourdain & Company Limited 1810–1860* (London: Newman Neame, 1961)

Muldoon, James, *Popes, Lawyers and Infidels: Church and the Non-Christian World, 1250–1550* (Philadelphia, PA: Liverpool University Press, 1980)

Mullings, Leith, ed., *New Social Movements in the African Diaspora: Challenging Global Apartheid*, The Critical Black Studies Series (New York: Palgrave Macmillan, 2009)

Mulloo, Anand, 'Isle de France under Mahé de Labourdonnais', in *Mauritius under French Administration*, ed. by S. N. Gayou (Moka, Mauritius: Mahatma Gandhi Institute, 1982)

Murphy, James Bernard, 'A Natural Law of Human Labor', *American Journal of Jurisprudence*, 39 (1994), 71

Musson, Anthony, and Chantal Stebbings, eds., *Making Legal History Approaches and Methodologies* (Cambridge: Cambridge University Press, 2012) www.dawsonera.com/guard/protected/dawson.jsp?name=https://idp.soas.ac.uk/entity&dest=www.dawsonera.com/depp/reader/protected/external/AbstractView/S9781139215046 [accessed 14 November 2012]

Napal, Dayachand, *British Mauritius, 1810–1948* (Port Louis: Hart Printing, 1984)

Napal, Dayachand, *Les Constitutions de l'Ile Maurice* (Port Louis: Mauritius Printing Coy Ltd., 1962)

Nederveen Pieterse, Jan, 'Empancipations, Modern and Postmodern', *Development and Change*, 23 (1992), 5–41

Nederveen Pieterse, Jan, *Empire & Emancipation: Power and Liberation on a World Scale* (New York ; London: Praeger, 1989)

Neveling, Patrick, 'A Periodisation of Globalisation According to the Mauritian Integration into the International Sugar Commodity Chain (1825–2005)', in *Global Histories, Imperial Commodities, Local Interactions*, ed. by Jonathan Curry-Machado (London: Palgrave Macmillan, 2013)

Nieboer, H. J., *Slavery as an Industrial System*, 2nd Edition (The Hague: Martinus Nijhoff, 1910)

Noël, Karl, *L'esclavage À l'Isle de France (Ile Maurice) de 1715 à 1810* (Paris: Editions Two Cities, 1991)

North-Coombes, Alfred, *La Découverte Des Mascareignes Par Les Arabes et Les Portugais : Rétrospective et Mise Au Point : Contribution À L'histoire de L'océan Indien Au XVIe Siècle* (Port Louis: Service Bureau, 1979)

North-Coombes, M. D., 'From Slavery to Indenture: Forced Labour in the Political Economy of Mauritius 1834–1867', in *Indentured Labour in the British Empire, 1834–1920*, ed. by Kay Saunders (London: Croom Helm, 1984)
North-Coombes, M. D., *Studies in the Political Economy of Mauritius*, ed. by W. M. Freund (Moka, Mauritius: Mahatma Gandhi Institute, 2000)
Northrup, David, *Indentured Labor in the Age of Imperialism, 1834–1922*, Studies in Comparative World History (Cambridge: Cambridge University Press, 1995)
Nunn, Kenneth, 'Law as a Eurocentric Entreprise', *Law and Inequality*, 15 (1997), 323
Nwulia, Moses D. E., 'The "Apprenticeship" System in Mauritius: Its Character and Its Impact on Race Relations in the Immediate Post-Emancipation Period, 1839–1879', *African Studies Review*, 21 (1978), 89–101
Nwulia, Moses D. E., *The History of Slavery in Mauritius and the Seychelles, 1810–1875* (Rutherford, NJ; London: Fairleigh Dickenson University Press; Associated University Presses, 1981)
Oliver, Paul, *Writing Your Thesis*, 2nd Edition (Los Angeles: SAGE, 2008)
Oppenheim, Lassa, *International Law: A Treatise. War and Neutrality*, 2nd Edition (London: Longmans, Green and Co., 1912), p. II
Orford, Anne, 'The Past as Law or History? The Relevance of Imperialism for Modern International Law', *IILJ Working Paper 2012/2*, History and Theory of International Law Series, 2012
Osterhammel, Jürgen, *Colonialism: A Theoretical Overview*, trans. by Shelley L. Frisch (Princeton, NJ: Markus Wiener Publishers, 1997)
Özsu, Umut, 'Ottoman Empire', in *The Oxford Handbook of the History of International Law*, ed. by Bardo Fassbender and others (Oxford: Oxford University Press, 2014)
Palmer, Vernon Valentine, Mohamed Y. Mattar, and Anna Koppel, *Mixed Legal Systems, East and West*, New Edition (Farnham; Burlington, VT: Ashgate, 2015)
Panton, Kenneth J., *Historical Dictionary of the British Empire* (London: Rowman & Littlefield, 2015)
Paquette, Robert L., and Mark M. Smith, eds., *The Oxford Handbook of Slavery in the Americas* (Oxford; New York: Oxford University Press, 2010)
Pearson, Michael N., 'Markets and Merchant Communities in the Indian Ocean: Locating the Portuguese', in *Portuguese Oceanic Expansion, 1400–1800*, ed. by Francisco Bethencourt and Diogo Ramada Curto (Cambridge: Cambridge University Press, 2007)
Peoples, Columba, 'Security after Emancipation? Critical Theory, Violence and Resistance', *Review of International Studies*, 37 (2011), 1113–1135
Perkins, John, and Roger Munting, 'Science versus Nature: The Cane–Beet Sugar Rivalry', in *White and Deadly: Sugar and Colonialism*, ed. by Bill Ashcroft, Roger Knight, and Pal Ahluwalia (New York: Nova Science Publishers, 1999), pp. 157–170
Phillips, Estelle M., *How to Get a PhD: A Handbook for Students and Their Supervisors*, 3rd Edition and updated (Buckingham; Philadelphia, PA: Open University Press, 2000)
Pitot, Genevieve, *The Mauritian Shekel: The Story of Jewish Detainees in Mauritius, 1940–1945* (Lanham, MD: Rowman & Littlefield, 2000)
Polanyi, Karl, *The Great Transformation: The Political and Economic Origins of Our Time* (Boston, MA: Beacon Press, 1944)

Porter, Andrew, 'Britain and the Empire in the Nineteenth Century', in *The Oxford History of the British Empire: The Nineteenth Century*, ed. by Andrew Porter (Oxford; New York: Oxford University Press, 1999), pp. III, 1–28

Porter, Andrew, ed., *The Nineteenth Century* Oxford History of the British Empire, vol. 3 (Oxford: Oxford University Press, 1999)

Porter, Andrew, ed., *The Oxford History of the British Empire: The Nineteenth Century* (Oxford; New York: Oxford University Press, 1999), p. III

Posner, Eric A., ed., *Law and Economics* (Aldershot: Ashgate, 2001)

Posner, Richard A., and Francesco Parisi, eds., *Law and Economics* (Cheltenham: Edward Elgar, 1997)

Prows, Peter, 'Mauritius Brings UNCLOS Arbitration Against The United Kingdom Over The Chagos Archipelago', *ASIL Insights*, 15 (2011)

Reddi, S. J., 'The Establishment of the Indian Indenture System 1834–1842', in *Indians Overseas – The Mauritian Experience*, ed. by U. Bissoondoyal (Moka, Mauritius: Mahatma Gandhi Institute, 1984), pp. 1–17

Renton, Justice Wood, 'French Law within the British Empire', *Journal of the Society of Comparative Legislation*, 10 (1910), 250–260

Rigney, Ann, 'History as Text: Narrative Theory and History', in *The SAGE Handbook of Historical Theory*, ed. by Nancy Partner and Sarah R. I. Foot (Los Angeles: SAGE Publications Ltd., 2013)

Rincon, Paul, 'UK Sets Up Chagos Islands Marine Reserve', *BBC News* http://news.bbc.co.uk/1/hi/sci/tech/8599125.stm [accessed 20 March 2015]

Rittich, Kerry, 'Between Workers' Rights and Flexibility: Labor Law in an Uncertain World', *Saint Louis University Law Journal*, 54 (2010), 565

Rouillard, John, ed., *A Collection of the Laws of Mauritius and Its Dependencies. Volume III: 3rd December 1810–16th November 1831* (Mauritius: Published by the Authority of the Government, 1866), p. III http://catalog.hathitrust.org/Record/011570339 [accessed 10 June 2015]

Saha, Panchan, *Emigration of Indian Labour (1834–1900)* (Delhi: People's Publishing House, 1970)

Said, Edward W., *Culture & Imperialism* (London: Vintage, 1994)

Said, Edward W., *Orientalism* (London: Penguin Books, 1995)

Salmon, Phillida, *Achieving a PhD: Ten Students' Experience* (Stoke-on-Trent: Trentham, 1992)

Salverda, Tijo, *Franco-Mauritian Elite: Power and Anxiety in the Face of Change* (New York: Berghahn Books, 2015)

Samuels, Warren J., 'Adam Smith and the Economy as a System of Power', *Review of Social Economy*, 31 (1973), 123–137

Sanadhya, Totaram, and Bernarsidas Chaturvedi, *My Twenty-One Years in the Fiji Islands & The Story of the Haunted Line*, ed. by John Dunham Kelly, trans. by Uttra Kumari Singh (Suva: Fiji Museum, 2003)

Sand, Peter H., *Atoll Diego Garcia: Naturschutz Zwischen Menschenrecht Und Machtpolitik* (Munich: Herbert Utz Verlag, 2011)

Sarat, Austin, ed., *Blackwell Companion to Law and Society* (Malden, MA: Blackwell Publishing, 2004)

Sartre, Jean-Paul, *Colonialism and Neocolonialism* (London; New York: Routledge, 2001)

Saunders, Kay, ed., *Indentured Labour in the British Empire, 1834–1920* (London: Croom Helm, 1984)

Scarr, Deryck, *Slaving and Slavery in the Indian Ocean* (New York: St. Martin's Press, 1998)
Selvon, Sydney, *A New Comprehensive History of Mauritius Volume 1: From Ancient Times to the Birth of Parliament* (Scotts Valley, CA: CreateSpace Independent Publishing Platform, 2012)
Selvon, Sydney, *A New Comprehensive History of Mauritius Volume 2: From British Rule to the 21st Century* (Scotts Valley, CA: CreateSpace Independent Publishing Platform, 2012)
Sheridan, Richard B., 'The West India Sugar Crisis and British Slave Emancipation, 1830–1833', *Journal of Economic History*, 21 (1961), 539–551
Shlomowitz, Ralph, 'On Punishments and Rewards in Coercive Labour Systems: Comparative Perspectives', *Slavery & Abolition*, 12 (1991), 97–102
Simnett, William Edward, *The British Colonial Empire* (London: G. Allen & Unwin, 1942)
Simpson, A. W. B., *Human Rights and the End of Empire: Britain and the Genesis of the European Convention* (Oxford; New York: Oxford University Press, 2001)
Simsarian, James, 'The Acquisition of Legal Title to Terra Nullius', *Political Science Quarterly*, 53 (1938), 111–128
Singer, Merrill, and G. Derrick Hodge, eds., *The War Machine and Global Health: A Critical Medical Anthropological Examination of the Human Costs of Armed Conflict and the International Violence Industry* (Lanham, MD: AltaMira Press, 2010)
Skinner, Quentin, 'Meaning and Understanding in the History of Ideas', *History and Theory*, 8 (1969), 3–53
Skouteris, Thomas, 'Engaging History in International Law', in *New Approaches to International Law: The European and American Experiences*, ed. by D. Kennedy and J. M. Beneyto (The Hague: T.M.C. Asser Press, 2012)
Smith, Adam, *An Inquiry into the Nature and Causes of the Wealth of Nations*, ed. by Edwin Cannan, 5th Edition (London: Methuen & Co., 1904)
Smith, Nicholas H., 'Three Normative Models of Work', in *Social and Critical Theory, Volume 13: New Philosophies of Labour-Work and the Social Bond*, ed. by Nicholas H. Smith and Jean-Philippe Deranty (Leiden: Brill Academic Publishers, 2011)
Smith Simmons, Adele, *Modern Mauritius: The Politics of Decolonization* (Bloomington, IN: Indiana University Press, 1982)
Smith Simmons, Adele, *Politics in Mauritius since 1934: A Study of Decolonization in a Plural Society* (Oxford: Oxford University Press, 1969)
Spalding, Roger, and Christopher Parker, *Historiography: An Introduction* (Manchester: Manchester University Press, 2007)
Spivak, Gayatri Chakravorty, *The Post-Colonial Critic: Interviews, Strategies, Dialogues* (New York; London: Routledge, 1990)
Springhall, John, *Decolonization since 1945: The Collapse of European Overseas Empires*, Studies in Contemporary History (Basingstoke: Palgrave, 2001)
Stanley, Amy Dru, *From Bondage to Contract – Wage Labor, Marriage and the Market in the Age of Slave Emancipation* (New York: Cambridge University Press, 1998)
Steinfeld, Robert J., *Coercion, Contract, and Free Labor in the Nineteenth Century* (Cambridge; New York: Cambridge University Press, 2001)
Storey, William Kelleher, *Science and Power in Colonial Mauritius* (Rochester, NY: University of Rochester Press, 1998)

Strauss, Kendra, 'Coerced, Forced and Unfree Labour: Geographies of Exploitation in Contemporary Labour Markets', *Geography Compass*, 6 (2012), 137–148

Strausz-Hupé, Robert, and Harry W. Hazard, eds., *The Idea of Colonialism*, The Foreign Policy Research Institute Series, no. 5 (New York: Praeger, 1958)

Sundararajan, Saroja, *From Bondage to Deliverance: Indentured Labour in Mauritius and British Guiana* (New Delhi: Allied Publishers, 2006)

Swartz, David, *Culture and Power: The Sociology of Pierre Bourdieu* (Chicago: University of Chicago Press, 1997)

Swinfen, D. B., *Imperial Control of Colonial Legislation, 1813–1865: A Study of British Policy Towards Colonial Legislative Powers* (London: Clarendon Press, 1970)

Tamanaha, Brian Z., *Realistic Socio-Legal Theory – Pragmatism and a Social Theory of Law* (Oxford; New York: Oxford University Press, 1997)

Teelock, Vijaya, *Bitter Sugar: Sugar and Slavery in 19th Century Mauritius* (Moka, Mauritius: Mahatma Gandhi Institute, 1998)

Teelock, Vijaya, 'The Influence of Slavery in the Formation of Creole Identity', *Comparative Studies of South Asia, Africa and the Middle East*, 19 (1999), 3–8

Teelock, Vijayalakshmi, *A Select Guide to Sources on Slavery in Mauritius, and the Testimony of Slaves in the Era of Sugar* (Bell Village, Mauritius: African Cultural Centre, 1995)

Teelock, Vijayalakshmi, *Bitter Sugar: Slavery and Emancipation in Nineteenth-Century Mauritius* (PhD Thesis) (London: University of London (SOAS), 1994)

Teelock, Vijayalakshmi, *Mauritian History: From Its Beginnings to Modern Times*, 2nd Edition (Moka, Mauritius: Mahatma Gandhi Institute, 2009)

Teelock, Vijayalakshmi, 'The Mauritius Truth and Justice Commission: "Eyewash", "Storm in a Teacup" or Promise of a New Future for Mauritius?', in *Emancipation and the Remaking of the British Imperial World* (Manchester: Manchester University Press, 2014), pp. 207–222

Teelock, Vijayalakshmi, Anwar Janoo, Geoffrey Summers, Marc Serge Rivière, and Sooryakanti Nirsimloo-Gayan, eds., *Angaje: Explorations into the History, Society and Culture of Indentured Immigrants and Their Descendants in Mauritius*, 3 vols. (Port Louis: Aapravasi Ghat Trust Fund, 2012)

Tinker, Hugh, *A New System of Slavery: Export of Indian Labour Overseas, 1830–1920*, 2nd Edition (Hertford: Hansib Publications, 1993)

Tomlins, Christopher, 'Historicism and Materiality in Legal Theory', in *Law in Theory and History: New Essays on a Neglected Dialogue*, ed. by Maksymilian Del Mar and Michael Lobban (Oxford: Hart Publishing, 2019)

Toorawa, Shawkat M., and Hassan Toorawa Trust, eds., *The Western Indian Ocean: Essays on Islands and Islanders* (Port Louis: Hassan Toorawa Trust, 2007)

Toussaint, Auguste, *History of Mauritius* (London: Macmillan, 1977)

Toussaint, Auguste, *Repertoire Des Archives de l'Ile de France Pendant La Régie de La Compagnie Des Indes (1715–1768)* (Mauritius: Mauritius Archives Publications, 1956)

Twaddle, Michael, ed., *The Wages of Slavery: From Chattel Slavery to Wage Labour in Africa, the Caribbean and England* (London: Frank Cass, 1993)

Twomey, Mathilda, 'The Parts That Make A Whole? The Mixity of the Laws of Seychelles', in *Mixed Legal Systems, East and West*, ed. by Vernon Valentine Palmer, Mohamed Y. Mattar, and Anna Koppel (Farnham: Ashgate, 2015), pp. 55–74

Uteem, Cassam, 'Chagos Archipelago: Beyond the UN Court Ruling', *Le Mauricien*, 25 March 2015 www.lemauricien.com/article/chagos-archipelago-beyond-court-ruling [accessed 25 March 2015]

Varma, Moonindra Nath, *The Making of Mauritius* (Mauritius: Editions Le Printemps, 2013)

Vaughan, Megan, *Creating the Creole Island Slavery in Eighteenth-Century Mauritius* (Durham, NC; London: Duke University Press, 2005)

Vaughan, Megan, 'The Character of the Market: Social Identities in Colonial Economies', *Oxford Development Studies*, 24 (1996), 61–77

Veerapen, Parmaseeven Pillay, 'Labour and the Truth and Justice Commission', *Le Mauricien*, 2 May 2015 www.lemauricien.com/article/labour-and-truth-and-justice-commission [accessed 21 February 2017]

Veeser, H. Aram, ed., *The New Historicism* (New York; London: Routledge, 1989)

Veracini, Lorenzo, *Settler Colonialism: A Theoretical Overview* (Basingstoke: Palgrave Macmillan, 2010)

Vine, David, 'Dying of Sorrow: Expulsion, Empire, and the People of Diego Garcia', in *The War Machine and Global Health: A Critical Medical Anthropological Examination of the Human Costs of Armed Conflict and the International Violence Industry*, ed. by Merrill Singer and G. Derrick Hodge (Lanham: AltaMira Press, 2010), pp. 179–206

Vine, David, *Island of Shame: The Secret History of the U.S. Militarybase on Diego Garcia* (Princeton, NJ; Woodstock: Princeton University Press, 2009)

Vine, David, 'Taking on Empires: Reparations, the Right of Return, and the People of Diego Garcia', in *New Social Movements in the African Diaspora: Challenging Global Apartheid*, ed. by Leith Mullings, The Critical Black Studies Series (New York, NY: Palgrave Macmillan, 2009), pp. 171–192

Ward, John Manning, *Colonial Self-Government: The British Experience, 1759–1856*, Cambridge Commonwealth Series (London and Basingstoke: Macmillan, 1976)

Weeramantry, Christopher, 'The Grotius Lecture Series', *American University International Law Review*, 14 (1999), 1515–1569

Wellington, Donald C., *French East India Companies: A Historical Account and Record of Trade* (Lanham, MD: Hamilton Books, 2006)

Wesseling, H. L., *The European Colonial Empires, 1815–1919*, Studies in Modern History (Harlow; New York: Pearson/Longman, 2004)

White, Hayden V., *The Content of the Form: Narrative Discourse and Historical Representation* (Baltimore, MD; London: Johns Hopkins University Press, 1987)

White, Nicholas J., *Decolonisation: The British Experience since 1945*, Seminar Studies in History, Second Edition (London: Taylor & Francis, 2013)

Willcox, Walter F., *International Migrations. Vol 1, Statistics* (New York: National Bureau of Economic Research, 1929)

Williams, Eric Eustace, *Capitalism & Slavery* (Chapel Hill, NC: University of North Carolina Press, 1994)

Williams, Patrick, and Laura Chrisman, *Colonial Discourse and Post-Colonial Theory: A Reader*, 1st Edition (New York: Columbia University Press, 1994)

Williams, R., *Keywords: A Vocabulary of Culture and Society*, Flamingo Edition and expanded (London: Fontana, 1983)

Winks, Robin W., and Alaine M. Low, eds., *The Oxford History of the British Empire*, vol. 5, Historiography (Oxford; New York: Oxford University Press, 2001), p. V

Young, Robert, *White Mythologies: Writing History and the West* (London: Routledge, 1990)
Zachariah, Benjamin, 'Postcolonial Theory and History', in *The SAGE Handbook of Historical Theory*, ed. by Nancy Partner and Sarah R. I. Foot (Los Angeles: SAGE Publications Ltd, 2013)
Zeuner, Lilli, *Cultural Sociology from Concern to Distance* (Copenhagen: Copenhagen Business School Press DK, 2003)

Reports, manuscripts and online materials

'Anti-Slavery Reporter', November 1828, No. 42 edition (Vol. II, No. 12)
Boudet, Catherine, 'Alex Boraine : "For Many, Mauritius Is Still Undemocratic and Racist"', *Analyse Sociopolitique de L'île Maurice*, 2010 https://catherineboudet.wordpress.com/2010/07/02/alex-boraine-for-many-mauritius-is-still-undemocratic-and-racist-2/ [accessed 26 June 2022]
'Britain Faces UN Tribunal over Chagos Islands Marine Reserve', *The Guardian*, 2013 www.guardian.co.uk/world/2013/jan/28/britain-tribunal-chagos-islands-marine-area [accessed 26 June 2022]
Bureau of Democracy, Human Rights and Labor, 'Country Reports on Human Rights Practices for 2015: Mauritius', *US Department of State* www.state.gov/j/drl/rls/hrrpt/humanrightsreport/index.htm?year=2015&dlid=252707 [accessed 26 June 2022]
Central Statistical Office, *1962 Population Census of Mauritius and Its Dependencies* (Mauritius, 1962)
Central Statistical Office, *Natality and Fertility in Mauritius, 1825–1955* (Mauritius: Central Statistical Office, 1956)
D-Maps.com, *Mauritius map* https://d-maps.com/carte.php?num_car=27487&lang=en [accessed 8 August 2021]
D-Maps.com, *Indian Ocean map* https://d-maps.com/carte.php?num_car=3255&lang=en [accessed 8 August 2021]
'Declarations Recognizing the Jurisdiction of the Court as Compulsory – United Kingdom of Great Britain and Northern Ireland', *International Court of Justice* www.icj-cij.org/jurisdiction/?p1=5&p2=1&p3=3&code=GB [accessed 26 June 2022]
Evidence of the Committee Appointed by the Supreme Government of India to Enquire into the Abuses Alleged to Exist in Exporting from Bengal, Hill Coolies and Indian Labourers, of Various Classes to Other Countries (Calcutta: G. H. Huttmann, Bengal Military Orphan Press, 1839)
Gentleman, Amelia, 'Home Office Tried to "Sanitise" Staff Education Module on Colonialism', *The Guardian* www.theguardian.com/politics/2022/jun/10/home-office-tried-to-sanitise-staff-education-module-on-colonialism [accessed 10 June 2022]
Gentleman, Amelia, 'Windrush Scandal Caused by 30 years of Racist Immigration Laws – Report', *The Guardian* www.theguardian.com/uk-news/2022/may/29/windrush-scandal-caused-by-30-years-of-racist-immigration-laws-report [accessed 29 May 2022]; notably, the Home Office has refused to make the report, compiled by a historian, available to the general public

Great Britain Parliament, House of Commons, *Select Committee Appointed to Inquire into the Working of the Apprenticeship System in the Colonies, the Condition of the Apprentices, and the Laws and Regulations Affecting Them Which Have Been Passed*, 'Colonial Laws as Examined by a Committee of the House of Commons in the Year 1836' (London: J. Haddon, 1837) http://0-www.llmcdigital.org.catalogue.ulrls.lon.ac.uk/docdisplay.aspx?textid=33097110 [accessed 26 June 2022]

'Legacies of British Slave-Ownership', 2013 www.ucl.ac.uk/lbs/ [accessed 26 June 2022]

Ministry of Finance and Economic Development – Statistics Mauritius, *2011 Housing and Population Census _ Republic of Mauritius* http://statsmauritius.govmu.org/English/Documents/publications/Housing/economics%20and%20social%20indicators/reports/2011VolIIPC.pdf [accessed 26 June 2022]

Ordonnance Ou Code Noir – Lettres Patentes En Forme d'Édit Concernant Les Esclaves Des Isles de Bourbon et de France, Décembre 1723, Publication No. 17 (Coromandel, Mauritius: Publication des Archives de Maurice, 2000)

Peerthum, Satyendra, 'Collective Resistance by Mauritian Slaves during the Early Nineteenth Century', *L'express*, 1 February 2008 www.lexpress.mu/article/collective-resistance-mauritian-slaves-during-early-nineteenth-century [accessed 26 June 2022]

Report of T. Hugon of Bengal Service upon the Subject of Indian Emigration to Mauritius (Port Louis, 1839)

Report of the Truth and Justice Commission (Mauritius, November 2011) www.usip.org/sites/default/files/ROL/TJC_Vol1.pdf [accessed 28 September 2022]

The Republic of Mauritius v. The United Kingdom of Great Britain and Northern Ireland – Procedural Order No.2 (The Hague: Permanent Court of Arbitration, 2013) www.pca-cpa.org/showpage.asp?pag_id=1429

Parliamentary Papers

PP 1823 (89)
PP 1826 (295)
PP 1828 (526)
PP 1829 (335)
PP 1829 (338)
PP 1829 (333)
PP XXV 1829 (337)
PP 1829 (335)
PP 1831–1832 (333)
PP 1831–1832 (381)
PP 1831–1832 (733)
PP 1835 (278-I) (278-II)
PP 1838
PP 1837–1838 (180) (232)
PP 1844 [530]
PP 1845 (641)
PP 1846 (229)
PP 1847–1848 (419)
PP 1889 [C.8706]

Archival materials

Public Records Office

CO 167 series
CO 167/141
CO 167/196
CO 168/16
CO 168/18
CO 170/1
CO 171/2
CO 171/4
CO 172/12
CO 172/28
CO 172/38
CO 172/39
CO 172/40
CO 171/41
CO 171/42
CO 172/43
CO 172/38
CO 172/62
CO 415
CO 882/2
FO 93/33/8
PC 1/4177

British Library

Add MS 41265
Add MS 38572
C.S.D.364/2
IOL 1947.b.250
IOL.1947.b.552
IOR H/MISC/701
IOR F/4/470–55506
IOR/F/4/1847/77655
IOR/H/701
X. 319/4471

Index

Note: Page numbers in *italic* indicate a figure and page numbers in **bold** indicate a table on the corresponding page.

For Product Safety Concerns and Information please contact our EU representative GPSR@taylorandfrancis.com
Taylor & Francis Verlag GmbH, Kaufingerstraße 24, 80331 München, Germany

www.ingramcontent.com/pod-product-compliance
Ingram Content Group UK Ltd.
Pitfield, Milton Keynes, MK11 3LW, UK
UKHW020141200926
475702UK00005B/844
* 9 7 8 1 0 3 2 3 2 2 0 1 8 *